Chats on Old E

Arthur Hayden

Alpha Editions

This edition published in 2024

ISBN : 9789366389080

Design and Setting By
Alpha Editions
www.alphaedis.com
Email - info@alphaedis.com

As per information held with us this book is in Public Domain. This book is a reproduction of an important historical work. Alpha Editions uses the best technology to reproduce historical work in the same manner it was first published to preserve its original nature. Any marks or number seen are left intentionally to preserve its true form.

Contents

PREFACE .... - 1 -
BIBLIOGRAPHY .... - 4 -
GLOSSARY .... - 7 -
CHAPTER I HOW TO COLLECT: A CHAPTER FOR BEGINNERS .... - 11 -
CHAPTER II EARLY WARE .... - 44 -
CHAPTER III ENGLISH DELFT .... - 55 -
CHAPTER IV STONEWARE .... - 76 -
CHAPTER V EARLY STAFFORDSHIRE WARE ..... - 93 -
CHAPTER VI SALT-GLAZED WARE—STAFFORDSHIRE .... - 115 -
CHAPTER VII JOSIAH WEDGWOOD 1730–1795 .... - 128 -
CHAPTER VIII THE SCHOOL OF WEDGWOOD 1760–1810 .... - 151 -
CHAPTER IX LEEDS AND OTHER FACTORIES .... - 171 -
CHAPTER X TRANSFER-PRINTED WARE .... - 192 -
CHAPTER XI STAFFORDSHIRE FIGURES .... - 218 -
CHAPTER XII SWANSEA AND OTHER FACTORIES .... - 242 -
CHAPTER XIII LUSTRE WARE .... - 260 -
CHAPTER XIV LATE STAFFORDSHIRE WARE .... - 271 -
FOOTNOTES: .... - 303 -

PREFACE

Five years have now elapsed since the publication of my volume, "Chats on English China," and in the interval a great number of readers have written to me suggesting that I should write a companion volume dealing with old English earthenware. It is my hope that this complementary volume will prove of equal value to that large class of collectors who desire to know more about their hobby but are fearful to pursue the subject further without special guidance.

It is a matter for congratulation in these days, when so many books have only a short life for one season, to know that, owing to the enterprise of my publisher in making the "Chats" Series for collectors so widely known, the volume dealing with old English China still retains its vitality, and holds its place as a popular guide to collecting with profit.

As far as is possible in the limits of this volume, the subject of old English earthenware has been dealt with in order to show how peculiarly national the productions of the potter have been. The collection of old English earthenware, in the main, is still within the reach of those who have slender purses. English china during the last decade has reached prohibitive prices, and there is every likelihood that old English earthenware will in the near future become of unprecedented value.

I have carefully refrained from confining my treatment of the subject to rare museum examples which are unlikely to come under the hand of the average collector. It is necessary to have the ideal in view, but it must be borne in mind that such specimens must always be ideal to the larger number of collectors. I have, therefore, without belittling the old potters' art, given considerable attention to the golden mean in the realm of old earthenware to be collected.

The two volumes—"Chats on English China," which mainly consists of an outline history of English china, with hints as to its collection, and the present volume, "Chats on English Earthenware," with a faithful *résumé* of the work of the old English potters—together form a record of what has been done by the potter in England, and are intended to be practical working handbooks for the collector of old English china and English earthenware.

The illustrations in this volume have been carefully chosen to illustrate the letterpress, and to enable readers to identify specimens that may come under their observation.

Lists of Prices accompany the various sections whenever it has been thought that they may be of practical value. I am indebted for the accuracy of these prices to that useful and authoritative quarterly publication, "Auction Sale Prices," which is a supplement to the *Connoisseur*, and forms the standard record in the collectors' world of the prices realised at auction.

A *Bibliography* of works on the subject has been given, in order that those who may wish to delve deeper may consult special volumes dealing in detail with special sub-heads of old earthenware.

I must here record my thanks for the generous aid I have received from possessors of fine examples who have willingly placed their treasures at my disposal, and by so doing have enabled me to present them as illustrations in this volume. To Colonel and Mrs. Dickson I am especially indebted for many specimens from their interesting collection. Miss Feilden has been good enough to select some typical examples from her fine collection of old earthenware of exceptional interest, and they are here reproduced by her courtesy, and to Mr. Richard Wilson I owe my gratitude for kindly allowing illustrations of some examples of Leeds cream-ware from his remarkable collection. Mr. Robert Bruce Wallis, with fine enthusiasm, has spared no trouble to enable me to present some of his rare examples, and Mrs. Herman Liebstein has kindly supplied some fine pieces from her collection. Mr. W. G. Honey has also kindly contributed several excellent illustrations of specimens in his collection.

The illustrations of specimens in the Victoria and Albert Museum are reproduced by permission of the Board of Education, and similar permission has been accorded me by the authorities of the British Museum to illustrate some of the rare examples in that collection. By a like courtesy I am enabled to give an illustration of an exceptional piece of marked Wincanton Delft, and some other examples from the collection at the Royal Scottish Museum, Edinburgh.

Messrs. Josiah Wedgwood and Sons, of Etruria have afforded me the pleasure of illustrating some fine specimens in their museum, including examples of the celebrated service made for the Empress Catherine II. of Russia. I am especially indebted to their courtesy in giving me facilities for the reproduction of a fine series of photographs showing the various stages in the manufacture of earthenware, which illustrations should be of practical advantage to the student and of no little interest to the general collector. It should be mentioned that these illustrations have been specially selected to represent the stages through which a piece of old earthenware passed in the hands of the Staffordshire potters.

In regard to the illustrations of the rare examples of Leeds and other pieces decorated at Lowestoft, and for the latest details known of this class of ware, I have to acknowledge the particular kindness of Mr. Merrington Smith, fine art expert of Lowestoft, who is known in connection with the excavations conducted a few years ago on the site of the old Lowestoft china factory, and whose detailed research regarding that factory has dissipated many erroneous theories and thrown so much light on its history and achievements.

To Mr. Rudd, fine art dealer of Southampton, I am indebted for a considerable fund of information relating to some of the exceptional examples of old English earthenware which have passed through his hands, and I am under a similar obligation to Mr. S. G. Fenton, who has contributed some fine pieces as illustrations to this volume.

Mr. James Davies, of Chester, has given me access to his collection, and has added some fine examples which are here included as illustrations. Mr. F. W. Phillips, of Hitchin, has from his fine collection made a generous selection of noteworthy specimens.

Mr. A. Duncan, of Penarth, has included photographs of some especially fine Swansea ware.

By the kindness of Mr. Hubert Gould, I am reproducing some typical examples of transfer-printed jugs from his collection of old earthenware.

To other friends who have generously forborne with my inquiries, and lent me their practical aid in various directions in assisting me to prosecute my researches in attempting to arrive at definite conclusions in regard to points not hitherto determined, I tender my warm appreciation of their kindness.

I may say, in conclusion, that a good photographer is a treasure, and no trouble has been spared by Mr. A. E. Smith, the well-known art photographer, to render difficult subjects pictorially attractive in conditions exceptionally detrimental to his art.

ARTHUR HAYDEN.

March, 1909.

BIBLIOGRAPHY

GENERAL.

- Catalogue of British Pottery and Porcelain. By T. Reeks and F. W. Rudler. 1876. (Out of print.)
(Formerly in the Museum of Practical Geology, Jermyn Street.)

- Marks and Monograms on Pottery and Porcelain. By W. Chaffers. 12th Edition. 1908.

- Ceramic Art of Great Britain. By Llewellyn Jewitt. 2 vols. 1878. 2nd Edition. 1 vol. 1883.

- English Earthenware (made during the 17th and 18th centuries). By Professor A. H. Church, F. R. S. 1905.

- History of Pottery and Porcelain. By J. Marryat. 1857.

- History of English Earthenware and Stoneware (to the beginning of the 19th century). By William Burton, F. C. S. (Cassell & Co.) 1904.

- Catalogue of British Pottery, &c., at the British Museum. By R. L. Hobson. 1903.

- Art of the Old English Potter. By M. L. Solon. Folio. 2nd Edition. 1885.

- Old English Pottery. By Mr. and Mrs. Frank Freeth. (Morgan, Thompson, & Jamison.) £2 12s. 6d. net.

- Catalogue of Pottery and Porcelain. (Willett Collection, at Brighton Museum.) 1905.

- Pottery and Porcelain. A Guide to Collectors. F. Litchfield. 1900.

- English Pottery and Porcelain. By E. A. Downman. 1896.

- History of the Staffordshire Potteries. By S. Shaw. (Hanley.) 1829. Reissue by the *Pottery Gazette*. 1900.

- The Chemistry of Pottery. By S. Shaw. (London.) 1837. Reissue by the *Pottery Gazette*. 1900.

- Catalogue of English Pottery and Porcelain. (Alexandra Palace.) By R. H. Soden Smith. Destroyed by fire. 1873.

- Transfer Printing on Enamels, Porcelain, and Pottery. By William Turner. 1907.

- Examples of Early English Pottery. By J. E. Hodgkin and E. Hodgkin. 1891.
- Staffordshire Pots and Potters. By G. W. Rhead and F. A. Rhead. 1906.
- Catalogue of a Collection of English Pottery Figures deposited on loan by Messrs. Frank Falkner and E. J. Sidebotham at the Royal Museum, Peel Park, Salford. (Manchester.) 1906.
- Chats on English China. By Arthur Hayden. (T. Fisher Unwin.) 4th Edition. 1909.

(The concluding chapters contain an outline history of English Earthenware.)

PARTICULAR.

Staffordshire.

- Pre-Wedgwood English Pottery. (Solon Collection.) *Connoisseur*, December, 1901; February, 1902.
- William Adams, an old English Potter. Edited by W. Turner. 1904.
- Josiah Wedgwood. By Miss E. Meteyard. 2 vols. 1865–6.
- Wedgwood and his Works. By Miss E. Meteyard. 1873.
- Memorials of Wedgwood. By Miss E. Meteyard. 1874.
- The Wedgwood Handbook. By Miss E. Meteyard. 1875.
- Josiah Wedgwood, Master Potter. By Professor A. H. Church. 1903.
- Old Wedgwood (1760–1795). By F. Rathbone. Folio; 65 plates in colour. 1896.
- Catalogue of Loan Collection of Wedgwood Ware, Liverpool Art Club. (Liverpool.) 1879.
- Josiah Wedgwood. By Llewellyn Jewitt. 1865.
- Handbook to the Tangye Collection of Wedgwood Ware. (Birmingham.) By F. Rathbone. 1885.
- Wedgwood, Josiah—his Catalogue of Cameos, Intaglios, Bas-reliefs, Busts, and Small Statues, with a General Account of Tablets, Vases, Escritoires, and other Ornamental and Useful Articles. (London.) 1787.

- Wedgwood, Josiah—his "Catalogue" (as above). Edited by Miss E. Meteyard. 1873.

- John Wesley Busts in Staffordshire Pottery. By C. S. Sargisson. *Connoisseur*, September, 1907.

- Catalogue of the Museum at the Etruria Works, Messrs. Josiah Wedgwood & Sons, Ltd. By Frederick Rathbone. 1909.
(Mr. Rathbone has arranged the collection of Flaxman's designs, Wedgwood's original pattern models and experimental "trials.")

Bristol.

- Two Centuries of Ceramic Art in Bristol. By H. Owen. 1873.

Derby.

- The Pottery and Porcelain of Derbyshire. By A. Wallis and W. Bemrose. 1870.

Liverpool.

- The Art of Pottery, with a History of its Progress in Liverpool. By J. Mayer. (Liverpool.) 1873.

- The Liverpool Potteries. By C. T. Gatty. (Liverpool.) 1882.

Leeds.

- Old Leeds Pottery. By J. R. and F. Kidson. (Leeds.) 1892.

- Catalogue of Exhibition of Works of Art in the Cartwright Memorial Hall, Bradford. 1904.

- Old Leeds Ware. By Henry B. Wilson. *Connoisseur*, 1904.

Swansea.

- The Ceramics of Swansea and Nantgarw. By William Turner.

GLOSSARY

- **Agate Ware.**—Earthenware made either "solid" or in "surface" decoration to resemble the veinings of agate and other natural stones. The "solid" agate ware is produced by layers of different coloured clays being twisted together and cut transversely. The "surface" agate ware is splashed and grained decoration on an ordinary cream body.

- **Astbury Ware.**—A generic term applied to specimens in the manner of the Astburys, with raised floral decoration of white on a red unglazed body.

- **Basalt.**—Black Basalt, or "Egyptian" ware, is a solid black stoneware of great hardness, made by Wedgwood and by his school of followers.

- **Biscuit.**—This term is applied to earthenware and porcelain when it has been fired once. It is after the biscuit stage that decorations in colour are applied, and the specimen goes to the oven a second time (see Chapter I.).

- **Body.**—The body of a piece of earthenware is the clay of which it is composed irrespective of the nature or colour of decoration applied to its surface.

- **China.**—This term is applied to porcelain of all classes, whether true porcelain of hard paste, *e.g.*, Chinese, Japanese, Meissen, Plymouth, Bristol, &c., or artificial porcelain of soft paste, *e.g.*, Sèvres (*pâte tendre*), Worcester, Chelsea, Bow, Lowestoft, &c.

- **China Clay.**—The whitest clay known. Obtained in England from Devon and Cornwall. Used for porcelain, and also for light-coloured earthenware.

- **China Stone.**—Known also as Cornish stone; used in conjunction with the china clay for porcelain, and employed for stoneware bodies.

- **Cream Ware.**—This term applies to all light-coloured English earthenware from about 1750 to the present day. It varied in character from the Queen's Ware of Josiah Wedgwood, 1760, to the "chalk body" used by Wilson at the end of the eighteenth century. Cream ware of later date when broken shows a pure white body—a puzzling fact to beginners in collecting.

- **Delft Ware.**—A generic term given to earthenware with tin enamelled surface. True Delft ware was made at Delft in Holland after 1600, but it was successfully imitated at Lambeth, Bristol, Liverpool, &c.

- **Earthenware.**—All ware may be termed earthenware which when in the *biscuit* state is too porous for domestic use but requires a coating of glaze. As a rule, earthenware is opaque, differing in this respect from porcelain, which is translucent.
- **Enamel Colours.**—The colours applied either in painted or printed decoration *over* the glaze.
- **Elers Ware.**—A generic term used in regard to unglazed red stoneware with applied decoration in the style of the Elers brothers.
- **Glaze.**—The glassy coating applied to earthenware and porcelain.
- *Lead-glaze.*—The earliest form used in England was known as *galena glaze*, when sulphide of lead was in powder form dusted on the ware. Later liquid lead glaze was used, into which the vessels were dipped.
- *Salt-glaze.*—Common salt was thrown into the kiln, and the resultant vapour deposited a fine layer of glaze on the ware.
- *Over-glaze.*—This term applies to painted or printed decoration done *after* the glaze has been applied to the object—*i.e.*, over the glaze.
- *Under-glaze.*—This applies to decoration, painted or printed, done *before* the glaze is applied to the object—*i.e.*, when completed the decoration is under the glaze.
- **Ironstone China.**—An earthenware for which Mason took out a patent in 1813. The body contains a large proportion of flint and slag of ironstone.
- **Jasper Ware.**—A fine hard stoneware used by Wedgwood, and imitated by his followers. It is unglazed.
- **Lustre Ware.**—Earthenware decorated by thin layers of copper, gold, or platinum (see Chapter XIII.).
- **Marbled Ware.**—Ware of a similar nature to agate ware, having its surface combed and grained to imitate various natural marbles or granites.
- **Marks.**—In earthenware these makers' names or initials or "trade marks" were usually impressed with a metal stamp. Obviously this must have been done when the ware was in plastic state; therefore it is impossible to add such marks after the ware is made, and when present on old ware they are a sign of undoubted genuineness. Of course a copy can be made bearing an impressed mark.

Painted or printed marks sometimes occur on earthenware usually of a later date. Such marks may be under-or over-glaze; the former are not likely to have been added after the piece has been made.

- **Modern.**—English earthenware may be termed "modern" when it is of a later date than 1850. Though, as is indicated in Chapter XIV., the modern renaissance in earthenware should be of especial interest to collectors.

- **Over-glaze.**—See *Glaze*.

- **Oven.**—The "oven," as the potter terms it, is a specially-built furnace in which the "saggers" containing the ware are placed during the firing (see Chapter I.).

- **Paste.**—This is another term for the "body" of the ware.

- **"Resist" Pattern.**—A term in silver lustre ware. For detailed description see Chapter XIII.

- **Sagger.**—A fire-clay box in which the earthenware is placed when being fired in the oven (see Illustration, Chapter I.).

- **Salt-glaze.**—See *Glaze*, and see Chapter VI.

- **Semi-china. Semi-porcelain.**—Terms applied to early nineteenth century earthenware having a very white or chalk body, and having the outward appearance of china or porcelain. Strongly imitative and false to the true qualities of earthenware. It is always opaque. Sometimes it is naïvely termed "opaque china."

- **Slip.**—A thick semi-solid fluid composed of clay and water.

- **Spurs. Spur mark.**—During the glazing of earthenware "spurs" or "stilts" of fire-clay are used to support the articles and keep them from touching each other. "Spur" or "cockspur" marks are found on the ware where it has rested on these supports (see Chapter IX., p. 298).

- **Stoneware.**—A variety of pottery distinct from earthenware, and more nearly approaching porcelain in its characteristics. Earthenware, as has been shown, needs a coating of glaze to protect its porous defects. Stoneware is a hard body needing no glaze. Glazed stoneware is frequently found, and the glaze employed is usually salt.

- **Throwing.**—The art of fashioning shapes on the potter's wheel (see Illustration, Chapter I.).

- **Transfer Printing.**—Printing employed as a decoration on ware by means of paper which had received a design from a copper-plate, and was transferred to the surface of the ware (see Chapter X.).

- **Under-glaze.**—See *Glaze*.

- **"Wedgwood."**—This has become a generic term for one or two classes of ware—*e.g.*, jasper and black basalt, which were made by most of the potters succeeding Josiah Wedgwood. The word has, in common with Boule and Chippendale become popularly and erroneously used.

- **Whieldon Ware.**—A generic term covering all classes of ware of a mottled, cloudy, or splashed character—*e.g.*, tortoiseshell plates, vases, figures, &c.

CHAPTER I
HOW TO COLLECT: A CHAPTER FOR BEGINNERS

Reasons for collecting—What is earthenware?—How earthenware is made—What to collect—Method of studying old earthenware—Forgeries—Table for use in identifying old English earthenware.

To attempt to advance reasons for collecting old English earthenware is seemingly to commence this volume with an apology on behalf of collectors. But there are so many persons ready to throw a stone at others who betray the possession of hobbies differing from their own, that it is necessary to state that the reasonable collection of old earthenware is based on sound premisses.

Similar reasons may be given for the collection of old English earthenware to those that may be advanced for the collection of old English china. Earthenware may be approached mainly from the æsthetic side and studied with a view to show the development of decorative art in this country and the foreign influences which have contributed to its evolution. The art of the old English potter is of especial interest to students of ceramic art, as many processes were invented in this country, and, in spite of periods of decadence, English earthenware has won for itself a considerable reputation on the Continent from a technical point of view.

It may be collected as an adjunct to old furniture by lovers of old furniture who are precisians in regard to harmony in schemes of decoration. They prefer to see china and earthenware of the same period as the furniture. A modern set of vases adorning a Georgian cabinet is like putting new wine into old bottles. So that concomitant with the love for old furniture, old pictures, and old prints is the accompanying regard for contemporary china and earthenware.

The "drum and trumpet history" relating the personal adventures of princes and nobles, and the pomp of courts, or the intrigues of favourites, sets no store on the apparent trivialities which mark the social and intellectual progress of a nation. But the scientific student of history cannot afford to ignore the detailed study of social conditions which are indicated by the china-shelf. The due appreciation of the development of costume, of furniture, and of the domestic arts gives life and colour to the written records of byegone days. A mug or a jug with an inscription may tell a story of popular party feeling as pointedly as a broadsheet or a political lampoon.

EXTERIOR OF WORKS, ETRURIA: THE MARL BANK.

By the courtesy of Messrs. Josiah Wedgwood & Sons.

The ordinary man sees in the collection of china and earthenware an interesting hobby. He reads of the prices remarkable specimens bring under the hammer, and he begins to think that his education has been partly neglected since he knows little or nothing concerning these art treasures, which seemingly are attractive to other men of culture and means.

"Collecting for profit" is a phrase that tickles the ears of many others. Undoubtedly there have been many who have entered the field of collecting and regarded their purchases solely as investments. It must be borne in mind that this class of collector is not to be despised, inasmuch as when he has mastered his subject (and as there is money in it he very speedily sets to work to do this) he is a very formidable rival.

It is absurd to imagine that an amateur, after having given especial study to a subject such as old earthenware, is not in a better position to enter the market as a buyer or a seller than he who comes with little or no training.

It is only reasonable that a man should take an intelligent interest in the evolution of the ware in everyday use. But it is to be feared that long rows of cases at the museum with specimens of earthenware behind glass doors must necessarily be a valley of dry bones to the spectator unless he bring the seeing eye and the understanding heart to quicken these dry bones into life.

Enough, perhaps, has been said as a prelude to this volume to show that various reasons may be advanced to account for the new spirit of collecting which has become so infectious. It is the hope of the writer that the following chapters, as an outline of the subject of collecting old English earthenware, may point the way to a better appreciation of what is really of value in this field, and will enable the collector in his search to sift the wheat from the chaff, and him who already possesses *lares et penates* of uncertain age to identify them.

What is Earthenware?—To know what is earthenware always puzzles the beginner. A rough-and-ready means of determining the difference between earthenware and porcelain is to apply the light test. Porcelain more nearly approaches glass and is translucent—that is, it clearly shows the shadow of the hand holding it when placed up to the light. But there are occasions when this test fails; for instance, a block of porcelain may, as in a heavy figure, be so thick as to render this experiment impossible. On the other hand, fine stoneware may be partly translucent in the thinner parts. In early nineteenth-century days a class of ware, such as that of Mason, is stamped "ironstone china" or "stone china." This is earthenware of a peculiar nature, having certain of the properties of porcelain. Similarly, at various times earthenware has been made which nearly approaches porcelain in its constituents. Dwight with his stoneware busts and Wedgwood in his jasper ware produced earthenware of such character as to come close to the border line dividing earthenware from porcelain.

The potter's art is divided into two sub-heads—porcelain and earthenware—which latter, for purposes of simplification, includes stoneware.

A CORNER OF OLD ETRURIA WORKS.

By the courtesy of Messrs. Josiah Wedgwood & Sons.

Earthenware is of soft body, is opaque—that is, it cannot be seen through. Its thinness or its thickness has nothing to do with its title. Stoneware is equally opaque, but it is as hard as porcelain. It may be as thick and heavy as a German beer-mug or a stone ginger-beer bottle, or it may be cream in colour, and thin as a Passover cake, as in salt-glazed Staffordshire ware, or white and heavy, as in later stone china. Porcelain may be hard or soft and possesses properties equally its own, but is outside the scope of this volume.

Practically earthenware is of such porous clay that when fired in the kiln it is unfit for use, as it is still too porous until it receives a coating of glaze. Unglazed stoneware, Egyptian black, and Wedgwood's jasper ware differ from earthenware in this respect, as they do not receive any glaze, since they are of dense enough body to be used in "biscuit" or unglazed state.

Its appearance. In colour earthenware may be brown or white in exterior, or brown or white in body as shown when broken. At its best its style to the beginner may not be suggestive of great difference between earthenware and porcelain. Similar figures were attempted in the one material as in the other. In France at Niderviller, at Marseilles, and at Scieux the potters deliberately set themselves to make objects in earthenware as delicate and fanciful as were produced in hard porcelain at Dresden or in soft porcelain at Vincennes. Clocks, vases, sweetmeat-boxes, and elaborate dinner services lavishly decorated in over-glaze enamels and gilded, emulated the best work of the porcelain factories. In Staffordshire the story has been repeated. So that form is no guide as to what kind of ware a piece may be. In weight earthenware is lighter than porcelain as a general rule, though variations in the body make this rule an elastic one. In stoneware, and ware approximating to this in character, the weight is heavier than porcelain. All ironstone ware is exceedingly heavy.

Reasons for its appearance. The earlier earthenware was brown in body. The Dutch potters in the seventeenth century covered their ware with an opaque white tin enamel to conceal the dark earthen body and to enable them to paint on its surface in imitation of Chinese porcelain. Stoneware, such as the jugs of early type known as Bellarmines, is of very vitreous earthenware fired so hard as to resist acids or the use of a file when applied to the surface. When glazed this class of ware has salt glaze. Dwight, of Fulham, introduced white, or nearly white, stoneware into England in his statuettes, which induced him to claim that he had discovered the secret of making porcelain. Cream ware followed later, and, perfected by Wedgwood, it was adopted as the standard earthenware of Staffordshire. It was the last note in earthenware till the beginning of the nineteenth century, when the Staffordshire potters invented an earthenware with a white body more nearly approaching porcelain in appearance. For fifty years experiments had been carried on, and this cream ware was whitened by a process called "blueing" by the use of cobalt to whiten the lead glaze. But the final invention was by Mason with his patent ironstone china, in which he produced a hard, white body.

How Earthenware is made.—A good deal of theory has found its way into print, but it is not every one, even among collectors, who has actually seen the various stages through which a lump of clay passes before it finally takes its place on the table as a teapot or a breakfast cup.

MILL FOR GRINDING RAW MATERIALS.

By the courtesy of Messrs. Josiah Wedgwood & Sons.

It has, therefore, been thought of interest to illustrate a few steps in the process of this transformation of clay into vessels of utility and beauty. By the kindness of Messrs. Josiah Wedgwood and Sons, of Etruria, this series of illustrations appears, and the subjects have been chosen with a view to showing those processes of the potter which are practically the same as in the days of the great Josiah.

The first illustration (p. 37) shows an *Exterior View of the Etruria Works*, with the Cornish stone and the ball clays from Dorset and Devon and the flints lying in heaps exposed to the sun and frost in order to "weather." This exposure is considered advantageous, as the longer the clay is in the open the better it will work when required for use.

The second illustration (p. 41) shows a *Corner of the old Etruria Works*. The structure is practically the same as in the early days, and the bottom windows on the right have remained unaltered. The farthest at the bottom corner on the right was the room of old Josiah.

The third illustration shows the *Mill for grinding raw materials*. The clays are put into this vat and crushed between two stones. There is nothing different now from the early days. The old oak beams tell their story. It is true that steam is now used, but that is all to make this process differ from that employed a century and a half ago—first when wind-power was used, as in flour mills, and later when a horse was substituted.

This grinding is done with water, and the mixture comes out a thick liquid. The mixing-tank is the next stage. These liquid constituents, such as ball clay, china clay, flint, &c., according to the formula of the pottery, are carefully admitted into the tank in correct proportions and thoroughly "blended" together. The body is now in its "slip" state, and is pressed and dried to make it more malleable when not required for casting. In its later stage, in more solid form, it is ready to be thrown on the potter's wheel.

The Potter's Wheel.—We illustrate (p. 40) the ingenious potter who is known as "The Thrower." It is he who, on a little revolving table between his knees pressed with his hands, magically transforms the lump of clay into beautiful shapes. Unfortunately, modern methods are eliminating the work of "the thrower," whose art dates back to the remotest past in the East when man first made clay into objects of beauty. We find the prophet Jeremiah saying, "Then I went down to the potter's house, and behold he wrought a work on the wheel. And the vessel that he made of clay was marred in the hands of the potter, so he made again another vessel as seemed good to the potter to make it."

Old Omar Khayyam brings a moral to bear on the potter and his wheel:

"Surely not in vain

My substance from the common Earth was ta'en

That He who subtly wrought me into shape

Should stamp me back to common Earth again."

And Shakespeare, not to miss a good simile, makes one of his characters say, "My thoughts are whirled like a potter's wheel."

THE THROWER.
Showing the Potter's Wheel.

By the courtesy of Messrs. Josiah Wedgwood & Sons.

The Pottery Kilns.—The next stage is to convert the vessel thrown in soft clay, and put aside to dry, into being as a piece of pottery. There are three ovens, termed the "biscuit," the "glost," and the "enamel." In the illustration (p. 53) it is seen how the vessels are put into "saggers," which are boxes of fire-clay piled upon one another. The doorway is bricked up and plastered, and gradually the furnace is heated. Practically this "oven" illustrated is typical of the "biscuit" or the "glost" oven, the difference being in the temperature applied, the latter being at a much lower temperature.

It may be interesting to mention that a quick oven is three days in firing and three days in cooling before the ware is removed. For ornamental and important specimens of a very special nature as long a period as a month may be taken to fire and half that time to cool. But of course this is only in exceptional circumstances.

It conjures up a picture of the awful anxiety of some of the great master potters at the critical moment when the doorway is pulled down and the contents of the oven are drawn. It is here where the triumph or the failure of the potter manifests itself.

When taken out of the first oven the ware is termed "biscuit." It is now ready for glazing. Of course, in such ware as jasper or unglazed stoneware, basalt, and similar kinds, the "biscuit" state is the final one, the object being completed.

The Dipping-house.—In the illustration (p. 57) it will be seen that the ware in its "biscuit" state is dipped in liquid glaze in a very deft manner, after which it proceeds to the "glost" oven to harden this glaze on its surface.

It is here that great care has to be exercised in keeping the pieces from coming in contact with each other; spurs and tripods are placed between each piece to obviate this. The "saggers" in which this newly-glazed ware is placed are dusted with material infusible at the lower heat to prevent the pieces adhering to these "saggers." In fact, as is readily seen, a fine specimen may be easily ruined at any stage.

In undecorated ware, as in the cream-ware examples illustrated (p. 225), this ends the process, and they are complete. But in ware that is to be decorated *over* the glaze there is yet another stage before they are finished.

It will be observed that we are alluding to *over-glaze* decoration. But ware may be painted before being glazed,—that is *under-glaze*. In order, however, not to confuse the beginner at the outset, this has been described in a later chapter (p. 326).

The Enamel Kiln.—After the decorations have been painted upon the glazed ware it has to be fired in the enamel kiln. A far lower heat than that of the "glost" oven is required; the flames do not pass inside the kiln, as in an oven, but are led in flues all round the kiln. We give an illustration (p. 61) of this for firing colours or gold *over* the glaze. As will be seen, the pieces are carefully protected from contact with each other, and at this last stage it is quite possible to undo all the patient labour previously employed and irretrievably ruin a piece.

In this hasty outline of the various processes of the potter much has been omitted; but, in the main, these illustrations should serve to kindle a more intelligent interest, even among collectors, in the earthenware and china which has passed through so many critical periods in its life-history.

THE OVEN.
Showing the "saggers" containing ware ready for firing.

By the courtesy of Messrs. Josiah Wedgwood & Sons.

What to Collect.—This is largely a question of personal predilection. In general the field of English earthenware may be divided into nine classes, and the collector who wishes to specialise will have his individual taste for one or more of these, according as its technical or artistic qualities appeal to him. This arrangement is mainly chronological, but obviously one class will overlap others in point of time. These classes are further summarised in detail in the table intended for use in identifying old earthenware given at the end of this chapter.

I. Early English pottery.

II. Delft ware.

III. Stoneware (including Staffordshire salt-glaze ware). Prior to the inventions of Josiah Wedgwood.

IV. Variegated ware—agate and clouded ware.

V. Cream ware—

- (1) Plain.
- (2) Decorated by painting.
- (3) Transfer-printed.

By far the largest variety of English earthenware, including domestic ware and figures. Made by all potters.

VI. Classic ware—the school of which Josiah Wedgwood is the founder.

VII. Figures (mainly Staffordshire).

VIII. Lustre ware.

IX. Opaque china }
Semi-porcelain } Nineteenth century.
Ironstone china }

Method of studying old Earthenware.—To those readers who peruse this volume without any definite idea of the standpoint of the collector it should not be left unsaid that the proper study and collection of old English earthenware require a considerable amount of reading and, what is of much greater importance, a very practical examination of some hundreds of specimens. It is this practical experience which alone can give the beginner the training he requires. It is a complex subject bristling with unexpected difficulties in regard to technical points and crowded with apparent contradictions. The bibliography given on pp. 23–25 will enable readers to pursue special studies in greater detail.

The next best thing to handling the actual specimens is to see them. It cannot here be impressed upon the beginner too strongly that it is absolutely necessary, in order to educate his eye, that the finest known examples in the particular classes should be frequently seen. The national museums, the Victoria and Albert and the British, in London, both contain splendid collections classified in a very thorough manner. In the provinces, the following museums among others contain fine collections, often of richer interest in special subjects than the aforementioned. For instance, the Public Museum at Liverpool contains the most representative collection of the various classes of Liverpool ware. The fine Art Gallery at Leeds is rich in typical examples of the finest productions in Leeds earthenware. At the Royal Scottish Museum, Edinburgh, and at the Science and Art Museum, Dublin, there are finely arranged collections of pottery. At the Castle Museum, Nottingham, at York, at Norwich, at Bath, at Bristol, at Swansea, at Cardiff, at the Weston Park Museum, Sheffield, at the Pitt-Rivers Museum, Farnham, North Dorset, at the Grosvenor Museum, Chester, at Maidstone, at Bury St. Edmunds, and at Saffron Walden, there are collections which can be studied.

THE DIPPING HOUSE.
Showing how the ware is glazed.

By the courtesy of Messrs. Josiah Wedgwood & Sons.

In the district of the Potteries itself the following museums have representative collections of special varieties of Staffordshire ware. At Hanley, at Tunstall, at Burslem, at Stoke-on-Trent, and at Etruria, with its Wedgwood Museum, there is material enough to be seen, so that it may be said that there is little need for the beginner to be starved for want of opportunities to see fine examples.

Hints as to Prices.—It is impossible in such a complex subject as old earthenware to lay down any hard and fast rules as to prices to be paid. Specimens vary very considerably in quality, and according to demand prices fluctuate as in other markets.

If the beginner will make a point of learning his subject and will keep in touch with a few dealers, he will find that they will readily assist him to identify his own specimens and systematically aid him in adding judiciously to his collection. A great deal of offensive nonsense has been written by fashionable lady journalists, declaiming against the professional dealer and crediting him with every conceivable trick under the sun. But the greatest and the wisest of collectors number a host of dealers as personal friends. A continuous stream of good things passes through the hands of the dealers who, by incessant handling and practical study, are able and willing to help the collector and to solve his difficulties.

Dealers' prices are in many cases surprisingly low considering the great trouble they have taken to acquire the pieces. It is far better to procure bargains in this manner, with one's personal knowledge supplemented by the friendly suggestions of one's favourite dealer, than to attempt to obtain through private sources "great bargains" from amateur dealers whose possessions would not, in many cases, bear the light of day in the open market.

Forgeries.—There are many "faked" pieces in existence, and there are many copies and a great quantity of productions of factories of to-day who reproduce their old patterns made a century or more ago. Some of this is made with intent to deceive, and much is merely a trade movement to supply a known want on the part of the public. But it is exactly here that the dealer who has a respect for his clients, and being a business man naturally does not wish to ruin his reputation, may be of inestimable value in advising the collector.

Mr. Solon, the eminent authority and a practical worker in artistic pottery, tells in his "Art of the Old English Potter" how, when he was searching for fine specimens to make his collection, he was deceived by some sham old slip ware bought at a high figure in a lonely cottage in a remote district. If the fabricator could lure so studious a collector into his net, it goes without saying that especial precautions should be taken by the beginner not to give large prices unless he has a guarantee or knows the seller's reputation.

Buyers of old delft ware should be careful in examining the decoration of their purchases. Plain ware, which is not so valuable and is comparatively common, is decorated in blue, or a coat-of-arms and a date added, giving a fictitious value to the piece. In fact, such genuine dated pieces are worth ten times the plain ones. Plain jars and jugs worth £2 or £3, with the fraudulently added word "Sack" and the initials "C. R." in blue, may tempt the unwary collector to give £20. It will thus be seen that this is the most dangerous of frauds, and difficult to detect unless the collector has handled many decorated pieces, for the delft itself is absolutely genuine.

THE ENAMEL KILN.
Showing the ware after being enamelled stacked ready for firing.
By the courtesy of Messrs. Josiah Wedgwood & Sons.

Similarly, plain pieces of genuine Staffordshire salt glaze are enamelled in colours in order to enhance the value, owing to the fashionable demand for coloured examples. As much as £50 has been paid by an unfortunate collector for a teapot quite worth this if genuine old colour work, but unhappily it was, although fine old salt glaze, quite recently coloured, evidently with fraudulent intentions.

Staffordshire figures that are modern tell their own story, or should do so, to the collector who has ever carefully examined the potting and the glaze of fine old examples. Nor is there much excuse for the blundering collector who cannot readily distinguish between the crude modern Toby jug with its blatant colouring, so smudgy and smeary with black stains to impart age, and its genuine prototype.

There are some fairly modelled Toby jugs, of modern origin, one in particular seated in a corner chair, with a salt-glaze surface. Another "fake" appeals to the lover of the Whieldon style, and has a mottled base and hat. But they are, as the expressive term goes, "hot from the oven." The "Vicar and Moses" was so well modelled by Ralph Wood that it shared the fate of George Morland's pictures which were copied by his contemporaries. Ralph Wood's "Vicar and Moses" was copied all through the late eighteenth and early nineteenth centuries, and to-day modern fabrications repeat the same model *ad nauseam*. Sham Voyez "Fair Hebe" jugs, made for foolish collectors, are frequently to be seen and avoided.

Leeds ware has engaged the attention of the imitator. Some of the ware is made in Germany and is unmarked. But other modern productions exist stamped "Leeds Pottery," and are imitations of the old Leeds patterns. There is a tobacco jar in pewter having a shield with the Leeds coat-of-arms, and raised medallions of a ship and of the patron saint of the woolcombers. This jar has been of late years copied in cream ware, and with its lid with twisted handle it has passed as "genuine old Leeds." But it is nothing of the sort.

In general, earthenware comes off better in regard to forged marks than porcelain. In the latter, of course, it is the easiest thing in the world to add the marks, especially when most of them were *painted*. But in earthenware the majority of marks were *impressed* in the ware and this cheats the "faker" of his quarry.

As a matter of fact, the mark should not lead the collector by the nose. Before seeing any mark a collector should begin to know his subject so well that the mark is an additional piece of information which serves to confirm his previous conclusions as to the specimen under examination. An unmarked example may show every evidence in modelling, in paste, in colour, and in glaze, of having been made by a certain potter at a particular date. The only confirmation lacking is the mark. It is here that marked ware becomes of paramount importance for purposes of comparison. And it is better to have a genuine marked piece in one's cabinet, from a business point of view, than a genuine piece equally fine that bears no signature or trade-mark. But this craving on the part of collectors for marks has led in the field of china to a disastrous state of things; marks of one potter have been added to the productions of another, and no fabricated Worcester china is worth its salt as a correct piece of forgery unless it bears the square mark or the crescent.

Happily, in earthenware the question of marks only affects the ware from Wedgwood's day onwards. The finest specimens of earthenware in the noted collections throughout the country, of Elers, and Dwight and Astbury, and Whieldon, and the whole salt-glaze school bear no mark, for the very simple reasons that the old potters had no "marks." But they signed their pieces all over, and the touch of these old masters is immediately intelligible to the trained eye of the collector.

How to identify old Earthenware.—The following Table roughly summarises the field under which English earthenware may be classified. It is the hope of the writer that possessors of earthenware which they are unable to identify will, by the help of this Table, be able to place their pieces under the sub-head to which they belong. The references given to the chapters dealing with the classes in detail are intended to point the way to a more extended examination of specimens.

A good general rule for beginners in attempting the proper identification is to commence by eliminating all the classes of ware to which the piece obviously cannot belong. Gradually the field becomes limited to one period, and finally it is narrowed to two or three factories. But it is only by practice that definite and accurate conclusions can be arrived at.

TABLE FOR USE IN IDENTIFYING OLD ENGLISH EARTHENWARE.

I.	**EARLY POTTERY.** Mediæval.	Early examples of green glazed pitchers and jugs of crude form, 13th, 14th, and 15th centuries.
	Domestic Vessels.	Costrels (*i.e.*, pilgrims' bottles), flasks with holes at shoulders for use of cord in carrying.

Ecclesiastical Tiles (15th-16th centuries).	Ecclesiastical tiles. Incised or impressed patterns, raised, inlaid, or with slip decoration. Floral, geometrical, heraldic ornamentation. Figures of men and of animals (see illustration, p. 85).
Slip Ware. (17th century.)	Loving-cups, or tygs, with several handles, posset pots with spouts. Lead-glazed, greenish in colour, with tones varying from purplish-brown to black (see illustration, p. 89).
Wrotham Ware (1612–1717).	Wrotham, in Kent, the seat of this ware of red body with slip stamped decorations or incised ornamentation. A great number of pieces of this class bear dates covering a century.
Toft Ware (Latter half of 17th century).	Dishes and posset pots of Staffordshire origin, Thomas Toft, 1660, Ralph Toft, Ralph Turnor, William Chatterly, Robert Shaw, William Tabor, John Wright, Joseph Nash, John Meir and other names appear on this ware, some being those of the potters, and others the owner's name.

(These varieties of Early Pottery are described in Chapter II.)

II. **DELFT WARE.**	*General Characteristics of Delft Ware.* In appearance it cannot be mistaken for any other ware. It has a brown or grey body, showing at crumbled

edges where the glaze is chipped off. The surface is white, and the painting upon it is more coarse than Dutch examples. English decorations are mostly painted under glaze in blue, yellow, or dull purple.

Lambeth.
Early examples, 1630.
Van Hamme, potter of Lambeth, 1671.

Dishes, plates, salt-cellars, puzzle-jugs, sack bottles, pharmacy jars and candlesticks are most ordinarily found. The enamelled surface of Lambeth delft has a pinkish tint. Plates with portraits and dates (1637–1702), Adam and Eve dishes, of large size, painted in blue with this and other Biblical subjects, "The Journey to Emmaus," "Jacob's Ladder," or with Oriental designs. Earlier specimens have a purplish or dull yellow lead glaze at back of dish.

Bristol.

Election and other plates dated 1740–1784. Painted tiles and plates with landscape subjects—Chinese figures, parrots. *Bianco sopra bianco* white enamel on greenish ground. Bowls with purple ground and white reserved panels with blue decoration.

Liverpool.

Early in 18th century, the principal trade of the city. Prior to 1762 all Liverpool delft, including tiles, was printed. Delft dishes decorated in Chinese style. Bowls with

	ships as decoration. Druggists' jars. Transfer-printed tiles by Sadler & Green, or later by Zachariah Barnes.
Wincanton.	Similar to Bristol in character. Up to the present very little is known of this factory. (See illustration, p. 127.)

(These varieties of Delft Ware are dealt with in detail in Chapter III.)

III.	**STONEWARE.** Early Bellarmine Jugs.	Mottled red-brown colour, mostly salt glazed, pitted surface like orange skin. Having dates and coats-of-arms in foreign examples; coarser style probably English.
	Fulham. John Dwight (1671–1703).	White busts and figures. Red, unglazed ware. Brown jugs and mugs. Marbling on vases and bases, and stamped ornaments in relief on teapots.
	Staffordshire. Elers Ware. John Philip Elers, David Elers (1690–1710).	A generic name for all unidentified red (unglazed) ware. Teapots, &c., with stamped ornament similar to Dwight. *Prunus* blossom and Chinese ornament, in relief. Turned on lathe and perfectly finished. Spouts plain, moulded by hand.
	John Astbury (died 1743).	Red, buff, orange, and chocolate body. Similar ware to Elers, with the ornaments

	in relief in white pipe-clay. Made early salt-glaze crouch ware.
Thomas Astbury (from 1725).	Followed same style. Little to distinguish his work from that of his father. *Astbury* is a generic term for all ware of this nature, with white stamped ornaments in relief. Many Staffordshire potters made this type of ware in latter half of eighteenth century, and it was imitated at Liverpool.
Nottingham. Early 18th century	As early as Dwight's day Morley made stoneware mugs, and Nottingham ware holds a high place. The jugs are sometimes with decorative pierced work, showing an inner shell which holds the liquid. The glaze is decidedly lustrous in appearance, and the colour of the body is a warm reddish brown. Discontinued at end of 18th century. *Bear Jugs* were a feature of this factory, and cruder examples were made at Chesterfield and Brampton.

(These varieties are described in detail in Chapter IV.)

Staffordshire Salt Glaze Astbury and Whieldon were the pioneers of this finer stoneware. Most of the	Finely potted thin stoneware, surface like skin of orange, almost as translucent as porcelain.

Staffordshire potters from 1725–1780 made salt-glaze ware. But this ware was supplanted by Wedgwood's cream ware, which seized the market in the last quarter of the 18th century.

- 1. Plain white or undecorated with raised stamped ornament.
- 2. Plain white body with incised ornament filled in with blue.
- 3. Enamelled in colours on a white body.
- 4. Body colour blue (rare examples by William Littler), enamelled decorations in black, white, or gold.
- 5. Pierced ware with decorations in colour, or undecorated.
- 6. Ware decorated by transfer printing.
- 7. Ware with raised ornament, touched with colour.

Some of this salt-glaze ware is in colour a slate grey. The sharpest cut designs and the highest type of the undecorated ware belong to the period from 1725–1740. The enamelling in colours was at its best from 1745–1760. Salt-glaze ware, in imitation of the Staffordshire potters, was also made at Swansea and at Liverpool.

(These varieties are described in detail in Chapter VI.)

Fulham.
(Eighteenth century.)

Fulham has been the seat of the manufacture of stoneware since the days of Dwight.

Early 18th century.

Blue and grey stoneware jugs and mugs, with initials of Queen Anne or those of George I., often dated.

Late 18th century.

The following are typical—brown stoneware jugs and mugs with bacchanalian subjects, or sporting scenes, in relief, inkstands, brandy flasks of grotesque shape.

In 19th century days "Doulton & Watts, Lambeth Pottery," is impressed on similar examples, and in middle 19th century days, under the guidance of Sir Henry Doulton, a revival of artistic stoneware took place, which traditions Messrs. Doulton carry on at the present day.

IV. **VARIEGATED WARE.**
Usually known under the generic term of *Whieldon ware*.

Marbled or agate wares (1740–1756), Dwight (of Fulham), John Astbury. The earlier surface marbling or combing supplanted by "solid agate" ware—a blending of layers of different coloured clays. Early tortoiseshell plates made by Whieldon. Tortoiseshell and mottled ware also made by Philip Christian at Liverpool, at Leeds, and at Castleford. *Wedgwood.*—Later developments of this ware—

vases and important classic pieces in imitation of coloured marbles.

The imitators of Wedgwood.— Palmer, Neale, and others made this marbled ware. Neale employed with great success sprinkled marbling, touched with gold, on a cream body. Both Wedgwood and his successors made "solid agate" and also surface-decorated ware of cream body.

(This ware is described in Chapter V. (Whieldon), and in Chapters VII. and VIII. in regard to Wedgwood and later developments.)

V. CREAM WARE. By far the largest variety of English earthenware. Made by all potters. The standard type of all subsequent domestic ware.	*Experimental Stage.*—Astbury (1725), Whieldon (from 1740), Warburton (Hot Lane), Baddeleys (Shelton). *Queen's Ware* perfected by Wedgwood (1765). Wedgwood, Turner, Warburton, (Leeds) Messrs. Hartley, Greens & Co., Liverpool, Swansea, Derby. *In colour creamy or yellowish white. In weight light.*
Plain or undecorated.	Many of Wedgwood's finest cream ware pieces are undecorated, and Leeds, at first largely imitative, developed a fine quality in design and potting, especially in designs after silversmiths' models.
Decorated by painting.	At first painting was sparely used. The style of enamelling

	used on salt-glaze ware was modified to suit the new cream ware. Later the colours began to emulate those of porcelain. Spode, in particular, copied the latter in earthenware, and cream ware became richly painted and gilded.
Transfer-printed.	As the invention of transfer-printing and the perfection of cream ware by Wedgwood were contemporaneous, the Liverpool printers decorated all the early cream ware. But cream ware was subsequently made as well as printed at Liverpool, and printed as well as made in Staffordshire and elsewhere.
Early Cream Ware.	*Wedgwood.* Enormous variety of domestic ware, *plain or undecorated*, as in perforated or basket patterns, fruit dishes, &c., *painted* in simple border designs, and *transfer-printed* in red, black, or puce, at Liverpool, for Wedgwood. Warburton, William Adams, John Turner, Spode, and many others made similar cream ware. *Leeds.*—Great variety of dishes, fruit baskets, centre-pieces, &c., made of undecorated cream ware. In addition painted and transfer printed decorations were also employed.

Transfer-printing in blue.
In imitation of Chinese styles, and in competition with the porcelain of Worcester, Bow, Plymouth, &c.

Liverpool made cream ware punch bowls finely decorated in blue.
Caughley produced for a few years earthenware of cream body decorated, in characteristic style, by Thomas Turner, who introduced the willow pattern in 1780, which appears together with similar Chinese subjects in his early Salopian *porcelain*.

Staffordshire.
(See Chapter X.)

John Turner (of Lane End) first introduced under-glaze blue into Staffordshire. Josiah Spode introduced "willow pattern" into Staffordshire, 1784. William Adams (of Greengates), 1787, fine under-glaze blue. Thomas Minton, 1793, fine under-glaze blue. Apprenticed to Thomas Turner (of Caughley).
Adams, Warburton, Spode, and other Staffordshire potters engaged largely in this deep blue printed ware.
Swansea had a similar cream ware, which had painted designs or blue-printed in imitation of Chinese style, with pagodas, &c. (See illustration, p. 405.)

VI. CLASSIC WARE.
Josiah Wedgwood

(born, 1730; died, 1795).

Thomas Bentley, in

Wedgwood. *Red ware* in imitation of Elers ware, chocolate ware with black ornamentation in relief. *White fine stoneware* used as plinths of marble ware and agate vases;

partnership with Wedgwood (1768–1780).

this was the experimental stage of Wedgwood's celebrated *jasper* ware. *Black basalt*, or Egyptian ware, fine unglazed stoneware, sometimes used for tea services, but mainly for busts, medallions, and vases. *Jasper ware.* Wedgwood's crowning invention. A fine, unglazed stoneware, white throughout. Produced either "solid" or "jasper dip," in blue (various tones), sage green, olive green, lilac, pink, yellow, and black. Used in classic vases, and on cameos, plaques, &c., with a ground of one of these colours and relief ornament in white. (See <u>Chapter VII</u>.)

William Adams (or Tunstall), pupil of Wedgwood (1787–1805).
Benjamin Adams (1805–1820).
John Turner (of Lane End) (1762–1786).
{ H. Palmer
{ (of Hanley),
{ from 1769.
{ Neale (1776–1778)
{ R. Wilson (1778)
{ Neale & Co.
{(1778–1787).
Jacob Warburton (of Cobridge) (1786–1826).

Contemporaries of Wedgwood. Adams, Turner, Palmer, Neale and Mayer, all made ware of a similar nature to above; all of fine quality. John Turner's "jasper" was really a semi-porcelain. Other potters whose stoneware in jugs and Pottery vases, &c., carried on the traditions of continued by sons. Wedgwood (though in the second flight), were Birch, Keeling, Clews, Hollins, Steel, Myatt, and many others, whose names are found impressed on ware, betraying the influence of Wedgwood. (See <u>Chapter VIII</u>. **for detailed list.**)

The *Castleford Pottery*, near

Leeds (1790–1820), David Dunderdale (D. D. & Co.) made black basalt ware in similar style.
(**See Chapter IX. for details.**)

At *Swansea* (1790–1817) basalt figures of fine style were made. Etruscan Ware (Dillwyn & Co.), 1845.
(**See Chapter XII. for marks.**)

VII.   FIGURES.
(Mainly Staffordshire.)

The body of Staffordshire figures by Ralph Wood, Neale and Palmer, Walton, Enoch Wood, Salt, and other potters, is of cream ware.

Leeds figures are similar, and are of the same body as the dessert centre-pieces and other cream ware.

Most of the Staffordshire figures are unmarked, but they can be identified as belonging to one of the following schools, by comparison with similar marked examples.

Salt-glazed Figures.

A class by themselves. Mainly small in size, and no marked specimen is known. Bears, cats, birds, and miniature figures of men, chief designs, and the kneeling camel modelled as teapot.

Whieldon School.
(1740–1780.)

Artistic blending of colourings and glazings. Animals, birds, sometimes classic figures, *e.g.*, Diana, Venus, and Madonna and Child. Miniature musicians, and satyr head moulded in form of cup. Early form of Toby jug. (See illustration, p. 179.)

Ralph Wood School.
Ralph Wood (died 1772).
Ralph Wood, jun. (born, 1748; died, 1795).

This represents the high-water mark of Staffordshire figures. *Vicar and Moses* group, *Toby Jug, St. George and Dragon, Haymakers, Charity, Neptune, Summer, Old Age*, &c., all remarkable for fine modelling and delicate colouring.

Wedgwood School.
Josiah Wedgwood.
{ Neale and Palmer.
{ Wilson.
{ Neale & Co.
Voyez, as a modeller, employed at Etruria, and by Neale and Palmer.
Lakin and Poole.

Many large figures, such as *Ceres, Diana, Juno, Prudence, Fortitude, Charity, Venus and Cupid*, &c., in cream ware delicately coloured. Other subjects of less classic taste were produced at Etruria, e.g., *Sailor with Cutlass, Girl playing Mandoline, Sailor's Farewell* and *Return* (a pair), *The Lost Piece* (after the Ralph Wood model), and *Elijah and the Widow*, a popular scriptural subject (a pair). *Fair Hebe* group modelled as a jug.

Wood and Caldwell School.
Enoch Wood (1783–1840).
Wood and Caldwell (1790–1818).
Enoch Wood and Sons (1818–1866).

Eloquence (or *St. Paul preaching at Athens*), *Descent from the Cross*, and other fine pieces display the powers of Enoch Wood at his best as a fine modeller. Other figures, some marked, are *St. Sebastian, Britannia,* Quin as *Falstaff, Antony* and *Cleopatra*, reclining figures (pair), *Fire, Earth, Air, Water* (set of four), *Diana* (similar to Wedgwood); group, *The Tithe Pig* (parson, farmer, and his wife and baby and pigs), with tree and foliage as background; *Leda and Swan*, *Jolly Traveller* (man, dog, and donkey), *Hurdy-Gurdy Player*, *Sportsman and Dog*, *Old Age* (pair), *Lovers* on garden bench, tree background, *Tailor and his Wife*, riding on goats (after the Dresden model). Busts were also a noteworthy production of this School. *Wesley*, *Whitfield*, *Wellington*, *Emperor of Russia*, *Napoleon*, *Miss Lydia Foote*, and several marked silver lustre busts and figures, e.g., *Mater Dolorosa*, *Boys Reading*, &c. The *Vicar and Moses* group and other earlier models were duplicated by this school, and many *Toby Jugs* were produced of bright colouring.

Walton School.
John Walton (of Burslem) (1790–1839).

Continuing the traditions of the Wood School, Walton and others produced a great number of *Toby Jugs*, following the Ralph Wood model, but growing more debased in form and colouring. *Girl* with lamb, *Boy* with dog, and simple figures largely made for popular markets.

Ralph Salt School.
Ralph Salt (of Hanley) (1812–1840).

Great fondness shown for village groups, with figures with tree background (imitation of Chelsea style). In character the work of this School differs little from that of Walton.

(See Chapter XI. for detailed description.)

Leeds School.
(1760–1825.)

Some of the Leeds figures are marked, *e.g.*, *Venus*, delicately coloured, slight oil gilding. Busts were made such as *Wesley*, and *Rhytons*, or drinking cups, in form of fox's head. Rustic figures of *Children*, and other miscellaneous subjects. *Lion* couchant, *Snuff bottle* in shape of Lady's head.

Liverpool School.
Herculaneum (1794–1841.)

Largely imitative of Staffordshire figures. Some excellent busts and figures were produced. Busts of *Wesley*, *Admiral Duncan*, and Mask Cup moulded with portrait of *Admiral Rodney*. *Toby Jug*, man standing upright holding jug of ale. *Lady* with bulldog at her feet.

Salopian.
Thomas Turner (of Caughley), about 1774.

Earthenware figures of fine modelling are attached to Caughley, but are unmarked. *Prudence* and *Fortitude* (large size), *Antony* and *Cleopatra* (recumbent), *Ceres* and *Apollo*, and others.
A figure of *Jacobin Pigeon* sitting

on nest in shape of sauceboat has the impressed mark **S**.

Swansea.

Cows and other small figures were typical of Swansea, but a recumbent figure of *Antony* is marked "G. Bentley, Swansea, 22 May, 1791."

Sunderland School.

Figures of *Seasons*, set of four female figures marked "Dixon, Austin & Co." *Shepherds* and *Shepherdesses* and *Bull Baiting* groups were also made here. The potting and colouring are crude, and the figures are of no artistic interest.

VIII. LUSTRE WARE.

Early Copper Lustre. Richard Frank at Brislington, near Bristol, crudely decorated in simple ornament.
Gold Lustre. Gold-purple or pink in colour. Wedgwood used this lustre in mottled and veined ware with rich effect. *As an adjunct to other decoration* this lustre has been widely used, crudely as at Sunderland, and with fine effect by Spode and other Staffordshire potters. Swansea employed it with great artistic skill.
Silver Lustre. *Plain.* Late 18th century. Thomas Wedgwood, E. Mayer, Spode, and others in imitation of silver designs. *Decorated.* 1. Silver lustre decorations painted on other coloured grounds in combination with subjects in

colours, birds, foliage, &c.
2. Silver lustre as a background with white, blue, or canary-coloured design. This unlustred ground, used as a pattern, is known as the "resist" style, and some of the most artistic effects are found in this, and in combination with painting in colours.
Copper Lustre. *Plain.* Early 19th century. Early and best style thin and well potted. *Decorated.* Red or blue or green in embossed floral design in combination with copper lustre frequently found.

(For details of makers and marks see Chapter XIII.)

IX. NINETEENTH CENTURY DEVELOPMENTS.

Spode's Felspar China, 1805.
Spode's Stone China.
Haynes' Opaque China (Swansea), invented end of 18th century.
Mason's Patent Ironstone China, 1813
Riley's Semi-China.
Minton's Stone China.
Meigh's Stone China.

Early Experiments.
Wedgwood's semi-porcelain, used at first for the plinths of his variegated vases. His *Pearl Ware.*

Nineteenth Century.
Josiah Spode the Second in 1805 introduced an opaque porcelain of ironstone body, which he termed *Felspar China, Stone China,* and on some of his marks, *New Fayence.* Spode's new ware received rich decorations in colour, in imitation of Derby and other porcelains.
Haynes, of the Cambrian Pottery, Swansea, invented a similar opaque china at the end of the 18th century.
At the Cambrian Pottery in

this new hard white earthenware, floral painting by trained artists was done in excellent style on enamelled grounds of chocolate.

Mason, with an earlier softer body, had followed the Japanese colours in his jugs, but when Charles James Mason, in 1813, patented his ironstone china, the jugs took a new form, becoming octagonal, and their corners were not easily broken as in the chalkier body.

Long dinner services of a great number of pieces were made in this ironstone china richly decorated.

Other Staffordshire makers made stone china, including Minton, Meigh, Riley, Clementson, Ridgway, Adams, Davenport, and many others. By the time the middle of the century had been reached, English earthenware had cast off its own characteristics and become what so many people to-day believe it to be—a poor imitation of porcelain.

(For details and marks see Chapter XIV.)

CHAPTER II
EARLY WARE

Mediæval Tiles (thirteenth to sixteenth centuries)—Slip Ware—Wrotham (Kent) (1656–1703)—Staffordshire Makers (1660–1700)—Prices of Early Ware.

As will be seen from the table at the end of the preceding chapter, the main body of English earthenware to which collectors can give their attention, belongs chiefly to the eighteenth and early nineteenth centuries. The beginnings of pottery and the first steps towards perfection in art are always interesting, but in the realm of English pottery the beginner had better push forward as the subject is a very complex one, and the general collector is perforce obliged to confine attention to the later periods.

It will therefore suffice if a hasty survey be made of the chief earthenware prior to the eighteenth century.

Mediæval Tiles.—From the thirteenth century to the dissolution of the monasteries the ecclesiastical tiles used in England were of a particularly noticeable character. The tiles vary in size, the earlier ones, as at Chertsey Abbey, were not more than three or four inches square. The earlier the tile, as a rule, the smaller is its area. The tiles were ornamented in various ways. They had incised, raised, inlaid, or painted patterns. The incised and relief tiles are the most uncommon, probably being the earlier. The designs are very numerous, and vary in character in the different abbeys at which they originated. Specimens have been found at Great Malvern, Denny Abbey in Norfolk, Castle Acre Priory, Jervaulx Abbey, Lewes Priory, St. Alban's Abbey, and at Chertsey Abbey, which latter had "one of the finest, if not the finest, inlaid tile pavement in existence" (Hobson). The Chertsey tiles are of different shapes, sometimes being round or half-circular to meet the exigencies of the design, and in general they are very quaint and original in their conception. The British Museum has some fine examples of these Chertsey tiles in composite pictures made up of many tiles.

The designs found on mediæval tiles consist of the figures of animals, mythical and heraldic, of birds, of human heads and grotesques, as well as conventional, floral, and geometric patterns. They are highly artistic and of great technical excellence.

It is generally believed that the monks made these tiles themselves in the great religious houses, and possibly some of them may have had foreign inspiration or have been made here by foreigners. But as the tiles at Malvern and at Chertsey are finer than any found on the Continent it opens up a field for conjecture. Mr. Solon says, "I have often thought that considering the

French pavements of the earliest periods have mostly been found in the provinces then under English domination, it would be worth while inquiring whether the art of tile-making had not been imported from England—a point which has never yet been sifted."

MEDIÆVAL TILES.
TILE FROM CHAPTER HOUSE, WESTMINSTER.
Probably of the reign of Henry III. (Thirteenth century).

TILE FROM VERULAM ABBEY.
Bearing arms and initials of Sir Nicholas Bacon (1510–1579).

(*By the courtesy of Mr. F. W. Phillips, Hitchin.*)

TILE FROM MALVERN ABBEY.
(English, fifteenth century.)

TILE FROM WHITMORE PARK, NEAR COVENTRY.
(Early fourteenth century.)

So here, then, is a subject ready to hand for the collector willing to specialise in a branch of ceramic study and collecting not greatly inquired into, and the way has already been pointed out by experts. There is every reason why these ecclesiastical tiles should be studied with as much assiduity as are the Bristol delft painted tiles and those of Liverpool.

Slip Ware.—This ware is peculiarly English and owes little or nothing to any foreign influences, as no ware like it has ever been made on the Continent. White or light-coloured clay was used in the form of "slip," that is, a mixture of water and clay of such consistency as to be dropped in fanciful pattern upon the darker body of the ware much in the same manner as the confectioner ornaments his wedding-cakes with sugar. Candlesticks, cups, tygs (drinking vessels having several handles for use in passing round), posset-pots, jugs, besides the large ornamental dated dishes by Toft and others were all made of this slip-decorated ware.

Wrotham, in Kent, claims superiority in the manufacture of this ware, of which many pieces exist. The earliest Wrotham specimen is dated 1656 (Maidstone Museum). There are other dated pieces, one as early as 1621, of red clay with more elaborate slip decoration than is found in Staffordshire and elsewhere, and in some cases with fine incised decoration cut through the white dip and exposing the red body beneath. But considerable doubt exists as to whether to ascribe some of this slip ware to Kent or to Staffordshire. It is probable that it was made at many other places, certainly in Derbyshire, in Wales, and in London. As some undoubted Wrotham pieces betray a slightly advanced type of decoration although prior in date to other pieces made elsewhere, it has been fairly conjectured that the style originated in Kent, and was brought thither by some foreign refugees from the Continent. But as it became practised more generally in England it assumed a national character entirely its own, and took to itself a quaint humour racy of the soil.

TOFT DISH, DATED 1671.
(*In the Grosvenor Museum, Chester.*)

By permission of the Proprietors of the "Connoisseur."

POSSET POT, STAFFORDSHIRE, DATED 1685.
Decorated in slip ware, yellow ground, with brown ornament.
Inscribed "William Simpson. His cup."

(*In the collection of Dr. W. L. Glaisher, Cambridge.*)

Toft Ware.—The names of Ralph Toft and Thomas Toft appearing on certain large dishes, usually about eighteen inches in diameter, decorated in slip in a somewhat crude manner, have given the name to this class of ware, which at best is peasant pottery. The Tofts had their works near Shelton in Staffordshire. Similar dishes were made at Derby and at Tickenhall. The following names occur on examples in the National and other collections with dates, Ralph Toft, Thomas Toft, 1671; Robert Shaw, 1692; William Chaterly, 1696; Ralph Turnor, 1681; William Talor, 1700; John Wright, 1707; initials S. M., 1726, *Dublin Museum* (possibly Samuel Mayer, of Derby); John Wenter, 1686; I. W., 1706. The manufacture of this slip ware continued, in more or less spasmodic manner, throughout the eighteenth century. Pots and jugs had illiterate inscriptions on them in halting verse, or pious mottoes.

Toft ware, that is, the large dish form, apparently was made solely for ornament. There is a remarkable Toft dish in the Grosvenor Museum at Chester, having the inscription in Toft's peculiar orthography, "Filep Heues, Elesabeth Heues" (Philip and Elizabeth Hughes), signed Thomas Toft and dated 1671. This is evidently a marriage plate. There is the royal arms above, a favourite design in Toft ware, probably copied from some of the more elaborate foreign Bellarmine jugs. The slip potters had a fondness too for royal portraiture which ended lamentably in becoming dreadful caricatures of the subject. As many as nine crowned heads are found on one dish by Ralph Toft, signed "Ralalph To." These have as much art as the Stuart stump-work pictures in needlework, which were contemporary with them, in which kings and queens were represented in no more pleasing manner than on a pack of cards. In speaking of Toft's portrait dishes in general, and of the Grosvenor Museum example in particular, Mr. Frank Freeth, no mean connoisseur, says, "It must not be forgotten that these dishes were ornamental, and intended to occupy a conspicuous place in the homes of loyal citizens, just as oleographs of the King and Queen, that one often sees in country cottages, are made for the purpose in the present day. The same idea has remained; but the form of its expression has changed."

Looking at slip ware as a whole, one must not be too critical in regard to its somewhat inartistic appearance. It certainly has a charm about it which cannot be denied. It is native to the soil, and this peasant industry (if one can appropriately term it such), is chiefly to be regarded from the standpoint of what might have been if it had been allowed to develop on natural and untrammelled lines. But it was pressed on the one side by stoneware, such as the Bellarmine jugs and mugs imported from Germany, and it finally succumbed to foreign delft, which was largely used here prior to the Englishman's determined attempt, at Lambeth, at Bristol, and at Liverpool (where it was the staple industry for some time) to make his own wares.

It is the same story with the fine stoneware, the salt glaze of Staffordshire, which was a magnificent outburst of English art of the highest order, which

fell before the cheapness of Wedgwood's and other cream ware, after a heroic struggle in its enamelled stage with the coloured ware of the new English china factories. These precedents might be continued further up to the present day, when German, Austrian, and Japanese competition have driven English potters into the position of attempting to hold their own against foreign art.

It is the opinion of the present writer that the coats-of-arms on the Toft dishes were a deliberate attempt to copy those frequently found on the belly of the Rhenish stoneware jugs. From the days of Elizabeth coats-of-arms and heraldic devices were a feature in these jugs used in this country. Among those at the British and the Victoria and Albert Museums, and in the fine collection at the Guildhall, the use of crests is seen to be a striking characteristic (see illustration, p. 135). As a conclusive proof that the maker of earthenware had his eye on these stoneware models, we give as an illustration a jug in *earthenware* (not stoneware) of Bellarmine form made in England, undoubtedly by an English potter. The arms on it are those of the

Earl of Dorset, not improbably those of the sixth Earl, Charles Sackville, who lived from 1637 to 1706, and was the author of the well-known song, running—

"To all you ladies now on land

We men at sea indite;

But first would have you understand

How hard it is to write"—

written in 1665, when he attended the Duke of York as a volunteer in the Dutch war, and this song he composed when with the fleet on the eve of battle.

EARTHENWARE JUG.
Copy of Rhenish Bellarmine or Greybeard form.
With the arms of the Earl of Dorset.
(Late seventeenth century.)
(*At the British Museum.*)

There is a sort of heraldic touch about some of these Staffordshire dishes of the Toft class. The same idea seems to have possessed the workers of the Stuart stump-pictures in needlework, which were contemporary with these dishes. Coins and medals and Stuart marriage-badges are evidently the source from which Toft and his school on the one hand, and the gentle needlewoman on the other, derived their inspiration in design. Various animals and birds are used symbolically with great freedom. The caterpillar and butterfly nearly always accompany needlework portraits of Charles I., and the unicorn was the device of his father James I. There seems some similarity to this idea in the use of the *Mermaid* in the dish by Thomas Toft. Another dish of his, entitled "The Pelican in her Piety," depicts that bird with her young, the idea being that the pelican used to feed her brood with her own blood. The Latins called filial love *piety*, hence Virgil's hero is always termed *pius Aeneas*. "Ralph Simpson" is another name found on this pelican dish.

We give an illustration of a fine posset-pot of Staffordshire origin, dated 1685, in slip ware, with yellow ground and conventional ornament in brown, with dotted work. It is inscribed, "William Simpson, His Cup." It has three handles and three loops, and is quite a typical piece of this class of ware. It recently sold for fifty-five pounds (p. 89).

Metropolitan Slip Ware.—There is a slight distinction between pieces made in London and found during excavations, and those discovered elsewhere. The slip decoration is lightly done and there is a tendency to incised decoration of conventional floral design. One noticeable feature in this type of ware is its inscriptions, written in doggerel, always of a pious nature. "When this you see, Remember me,—Obeay God's word"; or "Drink faire, Don't sware"; or "Be not hyminded but feare God, 1638." This class of ware savours strongly of the Puritan influence, and it is evident that the potters who made these pieces were of the "Praise God Barebones" order of visionary, not uncommon at a time when books with titles like the following appeared, "Some fine Baskets baked in the Oven of Charity, carefully conserved for the Chickens of the Church, the Sparrows of the Spirit, and the sweet Swallows of Salvation."

It seems absurd in regarding the productions of this school of English slip workers, from middle Stuart days down to the early years of the eighteenth century, to consider that Vandyck had painted his galleries of beauties; that Hollar, with his etching needle, had drawn a long procession of figures in costume, thousands of etchings which surely must have caught the eye of some Toft or some Simpson. There was Grinling Gibbons working his artistic profusion in wreaths of flowers and fruit carved in wood, and there were the treasures of the silversmith, to say nothing of the sumptuous furniture that was beginning to make its way in England. But these slip ware dishes seem to stand somewhat like the Jacobean chairs made in Yorkshire and Derbyshire, of the same date, apparently unaffected by any of the æsthetic movements of the period. Simply and naturally, and, be it said, crudely representing the artistic aspirations of the ordinary craftsman when he was left to himself, it is *naïve*, standing as it does for English native art at a time when Bernard Palissy, the French potter, had been dead a hundred years.

EARLY WARE PRICES.

	£	s.	d.

WROTHAM WARE.

	£	s.	d.
Loving cup, four handled, fine specimen, decorated in slip; initials W.L.R. and H.I.; dated 1656. Sotheby, January, 1906	56	0	0
Wine jug, brown with yellow slip, inscribed Samuel Hugheson and dated 1618; 8 in. high. Sotheby, June, 1906	10	0	0
Cradle, with inscription, "Mary Overton, Her cradle, 1729." Puttick and Simpson, May, 1908	17	0	0

TOFT WARE.

	£	s.	d.
Plate (17 in. diameter), with figure of soldier, in relief, with sword in each hand; trellis border; dated 1677. Warner, Leicester, March, 1906	86	0	0

SLIP WARE.

	£	s.	d.
Brown posset-pot, two handled with lid, inscribed "William and Mary Goldsmith," date incised "June ye 7th, 1697"; 9 in. high. Bond, Ipswich, April, 1906	15	0	0
Dish, bearing royal arms of England, inscribed "G. R. 1748"; 18½ in. diameter. Sotheby, June, 1906	21	0	0
Posset-pot, three handled, inscribed "Robert Shaw." Sotheby, June, 1906	35	0	0
Posset-pot, larger, inscribed "God save the Queen 1711." Sotheby, June, 1906	26	0	0
Posset-pot, two handled, inscribed "Iohn Taylor, 1690." Sotheby, November, 1907	12	15	0
Dish, slip decorated and salt glazed, inscribed on rim, "Joseph Mosson, the Best is not too good for You 1727." Sotheby, May, 1908	13	10	0

Dish, trellis pattern, on rim in brown and yellow slip, portraits of Charles II. and Catherine of Braganza; inscribed with maker's name "George Taylor"; 17½ in. diameter. Sotheby, May, 1908	53	0	0
Posset-pot, yellow ground, conventional ornament in brown, with dotted work, inscribed "William Simpson, His Cup." Dated 1685. Sotheby, December, 1908 (see illustration, [p. 89](#))	55	0	0

CHAPTER III
ENGLISH DELFT

What is Delft?—Its foreign origin—Introduction into England—Lambeth Delft—Bristol Delft—Liverpool Delft—Delft Tiles printed at Liverpool by Sadler and Green—Wincanton (Somerset)—Prices of English Delft

Delft, of all earthenware, is, so to speak, the most earthen, and presents an object lesson to the student. It accurately conforms to the technical definition as to what constitutes the difference between earthenware and porcelain. It consists of a porous body (in the case of Dutch delft very porous, as we shall see later), covered by a thick coating of white, opaque enamel.

The porous nature of its body makes it light in weight, and the tin enamel which covers the brown body enables the potter to paint upon this white surface designs, usually in blue. This decoration is over the enamel, if it were under this opaque enamel, that is, on the brown underneath body of the ware, the coating of this white enamel would obliterate the designs. After a piece has been fired to the biscuit state and dipped in white enamel and painted upon when dry, it is, to preserve the painting, fired a second time, when it receives a thin surface of transparent lead glaze.

Its Foreign Origin.—Its name is derived from the town of Delft in Holland. It was about the year 1602 that Dutch potters invented this class of ware in their attempts, in common with all the other European potters, to produce some ware as decorative as the porcelain which had been brought to Europe long before by the Portuguese traders, and now was being largely imported by the East India Dutch merchants.

This first employment of a white enamel on a brown earthenware was clearly due to the very natural desire on the part of the potter to procure some surface upon which his decorations in colour would show well in contrast. All primitive potters have passed through several stages of evolution. Brown ware was at first plain, then it received scratched or incised decoration. Searching for greater contrast the potter applied his ornament in relief in white, as in slip ware, or he added coloured glazes, as in the Tudor miniature jugs.

But it seems that sooner or later the light background for the painted decoration must have become an ideal to strive for. It is, in effect, the same necessity which induces the signboard painter to cover his brown panel with a white background prior to painting in letters of red or blue some attractive announcement. But with the models of the Chinese potter now constantly before him the Dutch potter commenced at once to imitate them.

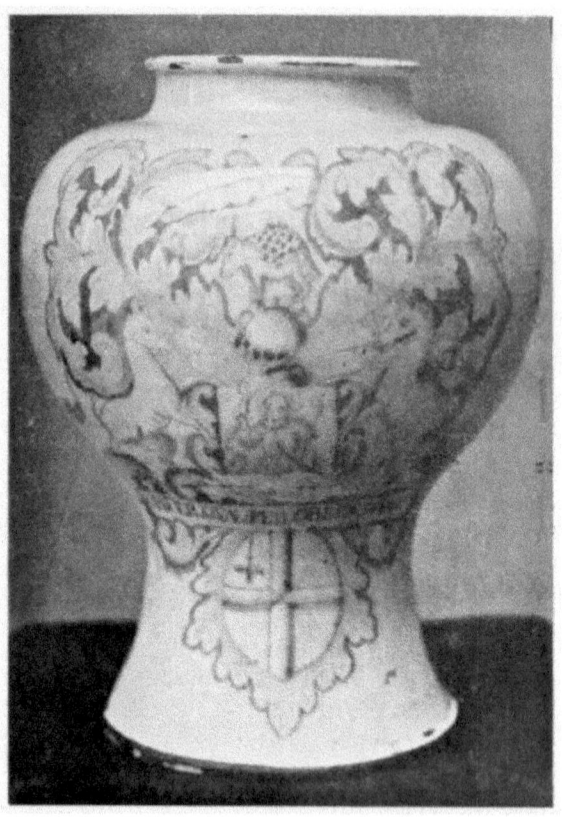

LAMBETH DELFT JAR.
Painted in blue, with arms of Apothecaries' Company with crest mantling and supporters. Motto—Opifer: Quæ: per: orbem: dicor; oval shield below with arms of City of London.
(11 inches high, 27¼ inches greatest circumference.)
(*In the collection of Mr. Robert Bruce Wallis.*)

But pleasing as is the Dutch delft in its fine colours, incorporated as they are with the enamel and glaze and giving the rich tone so much admired by collectors, and faithfully copying the form of the Nankin models, it falls short of these Oriental prototypes in many important respects. It is admittedly an imitation of the *appearance* of porcelain, and not an imitation of the qualities peculiar to porcelain. The Dutch potter in his delft did not, as in the case of other European potters, essay to copy the body of porcelain, and arrive at true hard white paste, as did Meissen. Apparently he took his earthenware, and with the limitations in technique in its working he produced a colourable imitation, in appearance only, of his blue and white Chinese models, and very fine some of these early seventeenth century Dutch delft pieces are, and highly prized by collectors.

But delft in comparison with porcelain may be said to be very similar to veneered furniture in relation to solid specimens. The veneer in the one case and the enamel in the other disguises something inferior beneath.

Introduction into England.—There is no doubt that, prior to its manufacture in this country, a great quantity of Dutch delft was imported and in general use in the middle years of the seventeenth century. In dealing with delft ware, in connection with the various types of earthenware at different periods of the history of the potter's art it must be borne in mind that delft was entirely of foreign origin. It owed everything to the inventiveness of the Dutch potters, and it gained very little when it became acclimatised in England, although it was manufactured here until the closing years of the eighteenth century, when Wedgwood's cream ware drove it off the market as a cheap and serviceable ware.

Naturally the close connection of the royal house of England with Holland accelerated the fashion of storing delft in closets and making considerable use of its rich colours as a decorative effect on sideboards and buffets. The lac cabinets and the fine blue and white delft jars at Hampton Court testify to the influence that the advent of William of Orange had on the taste of the country from the memorable year of 1688, when he landed at Torbay.

Delft was presumably being made in this country fifty years before that by Dutch refugees, but the thirties of the seventeenth century was not a very happy time to inaugurate the birth of a new branch of art in England. The rumblings of the civil war were in the air. It was in 1642 that Charles precipitated matters by going with an armed force to the House of Commons to arrest five members; and seven years later he lost his head in Whitehall. It is not until the last years of Charles II. that there appears to be any documentary evidence connected with the actual manufacture of delft in England. John Ariens van Hamme, evidently a Dutch refugee, a potter working at Lambeth, took out a patent for making "tiles and porcelain after the way practised in Holland." The word "porcelain" was used somewhat indiscriminately at this date and apparently meant anything having the appearance of the wares coming over in large numbers from the East, imported by our East India Company.

LAMBETH DELFT WINE BOTTLE.
Inscribed "SACK W^KE 1652."
(*At British Museum.*)

BRISTOL DELFT WARE.
(About 1784.)
Representing balloon ascent, two figures in car, with Union Jack flying.
(*In the possession of Mr. W. L. Yeulett.*)

Lambeth Delft.—To Lambeth must be accredited the best results of English delft ware. The glaze is thinner and whiter than is used elsewhere and the tone of the blue is less crude. It is difficult to differentiate between the work of Dutch refugees and of English born potters. Drug pots and sack bottles formerly imported from Holland began to be made at Lambeth. Some of these bottles are dated and the dates upon them range from 1649, the year of the execution of King Charles I., to 1664, during the early years of the reign of Charles II., the year in which New York, then New Amsterdam, a Dutch settlement, was surrendered to the English.

There are not a great number of these authentic dated sack bottles known. Lambeth must also be credited with the series of plates having dates and initials, and with some of the "blue dash" chargers or dishes. These are usually decorated with blue dashes clumsily applied round the edge, sometimes brown is used instead of blue. In the centre of the dish is generally a figure, often on horseback, and the foliage of the trees in the background is done with a sponge hastily applied. The range of colours used is not great—blue, green, orange, puce, and brown. Sometimes four colours are found on one dish, but not infrequently the decorator has been content with two, in addition to blue, which is nearly always present.

The following are among the subjects found on these dishes, which are usually about thirteen inches in diameter:—Charles I., Charles II., James II., William and Mary, William on foot or on horseback, Queen Anne, the Old Pretender, Duke of Marlborough, Duke of Monmouth, and the celebrated Adam and Eve dishes, in which Eve was represented as Queen Mary giving a kingdom to her husband, represented by an orange as a pun on his royal house. Although portraits of Charles I. appear in this series, they are not contemporary, and were probably not made at Lambeth until after about 1670, and their manufacture continued for a little over a quarter of a century, that is, until the opening years of the reign of George I.

That delft was made in England a little earlier than 1672 is proved by the fact that in that year a royal proclamation forbade the importation of "painted earthenware" to compete with the same production "but lately found out in England." Here is an instance of trade protection, but it should be borne in mind that at that date we were at war with the Dutch, who were in that year defeated off Southwold Bay.

Something should be said about the characteristics of this Lambeth delft. The body is fairly hard and the tin enamel or glaze is often found on the back of the piece; when this is not the case the back has received an application of yellowish lead glaze. The English clay being less spongy than that of Holland, did not take the enamel well, and often shows the colour of the body in pink lines through the glaze. English delft, owing to the glaze not being incorporated, is crazed on the surface. In regard to dated sack bottles, great caution should be exercised in buying them, as genuine examples of plain undated bottles have been skilfully redecorated by fraudulent hands, and the words Sack or Canary, together with a date, added.

There is an element of doubt about much of the Lambeth delft ware, as it is certain that some of the patterns were copied by the Staffordshire potters, and some of these copies are so faithfully done as to puzzle experts, but many of the cruder dash series of dishes and platters may safely be attributed to Staffordshire.

CANDLESTICK, LAMBETH DELFT.
Inscribed W E 1648.
(*At Victoria and Albert Museum.*)

OLD DUTCH BRASS CANDLESTICK.
(Seventeenth century.)
(*In the collection of the Author.*)

In the illustration of a dated candlestick, with the initials W.E. and coat of arms, and dated 1648, from the National collection at the Victoria and Albert Museum, it will be seen that the authorities attribute an earlier date to the manufacture of delft at Lambeth than the above-mentioned royal proclamation in 1672 would seem to warrant. But so learned an authority as Professor Church is of the opinion that "a considerable manufactory existed there at least as early as 1631." It is interesting to compare the style of this delft candlestick with a brass one of early Dutch manufacture, which at any rate shows that the design, as well as the method of manufacture, was derived from Holland.

Pharmacy jars, decorated in blue and plain white delft, were also made at Lambeth; of this latter there are many small jugs and puzzle jugs, and a variety of fancy pieces. We give an illustration of a very interesting Pharmacy Jar with the arms of the Apothecaries' Company, and with motto inscribed. A shield below has the arms of the City of London.

Bristol Delft.—There is no doubt that the delft of Bristol has not yet been thoroughly exploited. Farther removed from the influence of a constant stream of Dutch examples, the potters took some of their designs straight from Oriental models. Richard Frank and Joseph Flower are two potters who had works at Bristol. They are known to have manufactured delft as early as the opening years of the eighteenth century, contemporary with Lambeth, when the industry at this latter place was in full swing, and delft was made at Bristol until the middle of the reign of George III., after which delft was no longer fashionable.

It is not easy to distinguish between the productions of Frank and Flower, nor is it less difficult in some instances to state definitely whether a piece is Bristol, or Liverpool, or Lambeth, and we might add Staffordshire. There is a very interesting delft plate decorated in blue, representing a balloon ascent. In date this is about 1784 and it may be attributed to Bristol or Liverpool (see illustration, p. 107).

But as a rule it is held that Bristol delft is bluish in tint, and has a more brilliant and even surface. The ware is decorated with Oriental landscapes, and a considerable number of tiles were made and painted for use as pictures in the fireside in old Bristol houses a century and a half ago. Bowen, John Hope, Michael Edkins, and Thomas Patience are some of the painters who worked at the Frank pottery. There is one subject picture representing Hogarth's *March to Finchley*, and it was certainly executed more than once as there is one set consisting of forty-two tiles and another of seventy-two tiles of the same subject.

A peculiarity of some of the Bristol delft is the ground of powdered purple or brown with white panels, having a decoration in blue. We illustrate a bowl of this type of ware, which, although not having the white panel, is representative of this class as the fish is on a white ground with outline decorations in blue (see p. 115).

Another fine style of decoration is that known as *bianco sopra bianco*, that is, a pattern of foliage or sprays of flowers enamelled in white upon a dull, greenish-white ground (see illustration, p. 115).

BRISTOL DELFT PLATE.
Decorated in blue in middle and *bianco sopra bianco* around border.
(*At Victoria and Albert Museum.*)

BRISTOL DELFT BOWL.
Ground of powdered purple. Decorated with fishes in white and blue.
(*In the possession of Mr. S. G. Fenton.*)

There are many dated pieces of Bristol delft with initials, bowls, marriage and election plates, and sometimes tile pictures. At the Victoria and Albert Museum there is a fine plate with the initials E.M.B., and dated 1760, the initials being those of the painter, Michael Edkins, and his wife Betty. This was made at the factory of Richard Frank, and was presented to the National collection by the grandson of the painter.

In the collection of pottery at the Bristol Museum there is an example attributed to Brislington which in colouring is slightly duller than the Bristol examples. Connoisseurs of Bristol delft divide the ware into the earlier period prior to 1735, when the decoration followed Dutch prototypes, and they attribute much of the thinner or finer potted examples to Joseph Flower, but after that the Bristol potters struck out for themselves, and imparted more originality in their ware. Landscapes appeared on the ware, but not seen through Dutch eyes, and a slight variation was given to the form of the bases of the bowls and plates, falling into line with typical shapes employed by other English potters.

We illustrate a very remarkable piece of Bristol delft which is dated 1740, and bears the initials I.F., which may probably stand for Joseph Flower, whose factory was on the quay at Bristol. This plate, which is 13½ inches in diameter, has a painted illustration with the inscription in a medallion, "A Voyage to the Moon, by Domingo Gonsales from the Ile of Tenerife."

We do not know what is the particular story connected with the making of this plate, nor why such a subject should have been chosen. But there is no doubt that the painter of the plate took his design from a book entitled "The Man in the Moone, or a Discourse of a Voyage thither, By Domingo Gonsales, The Speedy Messenger." We give a facsimile of the title-page. This was a romance written by Francis Godwin, bishop of Hereford, and in the second edition of 1657, the title-page has the addition, "By F.G.—B. of H." There were many editions of this book, which became very popular. A French edition under the title of *L' Homme dans La Lune*, is dated 1671, and has the same illustration as the first English edition, with the exception of the inscription on the medallion.

This is not the place to give details of this interesting volume, which describes in language as faithful as that of Defoe, the voyage of Domingo Gonsales, a shipwrecked Spanish adventurer, from Teneriffe to the Moon in a car he invented, which was carried by a flock of wild geese he had trained in his solitude. After a stay of a year in that country, and meeting with adventures with the inhabitants of that kingdom, he sets sail for the earth and lands in China. He by great fortune hears of some Jesuit fathers hidden away in Far

Cathay, who welcomed him, "much wondering to see a lay Spaniard there," and by them his story is committed to writing.

Written in 1638, the following sentence in the *Preface* sounds quite modern, "That there should be Antipodes was once thought as great a paradox as now that the Moon should be habitable. But the knowledge of this may seem more properly reserved for this, our discovering age." There is no doubt that the book had a very considerable circulation, and it is not improbable that Swift knew of it and incorporated some of the ideas of the author in his "Gulliver's Travels," which appeared in 1726. But it is not easily explained why this delft plate, dated 1740, bears the inscription and illustration of a volume published nearly a century earlier.

BRISTOL DELFT DISH.
Inscribed "A Voyage to the Moon by Domingo Gonzales from the Ile of Tenerife."

REVERSE OF DELFT DISH.
Marked I F and dated 1740.
(Diameter 13½ inches.)
(*In the collection of Mr. W. C. Wells.*)

Liverpool Delft.—Collectors of Liverpool delft would like to ascribe many pieces to that city. But, unfortunately, the difference between this and the other English delft is not so defined. One has to take the style of subject largely as a guide for the origin. There is a large punch bowl at the Victoria and Albert Museum which may certainly be attributed to Liverpool. It was painted by John Robinson at Seth Pennington's factory. A similar bowl is in the Mechanic's Institution at Hanley. It is painted in blue with a three-masted man-of-war inside the bowl. The flag is touched with red. The exterior shows an array of military trophies. It is somewhat confusing to collectors to know that the fine punch bowls of Seth Pennington, with his renowned blue colouring, are of delft, earthenware, and of *china*. These latter are of great rarity and value.

Another maker of delft punch bowls was Shaw, but it is not easy to determine with exactitude to which factory to ascribe some of these delft bowls, and there is room for considerable inquiry and exhaustive research to be made into the early history of the Liverpool potteries in general, as much information is needed to settle controversial points.

Delft Printed Tiles.—It is here that Liverpool stands pre-eminent in the transfer printed delft tiles. As early as 1750 Sadler and Green discovered the transfer printing by means of adhesive paper placed on previously inked copper-plates and laid on the earthenware as a decoration in black or in red, and sometimes puce. The signature of the engravers appears on some specimens, *J. Sadler, Liverpool*; *J. Sadler, Liverpl.*; *Sadler, Liverpool*; *Green, Liverpool*; or *Green*.

The invention was invaluable as a decoration for china and earthenware in lieu of painting. The following affidavit was made in 1756 by John Sadler and Guy Green that they "without the aid of or assistance of any other person or persons, did, within the space of six hours, to wit, betwixt the hours of nine in the morning and three in the afternoon of the same day, print upwards of 1,200 tiles of different patterns at Liverpoole aforesaid, and which, as these deponents have heard and believe, were more in number, and better and neater, than one hundred skilled potmakers could have painted in the like space of time in the common or usual way of painting with a pencil, and these deponents say that they have been upwards of seven years in finding out the method of printing tiles, and in making tryals and experiments for that purpose, which they have now, through great pains and expense, brought to perfection."

There is no doubt that this invention revolutionised the decoration of all wares. In regard to the controversy which has arisen as to the prior claims of Battersea for its transfer decorated enamels, and of Worcester for similar decorations by Hancock, the whole matter has been exhaustively dealt with by Mr. William Turner in his "Transfer Printing on Enamels, Porcelain, and Pottery," in which the case for each claimant is minutely analysed.

TITLE PAGE AND ILLUSTRATION.
From volume, "The Man in the Moone," published in 1638.

(In Library at British Museum.)

Sadler and his partner Green conducted a large business in this transfer printing for other factories as well as, of course, for the Liverpool delft and other wares. Sadler apparently left the partnership somewhere between 1769 and 1774, so that the signature on the tiles by him gives the date of their printing. Green carried on the business until 1799, and so great was the fame of the firm that cream ware was sent from Etruria and by other Staffordshire potters to be printed at Liverpool, and up till 1799 Wedgwood's successors still continued the practice of having their cream ware printed by Green.

Liverpool tiles obviously differ from Bristol tiles inasmuch as the former were printed after 1756, but of course before that date Liverpool delft tiles must have been painted as they were elsewhere. There are many series of the

Sadler and Green period, one notable one being a number of actors and actresses, including Garrick, Foote, Mrs. Abington, Mrs. Yates, and others, in character.

Fable illustrations from Æsop and others were largely printed, and some of Wedgwood's plates have been decorated in red, with fable subjects some five inches square, which, in spite of the festoons in which they are set, cannot escape from seeming what they are—square tile-subjects applied to the decoration of a round plate—and the result is not pleasing.

Among the signed pieces of Sadler and of Green, if any difference in style can be discerned in the results, it is indicated by the subjects they chose. Sadler's name appears on pastoral subjects with luxuriant foliage and with dainty rustic scenery, while Green seems to have had a fondness for Oriental groups with a framework of fantastic furniture. The best collection of Liverpool delft in this country is in the museum at Liverpool.

At this museum may be seen the printed work on delft tiles of a later Liverpool potter, Zachariah Barnes, who was only twelve years of age when Sadler and Green commenced their tile printing, but who lived till 1820, and had a considerable business in printing wall tiles of fine character.

Wincanton Delft.—A delft factory existed at Wincanton (Somerset), and recent excavations have brought to light material proving the class of ware made there. Nathaniel Ireson is believed to have started the works about 1730. There are examples of this delft bearing the name "Wincanton," and dated 1737. One specimen has the name Nathaniel Ireson, and is dated 1748. One of these dated plates is in the National Scottish Museum at Edinburgh, which we are enabled to reproduce as an illustration. It is decorated in blue, with the arms of the Masons' Company, and inscribed "Js. Clewett," and dated 1737. At the back of the dish are painted sprays of blossom, and it is marked "Wincanton." This is a remarkable specimen.

Tudor Jugs.—Though earliest in date, we mention this last, as the ware is not true delft. This is a class of Elizabethan ware, mostly small jugs some five or six inches in height, of brown-and-blue mottled surface. The exterior has all the appearance of Cologne stoneware, but the pieces bear a closer relationship to delft; they have a tin glaze, whereas the stone Cologne ware has a salt glaze. They are exceedingly rare and valuable, and some of them are mounted with silver bearing Elizabethan hall-marks. They are disclaimed by continental authorities, who refuse to acknowledge them as belonging to their factories, and they apparently were made in England. A great deal of mystery surrounds their origin, and no doubt further research will at some future date determine the history of these specimens which, under various fancy names, such as "Tiger" pattern, due to their peculiar mottling, bring considerable prices under the hammer.

WINCANTON DELFT DISH.
With arms of Masons' Company. Inscribed "Js. Clewett 1737."

BACK OF DELFT DISH.
Showing the mark "Wincanton."
(*At the Royal Scottish Museum, Edinburgh.*)

To bring the story of English delft to a conclusion, it may be said that it had an ephemeral life as a ware for domestic use, until it was dethroned by Staffordshire salt glaze ware, which held the field until Wedgwood's cream ware drove this latter from the market.

DELFT PRICES.

LAMBETH.	£	s.	d.
Dish, octagonal, decorated in blue and white, bearing arms of Routledge family, with motto, *Verax atque probus*, dated 1637. Sotheby, February, 1906	7	0	0

Coronation mug, 3½ in. high, portrait of Charles II., inscribed and dated "C. 2nd R., 1660." Bond, Bristol, April, 1906	38	0	0
Set of six plates inscribed "What is a Merry Man," &c., all dated 1734. Sotheby, June, 1906	41	0	0
Vessel modelled in form of cat, painted in blue, dated 1657. Sotheby, June, 1906	20	0	0
Plaque, with arms of Apothecaries' Company in blue. Christie, November, 1906	9	19	6
Wine bottle, inscribed "Sack, 1650," in blue. Sotheby, May, 1908	15	15	0
Plate with blue decoration on border, and initials A EC, 1698. Sotheby, April, 1908	3	3	0

STAFFORDSHIRE.

Delft dish painted with tulip and with blue dash border, 13 in. diameter; another with head of Charles II., and inscribed "The Royal Oak"; another inscribed G L. 1680. Sotheby, December, 1908	1	12	0

BRISTOL.

Plates, small, ordinary style, from 7s. 6d. to	1	0	0
Dishes, larger size, ordinary style, from £1 to	2	0	0

Plates, small, with initials and dated, from £1 10s., upwards.

Dishes, larger size, with initials and dates, or of especial interest, from £2 to £5 and upwards.

LIVERPOOL.
(SIMILAR PRICES TO THOSE OF BRISTOL.)

Puzzle jug painted in blue, with verse. Puttick and Simpson, December, 1905	3	12	6

TUDOR JUGS.

These jugs vary in character, but are always of some rarity, and range in value from £10, as a minimum price, upwards. With hall-marked silver mounts, in date from 1530–1600, they are greatly sought after. The West Malling Jug is the most famous specimen that has been sold of recent years.

The description is as follows,—

Fulham delft or stoneware, splashed purple, orange, green, and other colours. With silver mounts, having London hall-mark, 1581. Height, 9½ in. Strong probability that it is nothing more than an old sack-pot. Sold at Christie's, February, 1903 £1,522 10 0

CHAPTER IV
STONEWARE

Cologne Ware and Bellarmines—John Dwight of Fulham (1638–1703)—The Brothers Elers, working in Staffordshire (1690–1710)—John Astbury (1679–1743)—Thomas Astbury—Fulham Stoneware—Nottingham Stoneware—Prices of Stoneware.

Stoneware in point of date is prior to delft in its beginnings, and it had in its subsequent development a longer life than delft. It has already been shown (Chapter II.) how broken is the history of the evolution of the potter's art in England in the Middle Ages. There are great gaps which divide the period of the mediæval tiles from the more or less peasant pottery known as slip ware. It is not until the seventeenth century had well advanced that the manufacture of stoneware took its place as an industry.

To the beginner it should be explained that stoneware is coated with a glaze by means of common salt. It is extremely hard, and has a surface in old and admired specimens like the skin of an orange being pitted with minute depressions, or in finer and thinner ware being like the surface of leather or chicken skin. The ordinary ginger-beer bottle is stoneware, and although serving in a humble capacity, is often found to be perfect in the technique of salt glazing. In old jugs of seventeenth-century manufacture, the mottled colouring and distinctly pleasing surface varying in tone from warm brown to reddish-yellow, is exceptionally attractive to collectors who import a love for technique into their hobby.

Undoubtedly the Bellarmine, or Greybeard, jug was in use in this country for a considerable period. References abound in old plays. Ben Jonson, in his "Bartholomew Fair" (Act IV.), makes Captain Whit say, "He has wrashled so long with the bottle here, that the man with the beard hash almosht streek up hish heelsh," in simulation of the speech of a man who has well drunken. But it must be concluded that this stoneware, or Cologne ware, was largely imported, and was never greatly made in this country until John Dwight, of Fulham, took out his patent in 1671. There are pieces bearing Elizabethan dates and coats of arms, as, for instance, the small brown cruche in the Schreiber Collection at the Victoria and Albert Museum, with the initials "E. R." and the date 1594; and the fine Bellarmine jug in the British Museum, with the arms of Queen Elizabeth, and dated 1594. We illustrate a fine stoneware Bellarmine jug, of the late sixteenth century, having a coat of arms with crown and Tudor roses. The character of some of these jugs differs from continental examples. This may have been due to a desire on the part of the consumer for vessels of that type, but there seems some likelihood that the commoner sorts were made here, and it is conjectured that Fulham was the chief place of their manufacture.

STONEWARE JUG. BELLARMINE OR GREYBEARD.
Having arms with Tudor roses. (Late sixteenth century.)
(*At British Museum.*)

STONEWARE JUGS WITH ROYAL ARMS AND PORTRAIT MEDALLIONS OF WILLIAM AND MARY.
The left-hand jug with portrait of Queen Mary is attributed to Dwight.
(*In the collection of Mr. F. W. Phillips, Hitchin.*)

In the group of fine Bellarmine jugs illustrated, the characteristics of the ware are shown. The decorations begin to assume a national feeling, and the jugs differ in form from the continental type. The fine specimen of grey stoneware with the portrait medallion of Queen Mary is attributed to Dwight. The inscription runs "Maria. D. G. Mag. Brit. Franc, et. Hib. Regina." The right hand jug in the group has a raised medallion portrait of William III.

The Bellarmine, or Greybeard or Longbeard, is so called from the head which appears on the neck of the jug, which mask is always referred to in a satirical manner as being the likeness of Cardinal Robert Bellarmin, who rendered himself obnoxious by his opposition to the reformed religion in the Low Countries.

These old examples of foreign stoneware, miscalled *grès de Flandres*, are known to have been made at Raren, at Siegburg, at Grenzhausen, near Coblenz, and later in the seventeenth century they were made at Namur.

The fact that they were imported and not made here appears from the petition of William Simpson, merchant (*Lansdowne MSS.*) to Queen Elizabeth: "Whereas one Garnet Tyne, a strainger living in Acon, in the parte beyond the seas, being none of her Majestie's subjects, doth buy up all the pottles made at Culloin called Drinkynge Stonepottes & he onlie transporteth them into this realme of England & selleth them; It may please your Majestie to graunt unto the sayd William Simpson full power & only license to provyde, transport, & bring into this realme, the same or such like Drynkynge pots"; the petitioner adds that "no Englishman doth transport any potte into this realme," he also gives a promise "as in him lieth" to attempt to "drawe the making of such like potte into some decayed town within this realme, whereby many a hundred poore men may be set a worke." Thirty years later Letters Patent were granted to Thomas Rous and Abraham Cullyn in 1626 for the sole making "of the stone pottes, stone juggs, & stone bottles, for the terme of fourteene years for a reward for their invention."

Here, then, are sufficient facts to show how largely the importation and manufacture was in foreign hands, and the finer specimens must undoubtedly be assigned to foreign potters.

John Dwight.—In 1671 a patent was taken out by John Dwight for "the mistery of transparent earthenware, commonly knowne by the names of porcelaine or China and Persian ware, as alsoe the misterie of the stoneware vulgarly called Cologne ware." It appears from this patent that he had "invented and sett up at Fulham, several new manufactories." There is no doubt that John Dwight was one of the greatest, if not the greatest of English potters. His magnificent life-size bust in stoneware of Prince Rupert, now in the British Museum, excites the wonder and admiration of modern potters. The technical excellence he displays in his fine stoneware, which is of a grey-white or pale fawn colour, and is salt glazed, is as remarkable a triumph of modelling as it is of skill in potting. To quote Professor Church in regard to Dwight's busts and figures, "They stand absolutely alone in English ceramics. They are the original and serious work of an accomplished modeller. The best of them are instinct with individuality and strength, yet reticent with the reticence of noble sculpture."

STONEWARE BUST OF JAMES II.
By Dwight, of Fulham. (About 1686.)
(*At Victoria and Albert Museum.*)

DWIGHT STONEWARE FIGURES.
Children reading.
(*At British Museum.*)

The illustration of the bust of *James II.* (p. 139) is not so well known as the famous *Prince Rupert*, nor is it of the same superlative power; but it is a fine example of stoneware.

The two figures illustrated of *Children Reading* have just been added to the national collection, and exhibit the mastery of Dwight over his medium.

There is no doubt that John Dwight is coming into his own. Among the fathers of English pottery there are Dwight and Elers, and Astbury and Whieldon, and Josiah Wedgwood, and the greatest of these is unquestionably Dwight. Dr. Plot, in his "History of Oxfordshire," published in 1677, passes this eulogy upon him: "He has so advanced the *Art Plastick*, that 'tis dubious whether any man since Prometheus have excelled him, not excepting the famous Damophilus and Gorgasus of Pliny." And yet this Dwight is reported to have destroyed most of his formulæ and many of his papers connected with his inventions in the hope that his descendants would not engage in so unprofitable a business.

It is not known when Dwight was born; 1638 is the conjectured date. He was M.A. and B.C.L. of Christ Church, Oxford, and was secretary to the Bishop of Chester. Between 1671 and 1676 he settled at Fulham. It appears that he had previously established a factory at Oxford with considerable success. He died in 1703, and the pottery was continued by his son Samuel, who died in 1737. The works were carried on by his widow, and subsequently by William White, who married her, and the pottery remained in the hands of the White family until 1862.

Of his portrait busts and statuettes, the Victoria and Albert Museum and the British Museum have about thirteen examples, and there is a fine statuette of *Jupiter* in the Liverpool Museum. Besides this class of ware, he certainly made stoneware jugs of the Cologne type, and red-ware teapots. He was known to use small raised ornaments on this ware, produced by the use of metal stamps. His vases have marbled decorations, and he was fully aware of the use of pounded flint, which gave his ware a porcellanous character, "a discovery which was not apparently known to the Staffordshire potters until about 1720."[1]

In relation to Dwight and his patents, new light has been thrown upon the originality of the work of the Brothers Elers in their secretly-guarded factory at Bradwell Wood. All earnest students are indebted to Professor Church for his recent researches to establish Dwight's reputation, which go a great way towards dethroning the two Dutch brothers Elers, who have been hitherto regarded as the pioneers of Staffordshire fine pottery.

**COFFEE POT, ELERS RED UNGLAZED WARE.
MUG, RED UNGLAZED WARE, PROBABLY MADE BY ELERS**

OR DWIGHT.
(*At British Museum.*)

ELERS RED WARE TEAPOT.
(*In the collection of Mr. F. W. Phillips, Hitchin.*)

Elers Ware (1690–1710).—There is a great deal of mystery surrounding the name and fame of the two Dutchmen, John Philip Elers and David Elers. They came to this country as did so many of their countrymen in the latter part of the seventeenth century. Earlier, Dutch refugees had fled hither on account of religious persecution, and later, when William of Orange came over, his court attracted many of his countrymen of distinguished birth. Martin Elers, the father of our two Dutchmen, had been ambassador to several European courts. John Philip his son was "the godson of the Elector of Mentz, after whom he was named, and was held at the baptismal font by Queen Christina of Sweden." [2]

There is no reason to believe that they had any patronage from the court themselves, but their sister was granted a pension of £300 a year by William, and she subsequently became the second wife of Sir William Phipps, founder of the house of Mulgrave, the title of Earl of Mulgrave is now borne by the Marquis of Normanby, whose family name is Phipps.

However aristocratic they were, it is certain that they had considerable practical knowledge in order to embark in business and carry on a pottery.

They prepared the red clay of Bradwell in a far more scientific manner than had any Staffordshire potters prior to that date, and by the lathe they turned forms far thinner than could be done on the wheel. Wherever they had gained their technical skill, they placed for the first time the wares of Staffordshire on the same plane as Böttcher's work of Meissen, or the models of the old Chinese potters.

We have already shown that they engaged some of Dwight's workmen from Fulham, and that they infringed Dwight's patents in respect to the Cologne jugs and red teapots. This does not accord with the fables hitherto industriously repeated in every succeeding volume dealing with china, that the Elers employed imbeciles in their factory, in order that their trade secrets might be jealously guarded. It is true that Twyford and John Astbury learned all that they wanted to know by gaining employment at the Elers pottery at Bradwell, and there is little doubt that in so doing they simulated a stupid indifference as to the new methods of stamping china ornaments by metal stamps and of the lathe work employed on the red teapots.

Both black and red teapots were made by Elers and ornaments in Chinese style added in relief. These ornaments were stamped with a metal die and laid on the vessel, several dies were used for portions of the same teapot. The connecting portions such as the stalks between two sprigs were finished by hand. This red ware was unglazed. As most people are familiar with Wedgwood's black, basaltes ware, it is useful to know that, except in colour, the wares are almost identical in point of external appearance and to the sense of touch. Some of this red tea and coffee ware or "old china," as it was called, is marked with a seal in imitation of Chinese marks. The red teapots of small dimensions sold for ten to twenty-five shillings apiece, and David Elers had a shop in the Poultry in Cheapside, where he sold them.

The Elers left Staffordshire in 1710, so that their pottery lasted only twenty years. In view of the fact that Dwight complained about their manufacture of stoneware jugs and mugs as being subsequent to his, it would seem doubtful if they can still be accredited with the invention of this old ware or with the introduction of salt glaze into England. Undoubtedly this early class of hard red stoneware, almost approaching porcelain in character, will have to be thoroughly reviewed with the object of assigning to Dwight what is his, and to the Elers, and to Aaron, Thomas, and Richard Wedgwood what is theirs, to say nothing of Richard Garner, and of John Morley, of Nottingham, who confessed to copying Dwight's "browne muggs."

The subsequent history of the Elers may be interesting in passing. John Philip is believed to have been in some way connected with the foreign glass works at Chelsea, established by Italian workmen, under the patronage of the Duke of Buckingham, as early as 1676. He afterwards, with the assistance of Lady Barrington, set up as a glass and china merchant in Dublin, and became successful. David Elers remained in London.

John Astbury.—We have seen that the Elers' secret became known in Staffordshire to Twyford, and to John Astbury, and this latter together with his son carried on the same style of manufacture. As a general rule it is held that the ware of the earlier Astbury is not so sharp in its details as was the careful work of the Elers. His ware is of red, fawn, chocolate, and orange colour. His ornaments followed the style of Elers in being stamped, but he made them of Devon or pipe-clay, which has a cruder effect in white upon the darker grounds. He died in 1743. His son Thomas Astbury commenced potting in 1723, and his work is so similar to that of his father, that considerable doubt exists as to which pieces may safely be attributed to the father. It is certain that the son experimented with the bodies of clays until he produced a "cream colour," afterwards improved by Josiah Wedgwood in his renowned cream ware. We illustrate (p. 149) an Astbury teapot in date about 1740, with an orange-coloured glaze body having design in relief in white. The other Astbury ware teapot is of slightly later date, and has a coffee-brown body with white and green floral ornaments in relief. The Porto Bello bowl in the British Museum, of red clay with white stamped ornaments in relief of a group of miniature ships in battle array, made to celebrate the capture of Porto Bello by Admiral Vernon in 1739, is held to be a typical example of the work of the elder Astbury.

As a rule, black or red specimens having the name of Astbury impressed upon them are attributed to Astbury the second. But it must be borne in mind that for want of more exact knowledge, all red ware with stamped ornaments applied in relief and with indications of plain engine turning has been generically termed *Elers ware*, and it is quite certain that later than Astbury junior's day red ware with wavy lines was made. Similarly the type of ware with white applied ornament in relief has been termed *Astbury ware*. The elder Astbury, in addition to the stoneware, made crouch ware, a term employed for the earlier forms of the fine delicate stoneware known as salt glazed. The younger Astbury introduced the use of flint into his ware in or about 1723. Collectors should be cautioned not to assign plates and dishes marked ASTBURY, to Thomas Astbury. They are cream ware, and decorated in blue with Chinese patterns, and belong to a much later period.

Mention should be made of Ralph Shaw, of Burslem, who made brown or chocolate ware dipped in white pipe-clay, which afterwards was worked upon with a tool to display the dark body beneath. There is a jug in the British Museum (Franks Collection) which is thus decorated with birds and foliage. Twyford, the colleague of Astbury the elder, when with the Elers, seems to have applied himself to the use of white decoration, sometimes the red and brown ware is wholly coated inside with pipe-clay, and this is supposed to be his work.

ASTBURY TEAPOT.
Orange glazed body, pattern in relief. (About 1740. Height 4 inches.)
(*At British Museum.*)

ASTBURY WARE TEAPOT.
Coffee brown body, white and green floral ornament in relief. (About 1750.)
(*At British Museum.*)

With the advent of Josiah Wedgwood came the strong classic influence upon his plastic art, and in his various classes of stoneware (dealt with in Chap. VII.) considerable variety was introduced both in design and in colouring. Among the most notable of the contemporaries and successors of Wedgwood who successfully produced high-class stoneware, the following may be mentioned: William Adams, Turner, Elijah Mayer, Neale, Palmer, Birch, Keeling, and Toft, Hollins, Wilson, Spode, Davenport, and Dunderdale of Castleford, and the Leeds Pottery and the Swansea Pottery both made basalt in black ware (see Chap. VIII., The School of Wedgwood).

Fulham Stoneware.—In the eighteenth century Fulham became noticeable for a type of mug similar to that illustrated (p. 153), bearing the initials "W.G." and the date 1725. Another series made at Fulham are the jugs usually marked with the initials "A.R." and "G.R." belonging to the days of Anne and of George I. A great many exist of the fuller-bodied shape, with initials inscribed "G.R." Formerly on museum shelves these were attributed to Fulham, but it is now generally held that this form was imported from the Continent, and belongs to the *Grès-de-Flandres* class. The true Fulham contemporary form is that which we illustrate (p. 153).

The manufacture of stoneware continued for a century, and in the nineteenth century many fine specimens were being made by various potters, and Messrs. Doulton, of Lambeth, still continue to make stoneware vases and jugs and other vessels of an ornamental character.

Nottingham Stoneware.—John Morley, of Nottingham, was cited in 1693, as one of the persons who infringed Dwight's patent for stoneware. Evidently the same family of potters carried on the business, for in 1726, Charles Morley was a maker of brown stoneware jugs and mugs. There is a brown bowl at the Victoria and Albert Museum bearing this date. The Castle Museum at Nottingham possesses some fine examples of brown stoneware. The dates of jugs and mugs vary from as early as 1700 to the last quarter of the eighteenth century. Nottingham ware is smoother in its surface than old Staffordshire, only slightly showing the orange skin texture so noticeable in the other stoneware. It is rich warm brown, sometimes inclining to red and sometimes to yellow in colour. Bear jugs are a feature of Nottingham stoneware, but they are not peculiar to that pottery, as they were also made in Derbyshire and Staffordshire. The Nottingham stoneware is excellently potted and, of course, is salt glazed, the glaze having a slightly lustrous appearance.

The examples most familiar to collectors belong to the late eighteenth and early nineteenth centuries. The bear jugs may be either of plain surface or may have the rough grained exterior formed by minute particles of clay. They frequently have a collar around the neck, and a chain to which is attached a rattle. A rarer form represents a Russian bear hugging Bonaparte, who wears a big plumed hat. Puzzle jugs with incised ornament, and tall loving-cups of large size, are another noticeable production; many of these are inscribed with names and dates.

FULHAM STONEWARE MUG.
(Dated 1725. Period of George I.)
With embossed ornament of dogs, &c., and medallion portraits.

FULHAM STONEWARE JUG.
Raised medallion with crown and G.R. (Period of George I.)
Incised decoration filled with blue.

STONEWARE—PRICES.

BELLARMINES.   £   s.   d.

The prices of this class vary in ordinary examples, plain, or
of slight decoration, from 15s. to   1   10   0

Bellarmines with English arms of especial interest are of
considerably greater value, though not always of English
origin. Exceptional pieces bring exceptional prices.

DWIGHT.

All specimens of Dwight are extremely rare. It is impossible to say what a Dwight stoneware figure or bust would realise at auction, but certainly a very high figure.

ELERS.

Elers teapots, &c., are rare. The smaller lighter coloured teapots of the true Elers ware are worth as many half-sovereigns as the later coarser examples are worth shillings.

ASTBURY.

A similar difficulty arises in attempting to state prices for Astbury stoneware. Fine examples rarely come into the market.

FULHAM.

G. R. jugs ascribed to Fulham may be bought from 15s. to £1 10s., according to condition and decoration. The large jugs and mugs with medallion busts of William and Mary, inscribed and dated, vary in price from £3 to £5 and upwards.

NOTTINGHAM.

Bear jugs of coarse type may be procured from £1 10s. to	2	10	0
Tall Loving Cups, inscribed with name and date, vary from £2 to	5	0	0

The Russian Bear model hugging Bonaparte is worth £5 or more.

Nottingham ale jugs, dated and inscribed, have realised £12 under the hammer.

CHRONOLOGICAL TABLE.
XVIIITH CENTURY.

Anne (1702–1714)	1704	Gibraltar taken by Sir George Rooke. Marlborough gained victory of Blenheim.
	1711–1714	Addison published the *Spectator*.
George I. (1714–1727)	1715	Rebellion in Scotland. The Old Pretender landed at Peterhead.
	1715–1719	Pope translated Homer's *Iliad* into English verse.
	1719	Defoe's *Robinson Crusoe* published.
	1721	The South Sea Bubble burst; thousands of families ruined.
George II. (1727–1760)	1742	Fielding's *Joseph Andrews* published.
	1748	Richardson's *Clarissa Harlowe*.
	1749	Gray's *Elegy in a Country Churchyard*.
	1750	Fielding's *Tom Jones* published.
	1755	Dr. Johnson's Dictionary published.
	1757	Clive laid the foundation of the Indian Empire.
George III. (1760–1820)	1759–67	Sterne's *Tristram Shandy*.
	1766	Goldsmith's *Vicar of Wakefield*.
	1768	Sir Joshua Reynolds first president of the Royal Academy.
	1775	The American War.
	1777	Sheridan's *School for Scandal*.
	1779	Gainsborough at the height of his fame.

1782	The Independence of the United States recognised.
1786	Gillray's caricatures commenced to appear.
1790	Burke's *Reflections on the French Revolution*.
1791	Burns's *Tam O' Shanter*.
1792	Thomas Paine's *Age of Reason*.
1795	War with Holland. Capture of the Cape of Good Hope.
1801	Union of Great Britain and Ireland.

CHAPTER V
EARLY STAFFORDSHIRE WARE

THOMAS WHIELDON:
HIS CONTEMPORARIES AND HIS SUCCESSORS

The forerunners of Whieldon—The position of Staffordshire Ware—Whieldon as a potter—Early Staffordshire Art—The rivalry with salt glaze—Form *versus* Colour—The last years of the Eighteenth century—The English spirit—Prices.

"Early Staffordshire" is a generic term used to include much of the unknown ware of the early period between about 1720 to 1760. It is not early enough to go back to the butter-pot days of Charles II. nor to include the school of Toft and his contemporaries, with their quaint native humour. But it is an important period when earthenware was in a transitional stage. It is, in fact, the period when Staffordshire may be regarded as the great nursery of potters in swaddling clothes who came into their majority later with full honours.

The chronological table at the head of this chapter shows the great events that were shaping the destiny of this country, and, in politics, in art, and in letters, it must be admitted that the age of Anne and the first two Georges was prolific enough in incident. It was during the greater portion of the first half of the eighteenth century that English earthenware was finding itself. Attempts at classification nearly always leave the borders overlapping. In trying to gather in our net a band of representative potters with work peculiarly illustrative of this period which was essentially English—as English as Toft—but progressing towards something that should stand as worthy of our art, several great potters, such as the Woods, have escaped, and will be treated separately later. It must be granted that the influence of the Whieldon school was not obliterated even by the great rise of the classic school of design as exemplified by Wedgwood, Turner, and Adams. The strong English robustness and the national insularity of design never wholly died out in the eighteenth century. It was eclipsed by classic frigidities from across the Alps, and it suffered discomfiture from the rococo insipidities from France first naturalised at Chelsea and at Derby. But it lingered in the hearts of the common people like the tunes of some of the old ballads in spite of the fashions of Gluck and of Handel. Thus it comes to pass that, side by side with the Iphigenias, the Andromaches, the Venuses, the Minervas, and the other esoteric personages from among the gods and goddesses of Olympus, with their accompaniment of foreign fauns and satyrs, there were the very English (founded on Gillray and Rowlandson), almost Rabelaisian, grotesques in the army of Toby Jugs and the sporting, rural, nautical, historic, commemorative, and satiric jugs and mugs and figures, with English doggerel and with idiosyncrasies enough to make our earthenware essentially national.

WHIELDON WARE CAULIFLOWER TEAPOT.
With vivid green and yellow colouring.

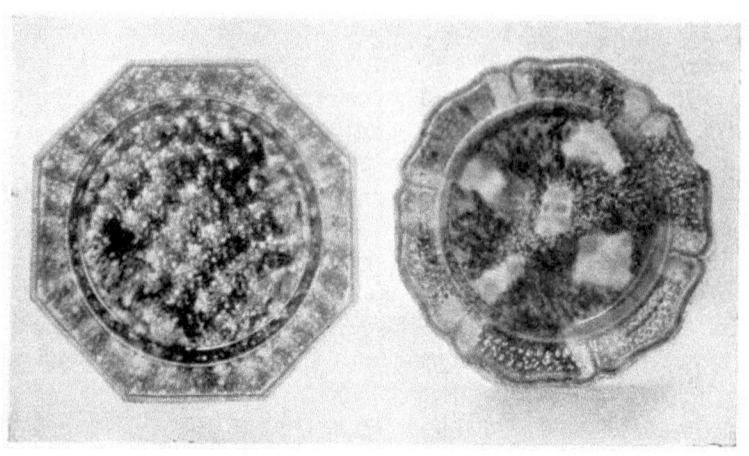

TORTOISESHELL WARE PLATES.
Richly glazed, producing clouded and mottled effects.
(*At Victoria and Albert Museum.*)

Unfortunately in the early days it is impossible with any degree of certainty to assign many of these older pieces to any particular potter. The collector can only lament "the iniquity of oblivion blindly scattering her poppy," as Sir Thomas Browne puts it. It is without doubt rightly believed that Thomas Whieldon had a great and lasting influence upon the potters of his generation, but his own actual work has been swallowed up by the covering phrase "Whieldon ware," which, like "Elers ware" and "Astbury ware," has come to mean a good many things, and these are names of types rather than persons.

The forerunners of Whieldon.—It is necessary briefly to recapitulate the events immediately from the commencement of the eighteenth century to the day when Whieldon established his status.

There was a continuous chain of potters working in Staffordshire from the days of the Elers (1690–1710), to the period when Josiah Wedgwood became a master potter on his own account in 1760; he was then thirty years of age.

Wedgwood's own estimate of the Elers is interesting. Speaking of what Elers did for Staffordshire he says, "It is now about eighty years since Mr. Elers came amongst us ... the improvements made (by him) in our manufactory were precisely these—glazing our common clays with salt which produced *Pot d'grey* or stoneware, and this after they had left the country was improved into white stoneware by using the pipe clay of this neighbourhood and mixing it with flint stones calcin'd and reduced by pounding in to a fine powder."

There is not a word about Dwight in all this; evidently Josiah seems not to have known of the legal action against Elers and one of his own kinsmen amongst others. The invention of flint is an allusion to Thomas Astbury about 1720, but Dwight also knew of this formula as his recorded notes prove.

To continue, "The next improvement by Mr. Elers was the refining of our common red clay by sifting and making it into tea and coffee ware in imitation of the Chinese red porcelain by the casting it in plaster moulds and turning it on the outside upon Lathes, and ornamenting it with the tea branch in relief, in imitation of the Chinese manner of ornamenting the ware. For these improvements—and very great ones they were—we are indebted to the very ingenious Messrs. Elers, and I shall gladly contribute all in my power to honour their memories and transmit to posterity the knowledge of the obligations we owe to them."

This is in respect to a jasper medallion portrait of John Philip Elers. Wedgwood is wrong in one or two particulars. The salt glaze question is open to doubt, and most certainly Elers never used moulds for their ware.

We give this as showing the continuity which existed between Elers and Wedgwood, the latter certainly owed his application of the ornamentation in relief to the method which Elers had introduced into Staffordshire. We do not say invented, because there is always Dwight standing in the background.

To give Elers his due he certainly set Staffordshire talking and wondering, and he unwittingly filled Twyford and Astbury with new ideas which they were not slow to adopt. Astbury comes as the echo which Elers left behind in Staffordshire, a substantial enough echo, for Astbury took his master's ideas and created a ware with white stamped ornaments in relief, to which his own name is given as a generic term. John Astbury the elder died in 1743, and Thomas, his son, commenced potting as early as 1723. And the Astburys rub shoulders with Thomas Whieldon, whose apprentice and sometime partner (1752–1758) was Josiah Wedgwood.

It will thus be seen that Thomas Whieldon (1740–1780) came upon the scene in the history of the Staffordshire potteries when the art was in a somewhat transitional stage. New fields were opening and new ideas developing that were shortly to bring English pottery into line with that on the Continent.

The position of Staffordshire Ware.—It is necessary to show the stage at which English pottery had arrived in order to place Whieldon aright and to show the various impulses which led to the outburst of potting which stirred Staffordshire. Stoneware in crude form or in highly finished foreign style in Cologne ware had been gaining ground since Tudor days. Later the use of delft had won favour and was still in full swing at Lambeth, at Bristol, and at Liverpool when Whieldon commenced potting. It had also become acclimatised in Staffordshire. Toft's and other slip ware was contemporary with delft as a native art. And now, looking forward, we see the oncoming triumph of stoneware, in its finely potted and highly artistic Staffordshire form, which was to overthrow delft and slip ware, and in turn be stamped out by the utilitarian cream ware of Whieldon's apprentice, Josiah Wedgwood, who built up his fortune at Etruria on this domestic ware.

The Whieldon period (1740–1780) was an important one in ceramic events. In 1744 Bow commenced to make porcelain. In 1745 is the earliest dated piece of Chelsea porcelain, the year that the Pretender won the battle of Preston Pans, near Edinburgh, and invaded England, bringing his army as far as Derby. In 1750, Derby made earthenware, and in 1751 commenced to make porcelain, which is the same year in which Worcester commenced a glorious record in the making of porcelain. Longton Hall, Bristol, and Liverpool continued the same story, and transfer-printing was practised at Worcester by Hancock on porcelain, and at Liverpool on delft tiles by Sadler and Green. Lowestoft opened a kiln in 1756. Leeds ware was made in 1760, and, finally, Wedgwood's queen's ware in 1762, and four years before Whieldon gave up his work Wedgwood had invented his jasper ware.

Whieldon as a potter.—Not a great deal is known of Whieldon's personality. He must have commenced in a small way of business as he tramped from place to place with specimens of his wares on his back in pedlar fashion. But he became of considerable importance as he held the office of High Sheriff of Staffordshire in 1786, some six years after he retired from his pottery. Whieldon numbered among his apprentices some young men who afterwards became famous. There was Josiah Wedgwood, who became his partner from 1753 to 1759, Josiah Spode, and William Greatbach, Edge, Heath, Marsh, and there was Aaron Wood, who was employed at Little Fenton for some time. On account of his apprentices having become famous, it has been suggested that he was probably indebted to them for much of his fame. On reflection it may possibly be seen that the opposite conclusion may very well be true, and it is not improbable that Wedgwood and Spode and Greatbach and the others owed a considerable debt to Whieldon for having received a highly technical training at his hands.

TEAPOT, TORTOISESHELL WARE.
Embossed with hawthorn pattern.
(*At the Royal Scottish Museum, Edinburgh.*)

BOWL AND COVER, TORTOISESHELL WARE.
Embossed with floral pattern.
(*At the Victoria and Albert Museum.*)

In regard to cream ware, undoubtedly this was in an experimental stage, and Whieldon in common with Astbury made those queer little figures with yellow heads and red or yellow bases, but the tortoiseshell flown colouring apparently denotes some of the specimens made by Whieldon. He made salt glaze, he made tea and coffee pots with the Astbury decorations, but with a strong leaning to the earlier Elers style in his avoidance of too strong contrast between white pipe-clay ornament on a dark body. Whieldon toned his ornaments with touches of his own in green and yellow and brown. His solid agate ware and his tortoiseshell and clouded wares, and his cauliflower ware have become so memorable in the cabinets of collectors that they have won him fame, and he has in consequence been credited with all specimens of these classes of ware. We illustrate (p. 161) an example of the Whieldon *Cauliflower Teapot* with vivid green and yellow colouring.

Of this early period, the fine group we illustrate (p. 171) with a *coffee-pot* of glazed red ware, a kaolin of deep cream colour decorated in red, may not unreasonably be attributed to John Astbury, while the little *Figure* of flown colouring, with red base and brown shoes, may be either by Whieldon or possibly by Thomas Astbury.

The "solid agate" of Whieldon is something far more artistic than the combed ware of earlier days or the very rough attempts at solid agate made by clumsier hands than his own prior to his experiments.

Surface decoration in imitation of agate had been produced by employing two different coloured clays on the surface of a vessel, and when in a wet state combing them to represent the desired veining of the stone to be simulated. "Solid agate" is another process of placing layers of clay of different colours and cutting them in section to show the bands of colour. In Whieldon's hands the layers were thin and the waves and twists, cut off the clay with a wire like cheese is cut, showed in the finished result something more artistic than had ever been attempted before. He made jugs and sauceboats, teapots, teapoys, and other table utensils of this ware, including knife handles. No two pieces are exactly alike, and there is a considerable variety in the breadth of the veining and in the ware, some being intentionally coarser in order to suit the subject potted.

There is no doubt that this ware, standing in a measure in a *cul de sac* of ceramic art, is highly effective, and Wedgwood used with great skill both the solid agate and the surface colour for his ornamental pieces and vases of classic type, in imitation of granite, Egyptian pebble, jasper, porphyry, and several kinds of agate. His range of colour was more extended than that of Whieldon, but there is little doubt that he gained his first knowledge of the properties and possibilities of this variegated ware when he was with Whieldon.

Casting about for something equally effective with possibly less technical difficulties, Whieldon evolved his celebrated clouded wares. Here he took advantage of the new cream ware as a body, the surface of which is splashed or sponged with various tints in imitation of tortoiseshell, although many of the colours introduced depart from tortoiseshell tones and introduce something fresh and original in earthenware decoration.

Group of Astbury Ware.

KYLIN.
Chiefly red and deep cream colour.

COFFEE POT.
Glazed red ware.

FIGURE.
Flown colouring, red base and brown shoes.

(*In the collection of Col. and Mrs. Dickson.*)

AGATE CAT. (4 inches high.)
Grey, with brown solid marbling, and splashed with blue on body and ears.

SALT-GLAZED BEAR JUG.
(Height 3⅛ inches.)

(*In the collection of Mr. Robert Bruce Wallis.*)

There is the patent taken out by Redrich and Jones, Staffordshire potters in 1724, for "staining, veining, spotting, clouding, or damasking earthenware, to give it the appearance of various kinds of marble, porphyry, and rich stones, as well as tortoiseshell." And Ralph Wood, of Burslem, made variegated ware of a particular kind which may well be termed "tesselated," as small pieces of tinted clay were affixed or inlaid on the surface of vessels to be decorated, and subsequently glazed. This mosaic work in imitation of granite was employed also at Leeds.

To return to Whieldon. There is no doubt that he found this variegated ware in a somewhat inchoate state in regard to technique, and the more scientific exactitude which he employed has gained for his wares their fame. We illustrate (p. 167) two fine examples of tortoiseshell ware, a *Teapot* embossed with hawthorn pattern design, and a finely decorated *Bowl and Cover* having a running floral pattern in relief.

The many coloured dessert plates, sometimes of octagonal shape, made by Whieldon in this later mottled manner, in which the surface only is decorated, are well known to collectors. In Whieldon's own examples the potting is more perfect than in those of other potters. His plates are to be recognised not only by their colour, but in the very subtle way he has handled it. The deft touch of blue or yellow or green, has in other hands become a patch of obvious crudity, striking a discordant note at once. The deep grey octagonal plates by him are loved by connoisseurs as exhibiting his subtlety at its best. We illustrate two examples of this class of Whieldon tortoiseshell plates with rich brown colouring flecked with green and yellow (see p. 161).

The mechanical mottling by his imitators, seemingly dabbed on in spots by a sponge, should not be easy to distinguish after having seen one of his best examples. In regard to the potting, Whieldon ware plates have a flat broad rim, which almost invariably has a border of applied strips laid crosswise.

But it must not be forgotten that, when once the fashion for "Whieldon ware" became general, other potteries came into line. At Liverpool this class of mottled and clouded ware was made, and also at the Castleford pottery, near Leeds, and consequently many unmarked examples may be attributed to these potteries. Some of the Castleford tortoiseshell plates are impressed "D.D. & Co."

Early Staffordshire Art.—Among the earlier figures of the Astbury pottery the elder Astbury worked from 1736 to 1743, and his son continued his traditions later. There are a number of quadrupeds and birds which are assigned by collectors to the elder Astbury, which are, although crude, extremely interesting as showing the experiments in coloured clays and in lead glazing. Agate figures of cats of intermingled clays, and diminutive figures of men, some six inches in height, with splashed or clouded decoration, all come into this indeterminate period. The figure in the group (p. 171) already referred to is a case in point.

In the illustration of a fine specimen of an agate cat, in height only 4 inches, the body colour is light grey with dark brown solid marbling, and the front and ears are splashed with blue. Another miniature animal figure belonging to this period is the salt-glaze jug in form of a bear, only $3^{1}/_{8}$ inches high (see illustration, p. 171).

WHIELDON TORTOISESHELL ANIMAL.
(*In the collection of Col. and Mrs. Dickson.*)

SPLASHED CREAM WARE ELEPHANT.
(Staffordshire, about 1750. Height 3¾ inches.)
(*At British Museum.*)

WHIELDON GROUP.
ST. GEORGE AND THE DRAGON.
Knight in green and cream; horse and base tortoiseshell.
EARLY STAFFORDSHIRE FIGURES.
Old Women Hucksters.

(*In the collection of Mr. James Davies, Chester.*)

We illustrate two animals, one of the tortoiseshell variety, a beast of formidable appearance and having considerable power in the modelling and strongly suggestive of the jaguar, but it must be remembered that beasts as depicted in contemporary books have an inclination towards heraldic monsters such as "never were on land or sea." The splashed cream ware elephant, only 3¾ inches in height, is fairly well modelled. But these, in common with the many diminutive figures of a like nature, belong to a period when Staffordshire was endeavouring to found an English school of potters, blindly groping along in almost untutored fashion—lame in design and feeble in inventiveness. From out of this chaos it seems impossible that there should arise soul enough to set the fashion later—nearly fifty years later—to the continent of Europe, and make English earthenware the formidable rival in point of cheapness, and often in point of beauty, to anything produced on the Continent. But the earthenware of Staffordshire was able to teach new points in technique concerning body and glaze to the continental potter.

In the illustration showing the group of *St. George and the Dragon* it will be seen that the modelling begins to assume a more pretentious character. The prevailing colours of the knight are green and cream, the horse and the base of the group are of the familiar tortoiseshell colouring. Beside this St. George are two early Staffordshire figures representing two old women as hucksters. Here the feeling is instinctively English, as national as are the Dutch beggars of the seventeenth-century Dutch etchers. Pity it is that this class of figure, recording national and local types, did not develop on uninterrupted lines. It is true, and of these we shall speak later, that the family of Wood in their types carried on the tradition, but the unfortunate classic influence monopolised the talents of the best modellers.

We illustrate two fine examples of *Toby Jugs* belonging to the Whieldon period. There is a strong family likeness between the two. The left-hand one is richly glazed and mottled in tortoiseshell markings. The other has the fine translucent colouring and glazing so noticeably prominent in this school. They are both remarkably good specimens of the Whieldon manner, and of unusual interest, as they represent the Toby jug in its earliest form.

The rivalry with Salt-glaze.—This "Whieldon ware" (of course it must not be forgotten that Whieldon made salt-glaze too) was contemporaneous with undecorated salt-glaze ware, which at its best exhibited in no small degree a complete knowledge of the strength and beauty of form unaided by colour. But in this school of Whieldon there is a distinct appeal to colour as a leading feature of the ware as opposed to form. There is a fine artistic blending of the colours and the variation of the glazes which palpitate with life and give extraordinary power to pieces possessed of the "Whieldon" touch. Not only on flat surfaces such as the well-known octagonal plates, but in figures and groups such as we have illustrated, these colour effects were employed with considerable dexterity. So that, in the contemplation of black-and-white illustrations of "Whieldon ware," everything is lost which gave the beauty and richness and mellowness which have an irresistible charm to those collectors who confine themselves to this early school of colourists.

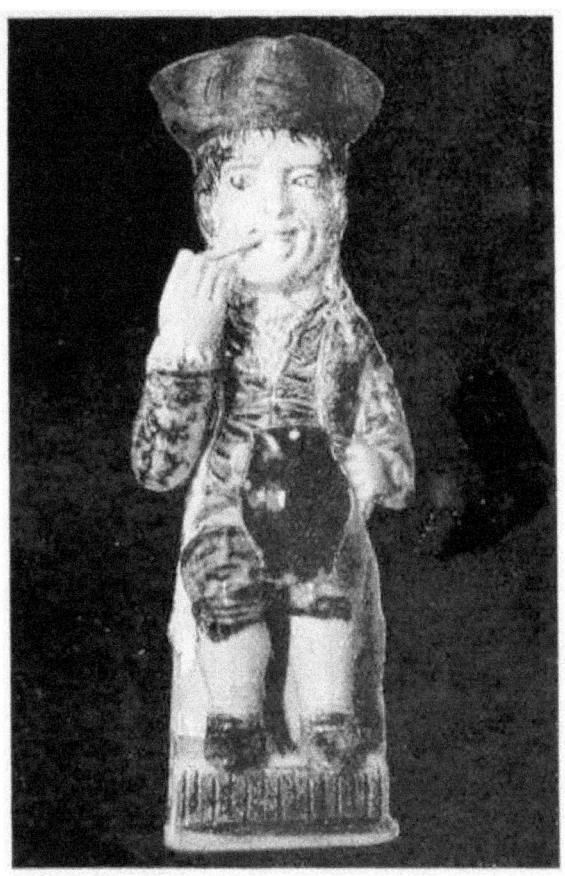

WHIELDON TOBY JUG.
Richly mottled and glazed.
(*In the collection of Col. and Mrs. Dickson.*)

WHIELDON TOBY JUG.
Fine translucent colouring and glazing.
(*In the collection of Mr. A. H. Baldwin.*)

Form *versus* Colour.—The salt-glaze potters, when they left their ideals of form and essayed to become colourists as well, made this attempt chiefly for two reasons.

(1) They had a very laudable desire to emulate the coloured porcelain made at Worcester, Bow, Chelsea, and Derby, which had become a serious competitor in their markets.

(2) They recognised a certain weakness in their ware in regard to its inapplicability to figures and groups. Unless the modelling is of the highest order the salt-glaze figures are insipid.

With regard to enamelled salt-glaze in general this is dealt with in another chapter, but it may here be remarked as touching the second point—the salt-glaze figure—that the salt-glaze potter brought himself directly in comparison with the figures and groups of earthenware of the later Whieldon school. Realising that if he must stand at all as a figure potter his modelling must be superlative, we find the salt-glaze figures, which are mainly small in size, taken direct from the antique or from porcelain models. But feeling the lack of colour he added touches here and there by applying reliefs of different coloured clays to heighten the effect. The salt-glaze potter rarely enamelled his figures in colours. In the illustration of a salt-glazed figure (p. 351) there are slight touches of blue.

So that in the contest between salt-glaze (the pre-eminent art of the Staffordshire potter in early eighteenth-century days) and its two great rivals, English porcelain and Staffordshire coloured earthenware, in other words—Form *versus* Colour—the first fall it received was at the hands of "Whieldon ware." The coloured and exquisitely clouded tortoiseshell plate, with its fine gradations of tone throbbing with colour, more than holds its own with the salt-glaze plate, even although its clear-cut arabesque designs and intricate patterns exhibit the excellence of its potting.

The Last Years of the Eighteenth Century.—Enough has been said to show that this typically English school had firmly established itself in Staffordshire. Whieldon, Dr. Thomas Wedgwood, Aaron Wood (block cutter to Whieldon), Josiah Spode the first, Greatbach, Enoch Booth, and many others, firmly adhered to their love of colour and their desire to see cream ware triumphant. The struggle for the supremacy of earthenware over English porcelain was still waging. And Wedgwood, with his marvellous invention of jasper ware and his equally stupendous innovation in the introduction of severe classic ornament, did not impose his style on all Staffordshire. We shall see in a later chapter how he had a crowd of followers and imitators, but at the same time many, very many, productions were potted contemporary with him that owed nothing in design to him, and on the face of them bear no traces of the classic influence.

It is this overlapping period, during which so many examples are unmarked, which is so puzzling to the collector. "Old Staffordshire," they certainly are, "Early Staffordshire" they may not be, but they exhibit a national and original feeling which it is impossible not to recognise and value.

GROUP OF EARLY STAFFORDSHIRE JUGS.
1. Jug. Pencilled floral decoration in blue. Inscribed "William and Mary Harrison. One Nother and Then."
2. Jug. Panel with *Miser* each side in relief.
3. Jug. Heart-shaped panel in low relief, *Children at Play*.
4. Jug. Panels of *Peacocks* in relief.

GROUP OF EARLY STAFFORDSHIRE JUGS.
1. Finely mottled granite jug.

2. Whieldon jug. Figures in coloured relief.
3. Jug. Moulded in form of satyr's head.
(*The above groups are in the collection of Mr. James Davies, Chester.*)

We illustrate two groups of jugs which belong to this period. In the top jug of the upper group, which is pencilled with blue floral decoration, the spout betrays a trace of Worcester and a tinge of classicism in the acanthus leaf ornamentation at its base. But the inscription drops at once into the homely vernacular, "William and Mary Harrison One Nother and Then." The quaint phonetic spelling tells its own story of the mission of the ale-house jug, with its invitation to another burst of hospitality.

The three jugs below are of the same species. The handles vary slightly, showing the inclination to adopt silver models. The left-hand one has a panel with figure of Miser in relief each side. The middle jug, with the heart-shaped panel, is decorated in relief with group of Children at play. Such subjects had not appeared on jugs before Wedgwood's day, but the idea might easily have been derived from contemporary prints of the pretty school of Bartolozzi and Angelica Kauffman. The right-hand jug, with its Peacocks in relief, is evidently derived from the exotic birds of Worcester.

In the other group of jugs, the uppermost betrays in the spout and neck distinct traces of its indebtedness to classic forms. It is translucent green in colour, and with coloured figures in high relief. At the front is Shakespeare, with figures of *Miser* and *Spendthrift* each side. Between these (one is just visible in illustration) are classic medallions. This is an incongruous style of decoration, and shows how little the Staffordshire potter who made it understood the meaning of ornament. He realised that the classic style was becoming popular, and so he half hesitatingly affixed two cameos to his otherwise harmonious production. The granite-ware jug, finely mottled, with two black-and-white bands as ornament round body, is the newer development of the early variegated ware. The right-hand jug is, in its gnarled and bulgy protuberances, known as the crabstock variety, the moulding, in the form of satyr's head crowned with vines, is an addition and is extraneous to the usual crabstock form. Obviously this is a welding together of the English and classic grotesque, and the combination is not too harmonious.

The early Staffordshire potters, apart from the splashed and variegated ware associated with Whieldon, made a variety of ware in pre-Wedgwood days and in the late eighteenth century. Obviously such a jug as that illustrated (p. 189) is an Oriental design taken straight from the contemporary English porcelain, or even from the actual Chinese original. But the Staffordshire potter was conservative in his shapes. Similarly, such jugs as that illustrated (p. 189) with the rustic design in crude painting, or seemingly in parts applied with a sponge, must have been general in the latter half of the eighteenth century. The scene is suggestive of Herrick and maypoles and haywains and rustic junketings, and such early cream-ware cider-mugs and ale-jugs are not uncommon. The *Mug* (illustrated p. 189) shows distinctive qualities. It is by Enoch Wood. It is decorated with translucent bands at top and base, and ornamented with a diaper-pattern stamped and coloured brown, with alternate lines of grey. These jugs and mugs are here illustrated to impress upon the reader the fact that in the Whieldon period (1740–1780) other forms than variegated ware were being made, and much unidentified early Staffordshire ware belongs to the later years of the eighteenth century.

The English spirit.—These forms—and the field is a great one for detailed study—were growing up in spite of foreign and un-English fashions, and long after Wedgwood's day they existed. It seems as though it was a dogged and obstinate attempt on the part of the potter to ignore classic models, and produce something "understood of the people." Obviously such ware did not rise to elaborate ornamental vases, but confined itself to mugs and jugs and useful articles in common use. So that, in spite of the enormous influence of Wedgwood, both in technique, but more especially in decoration, upon his contemporaries and his successors, it would seem that there was always an undercurrent of pottery which, even if crude, was extremely national. It appealed to no cosmopolitan *clientèle*, and the potters who made it were not important enough to issue price lists in three or four languages. Their message—as conveyed by their quaint inscriptions, "One Nother and Then," "I drink to you with all my hart, Mery met and mery part," and a host of other naïve sentiments—comes direct from the heart of the potter to his friend and neighbour who bought his wares. In a word, we may say that much that is native, much that is racy of the soil, in the long line of queer Staffordshire figures of animals and birds and of homely individuals, grotesque in their diminutive personality, owe direct kinship to Whieldon and the pre-Wedgwood school of potters, forgetful of the cold classic day, and, in the words of William Blake, snug by the glad sunshine of "the Alehouse so healthy and pleasant and warm."

CREAM WARE JUG.
Painted decorations in under-glaze colours. Typical example of Oriental influence on earthenware.
(*In the possession of Mr. W. L. Yeulett.*)

STAFFORDSHIRE CREAM WARE JUG.
Crudely painted in colours with English subject. Typical of earthenware of latter part of eighteenth century.
(*In the collection of Mrs. M. M. Fairbairn.*

BARREL-SHAPED MUG BY ENOCH WOOD.
Decorated with translucent green at top and base. Diaper pattern stamped and coloured brown, and alternate lines of grey.
(In the collection of Mr. Robert Bruce Wallis.

PRICES—EARLY STAFFORDSHIRE WARE.

WHIELDON.

	£	s.	d.
Teapoy, square, cream coloured, splashed with green, having female embossed figures, and inscribed "Abraham Randell, Alice Randell 1779," 5¼ in. high. Bond, Ipswich, April, 1906.	7	10	0
Plates, pair, foliage in blue on mottled ground, inscribed "LBC 1739." Christie, June, 1906	14	3	6
Teapot, agate ware, modelled with shells. Christie, June, 1906	12	1	6
Figures of musicians (three). Christie, November, 1906	13	2	6
Plaque. Portrait of Sarah Malcolm Saunders, executed in 1733 (very rare), taken from picture by Hogarth. Sotheby, November, 1906	2	10	0
Teapot and cover and milk ewer and cover, mottled. Puttick & Simpson, November, 1906	4	4	0
Figure of "Hope," with splashed and mottled base. Sotheby, February, 1907	1	15	0
Toy Teapot and cover, with vine-leaves and grapes in relief, decorated in rich translucent colours. Sotheby, February, 1907	2	18	0
Teapot and cover, agate ware, modelled with shells. Christie, April, 1907	5	15	6
Teapot, with roses in colours on blue ground, and another with rosebuds and strawberries on pink ground. Christie, April, 1907	27	6	0

Teapot, teacup, and two saucers, with flowers in colours in Chinese style. Christie, April, 1907	11	0	6
Group of two birds in tree, translucent colours. Sotheby, July, 1907	2	18	0
Teapot and cover, with peasant figures in colours. Christie, July, 1907	13	13	0
Figure of *Stag* at rest, mottled brown and white, on green pedestal (10½ in. high). Christie, November, 1907	10	10	0
Group of *Lovers*, pair, with birdcage, lamb, and dog (10 in. and 11 in. high). Christie, January, 1908	22	1	0
St. George and Dragon figure (11 in. high), and group nearly similar. Christie, January, 1908	10	10	6
Figures, pair, Peasant Boy and Girl, emblematic of Autumn and Winter, on octagonal plinths (7¼ in. high), and a Figure of *Man with Bagpipes* (8¼ in. high). Christie, January, 1908	13	13	0
"King David" Figure (12½ in. high), and "Neptune" (11½ in. high), on square pedestals, with medallions in relief. Christie, January, 1908	14	3	6
Cauliflower-pattern Teapot, cream-jug, and canister. Christie, February, 1908	11	0	6
Teapot and cover, solid agate ware, very large size. Sotheby, May, 1908	10	0	0
Teapot and cover, formed of leaves, with rabbit on cover. Sotheby, May, 1908	4	4	0

ASTBURY WARE.

Teapot and cover, dark buff body, decorated in relief with grapes, tendrils, and leaves in cream colour. Sotheby, November, 1907	3	10	0

Teapot and cover, brown hexagonal shape, with panels of
Chinese subject in relief, lid surmounted by rabbit.
Sotheby, November, 1907　　　　　　　　　　　　3　15　0

Astbury and early Whieldon figures, which are of small size as a rule, range in price from £4 to £10. Exceptional examples command much higher prices.

CHAPTER VI
SALT-GLAZED WARE—STAFFORDSHIRE

The originality of English Salt-glazed Ware—What is Salt glaze?—Early Salt-glaze—The classes of Salt-glaze—Its decadence and its extinction—Prices of Salt-glazed Ware.

The fine salt-glazed stoneware of Staffordshire which was made during the greater part of the eighteenth century is something in art of which the English potter may very justly be proud. It is remotely derived from the fine Flemish and Rhenish decorated stoneware, but the connection ends with the common qualities of being glazed with salt and of being extremely hard, almost so hard as to resist a file. But in the Staffordshire salt-glazed ware the body became almost of a porcelain-like quality. It was able to be made as thin as stamped silver, and in the thinnest portions of the pieces it is translucent like porcelain. Indeed, since the days of Elers (whom Dwight termed a silversmith) earthenware, or rather stoneware, took some of its details in form and in ornament from the worker in silver.

The applied ornament of Elers stamped with a brass die suggests the metal worker, and, with the models of the school of Astbury before them, Staffordshire potters followed the same methods. It is not astonishing to find the moulded designs with their intricate patterns in the newer school of potters of salt-glaze ware—which in its best period (1720–1740) relied solely on form and not on colour, being a dull, creamy white—emulating the fine work of the silversmith. It was only a natural striving in the new generation of potters of the Whieldon school, with fresh inventions in clays and glazes and moulds, to cast about them for better and worthier ideals than Toft had, and fresher models than stoneware Bellarmines which had been in circulation in the country since Tudor days.

Silver models provided many a fine shape for Wedgwood, his cream ware and his basalt teapots are bodily taken from Sheffield. But imitativeness has always been the curse of English potters. Wedgwood copied in jasper ware the cameo work of the classic world, and the whole of Staffordshire to a man commenced to pot on similar lines. Through the last decades of the eighteenth century, and well into the nineteenth, thousands of vases and jugs were turned out as echoes of Etruria in Staffordshire which, as its name denotes, was but an echo of something centuries earlier. Bow called itself "New Canton," and Worcester slavishly copied Chinese mandarins and exotic birds, coined in the brain of some Oriental potter. Chelsea copied Dresden, and Lowestoft copied the Bow and Worcester copies of Chinese originals, and the list could be prolonged *ad nauseam*.

SALT-GLAZED LOVERS' TEAPOT.
In the shape of a heart. Floral decoration slightly gilded.
(*At Victoria and Albert Museum.*)

SALT-GLAZED TEAPOT.
In the form of a camel.
(*In the possession of Mr. F. W. Phillips, Hitchin.*)

Indeed, this curse lies very heavy on the collector who has to devote a great portion of his energy to research in order to determine who first made certain models. This, unfortunately, tends to divert the study of old earthenware, its artistic qualities and its technical triumphs, into channels more or less contentious. The literature of English ceramics is rapidly becoming like many of the editions of Shakespeare, where a few lines of text stand as an oasis in a desert of commentators' controversial opinions.

It is, therefore, refreshing to find, as one does undoubtedly find in Staffordshire salt-glazed ware, one of the most remarkable and original outbursts in English art pottery that has taken place. This delicate stoneware is as thin as some of the Oriental porcelain, and possesses a grace and symmetry peculiarly its own. In some of its decorations it bears a likeness to Chinese work. This does not detract from its high place as a ceramic record. On the contrary, this similitude is a tribute to pay to its artistic excellence, for there is very little earthenware that came out of Staffordshire that will bear comparison with the work of the Chinese potter.

What is Salt glaze?—We know that many of the stoneware Bellarmines and Rhenish jugs were glazed with salt. It was a process known on the Continent at a very early date, some authorities place it as early as the twelfth century. But it was not until the second half of the sixteenth century that German and Flemish potters used this salt glaze to any great extent. We have seen, in the chapter on stoneware, that the appearance in the mottling and in the orange-skin-like surface is due to the action of salt glaze.

To cover pottery with an outer surface has been practised from earliest times either by the use of some glassy material or by powdered lead. Glazing with common salt was quite a new departure by the English potters. In order for this salt glaze to be used there must be a very high temperature, so high, as a matter of fact, that it would melt or soften in the kiln most English earthenware. This is where stoneware in its body differs from earthenware; it is what is termed "refractory," that is to say, it is not readily fusible. Stoneware is not always glazed. Elers did not glaze his red ware, and Wedgwood did not glaze his basalt or black ware. Stoneware can also be glazed with other processes than the salt glaze, but, as a rule, stoneware is associated with salt glaze.

Without entering too tediously into the exact steps by which salt glazing is performed, it may be roughly described as follows. Other glazes, such as lead, are applied to the surface of the ware prior to its entry into the kiln for firing, but in salt glaze the glaze is incorporated with the ware while it is actually in the kiln. Towards the end of the firing common salt (chloride of sodium) is thrown into the kiln, which is packed with the ware, through apertures in the kiln which has to be specially designed for salt-glaze use. At the high temperature of the kiln (about 2,190° Fahr.) the salt is volatised and its vapour penetrates the saggers (that is, the earthen vessels containing the pieces being made), which have perforated sides to enable this vapour to form on the surface of the pieces being fired. This vapour chemically unites with the silica largely present in the body of the stoneware, and forms a silicate on the surface of the ware. That is to say, the stoneware becomes coated with a thin layer or glaze of sodic silicate or soda-glass.

GROUP OF SALT-GLAZED WARE.
Jug enamelled in colours. Teapot blue enamel by Littler.
(*In the collection of Col. and Mrs. Dickson.*)

This chemical action taking place simultaneously with the final firing of the ware before its removal from the kiln incorporates the glaze with the body of the ware itself. It is this combination which causes the minute depressions or tiny pin-holes in all stoneware from Bellarmines down to the finely and nearly translucent salt-glazed Staffordshire ware which has a surface like that of leather. The same multitudinous pin-hole surface is characteristic of Oriental porcelain, which like stoneware is fired at a very high temperature, and the glaze and the body completed at one firing in the *grand feu*. Though, of course, this is not salt glaze, nor is the surface other than as smooth as glass to the touch, although under a strong glass or even to the naked eye these pin-holes are easily discernible.

At the present day salt glaze is mainly used for such ware as ink-pots, drain pipes, insulators for telegraphic instruments, and common ginger-beer bottles. The connection between John Dwight, of Christ Church, Oxford (Master of Arts), the creator of the magnificent bust of *Prince Rupert*, the glory of the ceramic collection at the British Museum, and between John Philip Elers, godson of Queen Christina, and this sad array of utilitarian nondescripts, is not a pleasing subject for reflection. It is sad to think that these triumphs have been won in vain by the genius of the old potters over the plastic clay. What an ignoble ending to the long chain of experiments! When Dwight destroyed his secret memoranda it is as though he foresaw the era of the drainpipe.

Early Salt-glaze.—The early stages of the manufacture of salt-glazed ware were crude and experimental. There is some connection between the finely potted lustrous stoneware of Nottingham and "Crouch ware," the undeveloped form of the later phase of finely-potted Staffordshire salt-glaze ware. This "Crouch" ware represents the transitional stage between the ordinary brown stoneware and the later drab or greyish white examples. Crouch ware at its earliest was not made in Staffordshire till 1690, and there is presumptive evidence to show that salt-glaze brown ware was made at some pot-works at Crich, near Matlock, Derbyshire; and that the same or similar clay was used by the Staffordshire potters who gave it that name, and there is proof that the Crich pottery existed as early as 1717, and Nottingham has dated pieces as early as 1700.

On the face of it, in spite of Josiah Wedgwood's letter in connection with the medallion to John Philip Elers, there is little evidence to go upon to credit the Elers with having made salt-glaze ware at all. Excavations on the site of their factory at Bradwell Wood have only resulted in the discovery of fragments of their unglazed red ware, "red porcelain" as it was called, and experts have pronounced their oven as being unfitted for salt-glaze operations.

On the whole, therefore, in accordance with the latest research, one is inclined to come to the conclusion that the Brothers Elers did not invent Staffordshire salt-glazed ware. If they made it at all, they made very few examples. The red ware is theirs as far as Staffordshire is concerned, although Dwight had something to say on that score when he charged them and Nottingham potters and others with infringing his patents.

SALT-GLAZED TEAPOT.
Enamelled in colours. Marked "John Toft."
(*In the collection of Col. and Mrs. Dickson.*)

Among the early makers of salt-glazed ware were Astbury and Twyford, and Thomas Astbury, son of the former, being associated with the introduction of ground flint into the body in 1720. Thomas Billing in 1722, and Ralph Shaw in 1732, made further improvements in the body. Dr. Thomas Wedgwood and Aaron Wood, and Thomas Whieldon and Ralph Daniel, of Cobridge, were all well-known makers of this ware, the latter having introduced plaster-of-paris moulds in lieu of alabaster, and being further notable for his enamelled decorations in colour, in the period 1743 to 1750, which attempted to vie with the contemporary coloured porcelain. William Littler, of Longton, used a similar blue to that which he used on the porcelain at Longton Hall.

At this date the ware became white in colour, and took its pleasing forms so dear to connoisseurs.

The Classes of Salt-glaze.—In its various styles salt-glazed ware may be roughly divided into periods. The experimental stage was over in 1720. From 1720 to 1740 the undecorated or white examples were made, depending on form for their beauty. These had applied ornamentation stamped with metal dies, or made in separate moulds and affixed to the body to be decorated (similar to the Elers style). It is during this period that some of the finest pieces were made with sharp, clear-cut designs. Later, when moulds were made of plaster-of-paris in place of alabaster, the design became blurred.

Among the most beautiful designs in this plain white ware having raised ornament are sauceboats, pickle trays, sweetmeat dishes, teapoys or tea canisters, and teapots; these latter are of a great variety of shapes, many having shell ornament, very exquisitely moulded, and others being of hexagonal shape divided into compartments. There is, too, a trace of the grotesque discernible in some of these teapots and a subtle humour too rarely found in English pottery. There are those of the camel form, such as the specimen illustrated (p. 197). The peculiar handle made by hand is very noticeable, usually such handles are snipped off at the end. Others are of the shape of a house, and many types of this design occur. Some are in the form of a squirrel. Then there are the heart-shaped teapots with the spout incongruously representing an arm resting on the neck of a swan. These teapots were supposed to have been made for lovers. We give an illustration (p. 197) of one of these heart teapots, and it will be seen how a slight touch of gilding has been added to heighten the effect on the embossed portions showing the fruit. Of course the cauliflower teapot exhibits a touch of humour, too, but this form is rarely found in salt glaze. The bright natural colours of that interesting vegetable were reproduced by Whieldon, who made this type as well as melon and pineapple teapots and coffee-pots. The vivid green and yellow glaze of this cauliflower ware is of the period when Josiah Wedgwood was with Whieldon and is held to be young Josiah's invention. He afterwards made similar ware himself.

The next stage was the slight use of colour in what is termed "scratched" blue. This style of decoration is the opposite of the relief ornaments. The pattern was incised with a sharp instrument on the piece, in the lines thus cut cobalt blue was applied with a sponge. Birds and foliage are the typical form of decorations to pieces of this style from 1740 to about 1750.

From 1745 to 1750 William Littler introduced his cobalt blue ware over which decorations in black or white were enamelled or gilded, and such pieces are rare. (See illustration p. 201.)

SALT-GLAZED VASE.
Enamelled in colours—turquoise blue, yellow. (Height 5¾ inches.)

SALT-GLAZED PUNCH BOWL.
Enamelled in colours, with portrait of the Young Pretender.
(Diameter 10 inches.)
(*In the possession of Mr. S. G. Fenton.*)

Then comes the period in which colour was in full swing. From 1740 to 1760 enamelling in colours was extensively used. It was employed on plain surfaces, or as a touch of colour to ornaments in relief. There is no doubt that some of these coloured examples are very beautiful. It is not necessary to dethrone the plain white ware from its place of honour. With later developments it was found that colour could be used with artistic advantage, nor is there any deterioration of the ware from an æsthetic point of view in this colour work when in the hands of skilled craftsmen.

Similarly transfer-printing was recognised as a suitable means of decoration, and pieces are found with printed designs of black or red or puce. The head of the King of Prussia is found on some specimens of this type. Of course this is later in date, and must have been subsequent to 1760, when Sadler and Green invented transfer-printing at Liverpool. Doubtless these pieces entered into competition with the new colour ware then in vogue, which drove the salt-glaze ware from the market, and killed the most artistic and original productions the English potter had ever made.

The industry had by this time grown to great dimensions, and apparently the Staffordshire potters were turning out this salt-glazed ware as fast as they could, no very good sign that good work was to last much longer. Nor is all the enamel work English; two Dutchmen were secretly employed at Burslem to do this enamelling in colour. But the secret spread, and we find two Leeds painters, Robinson and Rhodes, doing enamelling on the salt-glazed ware for the Staffordshire potters.

We are enabled to reproduce a very fine example of enamelled salt-glaze ware having the inscription "James and Martha Jinkcuson," and dated 1764. It stands as a fine specimen of its class. The colours of the flowers and insects are very rich, being, as is usual, enamelled over the salt-glaze ground. Dated salt-glazed ware is always uncommon, and an example of such fine colouring in such perfect condition stands as a rare and splendid specimen.

There is yet another style in salt-glaze in which the whole surface of the piece to be decorated is coated with a slip of another colour, and the decoration cut through it to show the white body beneath. This belongs to the last period, 1760 to 1780, as also does the basket work for which Aaron Wood, and R. J. Baddeley, of Shelton, are noted for their fine patterns. Incised work in imitation of Japanese work was also prevalent during the last period of salt-glaze work.

We illustrate another very important salt-glazed piece, a teapot enamelled in colours having what is known as a "crabstock" handle, spout, and lid. It is remarkable as being incised with the name "John Toft" (see p. 205). Undoubtedly this is a member of the celebrated Toft family, whose dishes, marked "Ralph Toft" and "Thomas Toft" in slip-ware, gave the generic name to a class of ware. It is not improbable that one of the Tofts modelled the celebrated salt-glaze "pew group" in the Victoria and Albert Museum. It exhibits the peculiarly quaint doll-like faces with beady eyes associated with Toft dishes.

SALT-GLAZED JUG.
Richly enamelled in colours, and inscribed 'James & Martha Jinkcuson 1764.'
(*In the collection of Mr. Frederick Rathbone, South Kensington.*)

In the group illustrated (p. 201) there is one enamelled jug. The two dishes show another type of plain salt-glaze. The teapot shows incised work on the broad band around it, but no indication of colour. The coffee-pot is the well-known squirrel form, and the dark teapot on left is enamelled in blue by Thomas Littler, and is a rare example.

In colouring the salt-glazed vase in bright turquoise blue and pink and green, with its Oriental design, strongly suggests the enamel work of Limoges (see p. 209). It stands in the eighteenth century in the same relationship to the metal enameller as does a modern French factory at Bordeaux, Messrs. Viellard & Cie., whose work in coarse earthenware simulates the *cloisonné* enamel.

The punch bowl illustrated has a portrait of the Young Pretender. In date it is, of course, not earlier than 1745, the year of the Rebellion in Scotland on behalf of the Pretender, and when his son Charles Edward landed and defeated the royal forces near Edinburgh. This punch bowl tells its story of stirring days, when Jacobites secretly met at night in quiet manor houses and drank a toast to the Stuart claimant. In public by a kind of subtle jest when they were driven to drink the health of "the king," they by a specious mental reservation flourished their glasses over any water on the table, the hidden meaning being "the King—over the water." But here is a punch bowl which was probably brought out for the sworn partisans to drink to the pious memory of the exiled Stuarts. There was always, even when the Stuart cause was a lost one, a tender recollection of "Prince Charlie," the "Young Chevalier." The lilting lines of Bobbie Burns in the last quarter of the eighteenth century, always awaken romantic associations, and bowls such as this were relics of something that had been, and without doubt in its day this same bowl has filled the glasses of a loyal company who drank the health of his Gracious Majesty George the Third.

As we have pointed out in the introductory note there are many monuments in clay on the collector's shelf which punctuate the sonorous phrases of the historian. Such pieces are exceptionally interesting in aiding the reflective mind to recreate the events of a former day which touched the life roots of the nation.

PRICES.

Salt Glaze.	£	s.	d.
Teapoy, square shaped, decorated with scratched flowers in blue. With female half-length figure (within a Chippendale frame), inscribed "Martha Saymore September ye 25th 1770" (5¼ in. high). Bond, Ipswich, April, 1906	11	0	0
Bowl and cover and milk jug decorated, rich blue ground. Sotheby, June, 1906	26	0	0
Teapot, brilliantly enamelled in colour with roses, auriculas, &c., with turquoise handle and spout. Sotheby, June, 1906	50	0	0
Teapot, crimson ground, with white panels with flowers in colour. Sotheby, June, 1906	26	0	0
Teapot and cover, modelled as house with royal arms over door. Sotheby, February, 1907	5	12	6
Teapot and cover, modelled as a camel. Sotheby, February, 1907	6	6	0
Jug and cover, hexagonal, with subjects in relief. Sotheby, February, 1907	4	4	0

Teapot, enamelled in colours, with portrait of Frederick King of Prussia; on reverse, spread eagle holding ribbon with inscription, "Semper Sublimis." Sotheby, March, 1907	21	10	0
Milk jug and cover, enamelled in colours in a continuous landscape with castle, obelisk, and other buildings. Sotheby, March, 1907	7	15	0
Vessel, modelled as a *Bear*, head forming cup. Sotheby, March, 1907	4	4	0
Basin with raised subjects in panels. Sotheby, July, 1908	13	5	0
Teapot and cover, enamelled in colours, with roses, &c. Sotheby, July, 1908	8	0	0
Teapot and cover, dark blue ground. Sotheby, July, 1908	8	5	0
Coffee-pot and cover (small), decorated in enamel colours with Chinese figures. Sotheby, July, 1908	14	15	0

CHAPTER VII
JOSIAH WEDGWOOD
1730–1795

Josiah Wedgwood's place in the ceramic world—His business abilities—Josiah Wedgwood's wares—Cream Ware and its invention—Jasper Ware and its imitation—The influence of Josiah Wedgwood—Wedgwood Marks—The Prices of Wedgwood.

The time is now ripe to form a mature judgment as to the exact niche in the temple of fame which Josiah Wedgwood is to occupy permanently. His immediate successors were in too close proximity to his own day to form an opinion as to his life-work in relation to what had gone before and what has succeeded him.

The inquiry into the origins of certain inventions attributed to him have been pursued of late years with a scientific thoroughness, and many facts have come to light which tend to raise the reputation of other lesser known potters who immediately preceded him or were his contemporaries.

John Dwight (of Fulham) has come into his own. The Elers (of Staffordshire) have been dethroned from the unique position they occupied as pioneers of salt-glaze ware. In regard to the Astburys, father and son, credit has been given them for great work, and Whieldon is held to have had an immense influence on his contemporaries. During the great outburst in salt-glazed ware, cream ware, its later rival and conqueror, was in a transitional stage. This transitional period embraces a great field of pioneer workers who experimented unceasingly with clays and glazes. The days of salt-glaze were drawing to a close, it had many obvious defects; the ware would not readily stand hot liquids—and this in an age when tea drinking was becoming fashionable. The artistic side for the moment was cast aside in these experiments, the uppermost question in the Staffordshire potters' minds was the invention of some ware that could hold its own against the competition of the new English porcelain factories.

It thus came about that this period of great technical activity (1720–1740) was immediately succeeded by an almost simultaneous exhibition of work, suggesting a renaissance of earthenware in England (1740–1800) and establishing the European reputation of Staffordshire.

Josiah Wedgwood with John Turner, of Lane End, and William Adams, of Greengates, stand as a trio of master potters who developed the classic spirit in jasper and kindred ornamental ware. In regard to developing the manufacture of cream ware and stone ware for domestic use, and in building up a continental and American trade which won for British earthenware the supremacy of the world's trade in pottery, Josiah Wedgwood takes an equal prominence together with Warburton and the Baddeleys and the Adamses and Turner.

In roughly detailing the stages which led up to the manufacture of the main classes of ware for which Wedgwood was famous, it will be shown how with a masterly mind for realising broad results he combined the patient industry of a practical potter. He commenced with a capital of twenty pounds and died worth half a million. In spite of his ill-health and the loss of his leg, his unflagging energy and his keen foresight enabled him to build up an important business which is still carried on by his descendants. His love of organisation and the system of control which he exercised over his own enormous output had a lasting effect on the methods of the Staffordshire potteries.

The genius of Josiah Wedgwood has won the continued admiration of succeeding generations. It may be that he has somewhat overshadowed many of his contemporaries, and his successors have been termed imitators. In order to adjust matters there is a tendency in some quarters to belittle the work of the great Josiah. But surely the pendulum has swung too far the other way when it is advanced that "Wedgwood himself was no artist, he was a tradesman pure and simple."

This is not the opinion of critics with nicer balanced judgment and of cosmopolitan taste. The epitaph upon his monument in the parish church of Stoke-upon-Trent, which bears the inscription that he "converted a rude and inconsiderable Manufactory into an elegant Art," has been assailed in order to prove it to be a "travesty of the fact," and to state that "what he *really* did was to convert an Art—rude it may be, and inconsiderable, but still an Art—into a manufacture. In other words, he inaugurated an entirely new order of things in the production of pottery, and a less desirable one."

The truth is that it is not necessary to belittle Wedgwood in order to put his great contemporaries in the order of their merit. The later and more corrected opinion may be arrived at quite judicially by crediting them with some of the artistic impulses he possessed. While he lived he worked harmoniously and in close friendship with his fellow potters, and a century after his death it should not be difficult to determine their relative positions without bespattering his epitaph with mud.

Wedgwood's business abilities.—He was undoubtedly a keen man of affairs. When in partnership with Whieldon he had travelled to London, to Manchester, to Birmingham, to Sheffield, and to Liverpool, which brought him into touch with silversmiths and metal workers in connection with the agate knife-handles and similar Whieldon ware. He evidently realised that Staffordshire was behind other districts in many respects. Although only a young man, he interested the influential people in the neighbourhood of the potteries and the roads were improved and water transit provided as an outlet for goods. He cut the first sod of the Trent and Mersey Canal.

In 1759 he was master potter, but he made most of his own models, prepared his own mixtures, superintended firing, and was his own clerk and warehouseman. Less than ten years afterwards, on the advice of the Duke of Marlborough, Lord Gower, and Lord Spencer, he opened showrooms in London in Newport Street.

A year after this the demand for his fine jasper ware and expensive ornamental productions had so increased that he found the greatest difficulty in finding sufficient workmen.

WEDGWOOD CREAM WARE DESSERT BASKET.
Showing fine pierced work.

By the courtesy of Messrs. Josiah Wedgwood & Sons.

WEDGWOOD CREAM WARE DESSERT CENTRE-PIECE.
Designed from Josiah Wedgwood's collection of shells.
(*In Museum at Etruria.*)

By the courtesy of Messrs. Josiah Wedgwood & Sons.

His catalogues were printed in several languages, and he had the shrewd common sense to add some forewords of his own to indicate the lines on which he was working as a potter and to bring the attention of likely buyers to his ware.

Wedgwood as a potter.—There is no doubt that Wedgwood always had in view the improvement of whatever ware he engaged to make. When with Whieldon he perfected the green glaze in the cauliflower and kindred ware, and when he became a master potter in 1759, he produced pieces which were eminently remarkable for their fine technique. There is no doubt that his connection with silversmiths induced him to follow their designs. Some of his early ware, such as teapots, have punched perforated ornament in the rims for which he invented tools. In the museum at Etruria are some six thousand trial pieces, some few inches in length, covering a wide period when Josiah was pursuing his way towards his crowning achievement, the invention of his jasper ware.[3]

He claims credit for great improvements, both as an inventor and as a ready and masterly adapter, quick to seize the salient points of a half-perfected ware and by a few touches of genius make it his own. He was made a Fellow of the Royal Society for his invention of a pyrometer, an instrument for registering high temperatures in the kilns. His experiments led him into new fields in connection with bodies, glazes, and colours, and he introduced for the first time in pottery certain minerals such as barytes in his pastes.

Josiah Wedgwood's wares.—It will be seen, in the enumeration of the various classes of ware which were produced by him, in what respect he added improvements which in their turn were improved upon by later potters, and to what extent his productions were entirely original, adding a new note in English pottery, creating an entire school, and leaving the mark of his genius on his successors for nearly a century.

Variegated ware.—The agate, the cauliflower, and melon ware, the clouded and mottled glaze, and the various imitations of marbling, came into vogue in the days of Whieldon. But Wedgwood was more ambitious in his designs. We have already seen, in dealing with Whieldon ware, how the "solid" agate ware was produced by means of fine layers of clays of different colours, which after careful manipulation produced a series of waves resembling the natural ornamentation of the stone. Wedgwood also employed "surface" colouring for this variegated ware, the body being of the common cream-coloured earthenware and the veining and mottling being applied to the surface. In such pieces the handles and the plinths were usually oil gilded; later he used a white semi-porcelain for plinths of such ware.

Two agate vases and ewers marked "Wedgwood and Bentley" belong to the period 1768 to 1780. The plinths of the agate vases show the white undecorated body. Wedgwood imitated Egyptian pebble, jasper, porphyry, and various kinds of granite speckled with grey, black, white, or green. Much of this is a flight higher than the agate ware.

Black basalt Ware.—In this ware, which was termed "Egyptian black," Wedgwood triumphed over his predecessors. We know the black ware made by Elers and by Twyford (two fine black Twyford teapots are in the Hanley Museum), but the ware into which Wedgwood infused his genius is worthy to be called what he termed it—"black porcelaine." With its rich black, smooth surface it was capable of varied use, including useful as well as ornamental ware. In the former, we find tea services and coffee or chocolate pots strictly adopting the severe Queen Anne silver shapes, and in vases he followed bronze prototypes. See illustration (p. 241) of two *Black basalt Teapots*. It was used in fine manner for life-size busts and for medallion portraits of "illustrious Ancients and Moderns."

This basalt ware Wedgwood further used in combination with other processes. He imitated the ancient Greek vase paintings by decorating the black surface with unglazed colours, or he had ornaments in relief in red. Another replica of classic art was his simulation of bronze, and this black ware formed the groundwork to which he added the bronze metallic colouring in his rare bronze examples.

The two black basalt ewers, entitled *Wine* and *Water*, designed by Flaxman, are well known. It is at once evident that they owe no inconsiderable debt to the metal worker. It requires no great stretch of imagination to believe them to be in bronze. Technically, as specimens of earthenware, they are perfect, but it is open to question whether the potter has not trespassed on the domain of the worker in metal. There are canons which govern the art of pottery; form and ornamentation strictly appropriate in metal are utterly unfitted for the worker in clay. Branched candelabra are false in porcelain though extremely beautiful in silver. In passing this criticism, which applies to some of Wedgwood's work, we are incidentally brushing aside the contention of those critics who find him unoriginal. As a matter of fact he was so original and so responsive to the suggestion of allied arts that he often undertook the creation of pieces in his kilns the like of which no potter had ever attempted before.

Red Ware.—It is not to be supposed that Wedgwood would allow the fine red Elers ware to stand as representative of the uttermost that Staffordshire had produced without attempting to emulate this early ware. Accordingly, we find in what he terms his *rosso antico*, a red ware of extraordinary beauty. Some of the engine-turned pieces of this red ware are exceptionally fine. There is in the Hanley Museum a coffee-pot of great technical and æsthetic value. Wine-coolers and other useful creations, with classic ornamentation in relief, show the wide range of this red terra-cotta or unglazed ware. The Elers style was simple, with applied stamped ornament of small dimensions and Oriental rather than classical in *motif*. The red stoneware of Böttcher, of Dresden, was by this time fairly well known, and Wedgwood had both Elers and Böttcher to serve as models, although he does not seem to have employed this red ware to any great extent. Nor did Wedgwood confine himself to red in this type of ware; he made chocolate-coloured examples, and in his cane-coloured and bamboo ware he made articles for domestic use, such as tea and coffee services as well as mugs and jugs of this type, which differed from the black basalt inasmuch as the basalt was an especially hard body, whereas these others were porous and soft. As was usual with Wedgwood, not only did he have a series of wares of different colours, but he often worked with a combination of these colours in the same piece.

Cream Ware.—Something must be said concerning the development of cream ware before it can be accurately determined how much Staffordshire was indebted to Wedgwood for its development. At the outset it must be granted that he did not invent the ware. But he improved it. Similarly it was further improved subsequent to his day by other potters who made it finer and whiter.

But to this day, a hundred and fifty years after the introduction of this cream ware, his descendants, still trading under the name of Messrs. Josiah Wedgwood and Sons, produce this cream ware exactly as it was then produced. Dinner services are made with Flaxman's designs on the border, essentially English in character and feeling. Last year Messrs. James Powell and Sons, of the Whitefriars Glass Works, near the Temple, which were flourishing in 1710, and still continue to produce the finest glass in England, held an exhibition of Wedgwood ware. Considerable interest was drawn to the subject of this revival of the old patterns of 1775 from the designs of Josiah Wedgwood's band of artists. Those connoisseurs who love old furniture and old eighteenth-century glass ware, as made by Messrs. Powell, welcomed the Wedgwood queen's ware designs as being something eminently fitted to strike the right note of harmony, and accordingly, by arrangement with the firm at Etruria, some of the finest patterns of the old ware are exclusively made for Messrs. Powell. The English dinner table may now be as English as it was in Georgian days, and, happily, this æsthetic revival has met with a warm response by the patronage of the royal family, the nobility, and by all those who love the old-world charm of the domestic art of our forefathers.

Before Wedgwood's day cream ware was made. Astbury used an addition of white clay and flint to his bodies about 1720. In 1726 the grinding of flint stones into powder for the potters' use became so important that Thomas Benson took out a patent for a machine to do this. In 1750 we find cream ware being largely made. Aaron Wedgwood and William Littler introduced about this time a fluid lead glaze instead of the old manner of using powdered galena (native sulphide of lead). Body and glaze were at this period fired at one operation. Enoch Booth improved this by revolutionising the method of glazing. He fired the pieces to a biscuit state and then dipped them in this fluid lead glaze (ground flint and white lead), and refired them at a lower temperature. At this date two other potters, Warburton (of Hot Lane) and Baddeley (of Shelton), followed Booth's practice, and cream ware may be said to have been in a fairly flourishing condition.

These facts are all important and cannot be ignored in arriving at a satisfactory conclusion. Wedgwood commenced as a master potter in 1759, that is, about nine years after the latest inventions in cream ware had brought the ware into something more than an experimental stage. In 1761 Wedgwood's cream ware, both by its variety of beautiful form and its finer glaze and body, had surpassed that of his rival potters.

In 1762 Wedgwood presented to Queen Charlotte a caudle and breakfast service of the ware; this was painted by Thomas Daniel and David Steele. The Queen and the King were so pleased with the ware that complete table services were ordered, and Wedgwood received the Queen's command to call himself "Potter to Her Majesty" in 1765, and from that date he termed the ware "Queen's Ware."

WEDGWOOD CREAM WARE PLATES.
Painted with English scenery. From service made for Catherine II. of Russia, 1774. Having green frog in reserve on each plate.
(*In Museum at Etruria.*) (*At British Museum.*)

WEDGWOOD BUSTS OF ROUSSEAU AND VOLTAIRE.
Enamelled in colours. (Height 6½ inches and 6 inches.)
(*At Victoria and Albert Museum.*)

Though the invention of cream ware may not be his, there must have been something essentially more pleasing in his productions to have made such strides in so short a time. Perhaps Wedgwood, "the tradesman pure and simple," had something to do with this achievement, but we prefer to think it was the master hand of Wedgwood the potter and Wedgwood the artist.

We cannot leave this *cream ware* question without referring to an old legal controversy. This brings us down to the year 1775 when Wedgwood, in company with John Turner (of Lane End) journeyed to Cornwall and jointly leased some clay mines. The reason for their visit was that the whole of the Staffordshire potters were up in arms. Salt glaze was coming to an end in spite of the enamelling in colours in emulation of English porcelain. And now Cookworthy, the potter of Plymouth, the maker of the first hard porcelain in England, had sold his patent rights to Champion of Bristol, who, in 1775, applied for a further patent for fourteen years to use certain natural materials for making porcelain. The Staffordshire potters elected Josiah Wedgwood and John Turner as their representatives and petitioned against the granting of this patent, and Wedgwood urged that

> "the manufacture of earthenware in Staffordshire has of late received many essential improvements, and is continually advancing to higher degrees of perfection; that the further improvement of the manufactory must depend upon the application and the *free use* of the various raw materials that are the natural products of this country."

He further adds that "the natural productions of the soil ought to be the right of all."

Incidentally, this controversy throws light on the position of Wedgwood as a maker of cream ware, and it had a lasting effect, as we shall show in the improvement of cream ware itself and upon the class of ware turned out in Staffordshire.

Champion, in his reply to the Staffordshire outburst in petitioning parliament not to grant his patent, pays Wedgwood a great compliment:

> "Mr. Champion most cheerfully joins in the general praise which is given to Mr. Wedgwood for the *many improvements which he has made in the Staffordshire earthenware*, and the great pains and assiduity with which he has pursued them. He richly deserves the large fortune he has made from these improvements."

Champion goes on to make a most vital point in upholding his claim to protection that he "has no objection to the use which the potters of Staffordshire may make of his or any other raw materials *provided earthenware only, as distinguished by that title, is made from it.*"

Here, then, is the reason of the visit of Wedgwood and Turner to the West, in search of the natural earths that half the potters in Europe had been hunting for since Böttcher, of Dresden, made his great discovery of white clay.

But the story of *cream ware* is not ended. Wedgwood to this printed "Reply" by Champion entered the lists with some printed "Remarks," which he circulated to members of parliament. In this—and we must bear in mind that he was holding a brief on behalf of all the Staffordshire potters—we find the following statement:—

"*When Mr. Wedgwood discovered the art of making Queen's Ware*, which employs ten times more people than all the china works in the kingdom, he did not ask for a patent for this important discovery. A patent would greatly have limited its public utility. Instead of one hundred manufactories of Queen's Ware there would have been one; and instead of an exportation to all quarters of the world, a few pretty things would have been made for the amusement of the people of fashion in England."

In spite of the opposition of Staffordshire, the Bill enabling Champion to obtain his patent rights passed both houses of parliament, and in the last stage a clause was inserted throwing open the free use of raw materials to potters for any purpose *except for the manufacture of porcelain*; practically this patent was to be enjoyed by Champion for nearly twenty-two years.

Two extraordinarily important effects upon the pottery industry in Staffordshire were the result of this controversy: (1) The Staffordshire potter confined himself to earthenware. (2) Growan stone and Cornish Kaolin were added to the cream ware body, which enabled earthenware to compete successfully with china.

It may have struck an inquiring spirit as singular that the Staffordshire potters as a body were content to imitate English porcelain and compete with it. At first, of course, the remoteness of the Potteries from the West accounted for this, but clay was brought by sea from Bideford to Chester and carried overland to Staffordshire, but not the growan stone nor Cornish kaolin. Chelsea and Bow did not have natural earths to hand. But the additional reason seems to be the one we have given—that practically Champion's patent precluded them from making porcelain. When, in or about 1769, cream ware was perfected there was no need to cast about for new bodies. Staffordshire earthenware had found itself, and all other improvements after that date, for fifty years, until early nineteenth-century days, mainly concerned enamelling, printing, glazing, and the *exterior*, or developments in mechanical production, or attempts at higher artistic effects.

In the illustrations we give of cream ware it will be seen that it was of varying form and it received a variety of decoration.

It was *plain or undecorated*, relying chiefly on its symmetry of form as an artistic asset. The cut and pierced designs and many other shapes followed those of the silversmith, and in dessert dishes and centre-pieces considerable beauty was exhibited in modelling—a style which was closely followed by the Leeds potters, who made excellent cream ware.

A beautiful example of the perforated basket ware is illustrated (p. 225). It is a dessert dish of most pleasing shape, and is a rare specimen of the pierced work in Wedgwood's cream ware.

Wedgwood, as early as 1775, still experimenting with a view to make his cream ware better, determined to make a whiter body by the addition of more china clay and flint and to kill the yellow tone by the use of blue (oxide of cobalt). This later white ware he termed "Pearl ware." Among the most noticeable productions in this whiter ware are the dessert services modelled from shells. We know that Wedgwood had a collection, although he was not a conchologist, yet it is not improbable that the contemplation of these beautiful forms suggested ideas and he derived many of his artistic shapes from the forms of shells. The use of shell forms was not unknown. Salt-glaze pieces repeatedly show the pecten shell design, and Plymouth porcelain had adopted shell designs in salt cellars and similar pieces. We illustrate (p. 225) a remarkable example of a centre-piece in the form of a nautilus shell. Some of the shell dishes have a faint wash in pink, and yellow radiating bands, hardly perceptible, but conveying the suggestion of the interior of the shell.

Queen's ware, when decorated, was of two classes: (1) painted; (2) transfer-printed in red or puce or black.

It is not necessary to go into details in regard to these two forms of decoration. It is interesting in regard to the enamelling in colour to know that Wedgwood sent his ware to Mrs. Warburton's factory at Hot Lane to be painted. He also employed a band of enamellers at Chelsea who had been trained in the china factory. We reproduce an illustration (p. 233) of two painted queen's-ware plates from the celebrated service executed for Catherine II. of Russia. The enamel painting of the views and borders cost Wedgwood over £2,000. In the centre of each piece is a scene representing some place of interest in the country. Each view in this series of British scenery is different, and there are some twelve hundred. The body is in pale brimstone and the view painted in a brownish purple; the border was a wreath of mauve flowers and green leaves, and, as will be seen in the illustrations, each plate has a green frog in a reserve. This design has puzzled many writers, but as the Messalina of the North intended to place this service in her palace of La Grenouillère, near St. Petersburg—Grenouillère meaning a marshy place full of frogs—explains the whimsical design of the frog on each plate.

This dinner and dessert service was completed in 1774 at a cost of about £3,000. It was exhibited in London, and set the town agog with amazement. The rooms in Greek Street, Soho, were thronged with fashionable people, and, as may be imagined, it gave a great impetus to the manufacture of Wedgwood's ware.

The other decoration employed by Wedgwood on his cream ware was transfer printing. He availed himself at once of the new style of printing by Sadler and Green on the glazed surface of his ware, which was periodically sent to Liverpool to be so decorated. In the earlier pieces the tile design is evident, quite unsuitable for a round plate, in spite of Wedgwood's addition of wreaths and ribbons in enamel painting to help out the incongruity. In early books illustrated by Bewick with square woodcuts a similar use of garlands and ribbons as an ornamental border is observed.

Nor was the cream body confined to strictly domestic ware. Among his multifarious productions Wedgwood made some fine coloured figures, remarkable for strong modelling and subdued and harmonious colouring. The large figures, such as Fortitude, Charity, Ceres, Juno, Prudence, and many others, are not always marked. "Fortitude" and "Charity" both bear the impressed mark WEDGWOOD, the latter belonging to the series Faith, Hope, and Charity designed for Wedgwood by Mrs. Landré, and a marked example is in the Willett Collection. Many small coloured cream-ware busts were made. We illustrate two typical examples (p. 233) of Rousseau and Voltaire. They were evidently intended for the French market, and are very dainty though somewhat highly-coloured likenesses of two great Frenchmen. Jean-Jacques is portrayed in Armenian costume, after the well-known portrait. The coat is a chocolate brown and the stand is marbled. Voltaire has a blue surcoat, a terra-cotta cloak, and lilac vest.

WEDGWOOD BLACK BASALT TEAPOTS.

WEDGWOOD JASPER WARE DICED PATTERN TEA SET.

By the courtesy of Messrs. Josiah Wedgwood & Sons.

Jasper Ware.—As early as 1773 Wedgwood was experimenting with a view to producing jasper body. It is here that his greatest triumph in the ceramic art was won. Nothing like it had ever been seen in pottery before, and the ware he produced in an endless variety of forms which were termed "ornamental" by him to distinguish them from the queen's ware, or "useful" ware. About 1775—a great date in Wedgwood's history—the jasper ware was perfected, and from 1780 to 1795 is the period when it was at its best, when he poured forth from Etruria, then filled with a highly-trained body of workmen and artists, his jasper ware, exquisite with grace and beauty of form and fascinating in its charm of dainty and subtle colour.

The spirit of classicism was in the air in the days of Wedgwood. Dr. Johnson had imposed his ponderous latinity on the world of letters. Alexander Pope was still writing when Josiah was apprenticed and known already as a "fine thrower." Homer's *Iliad* and *Odyssey* had appeared in many editions just prior to Wedgwood's manhood. The statues of naval and military commanders in Westminster Abbey were in Roman costume. The Brothers Adam were in the heyday of their popularity. From sedan chairs to silver-plate their style was the vogue. The classical mouldings, capitals, and niches, the shell flutings and the light garlands in the Adam style are welcome sights in many otherwise dreary streets in London. In furniture, the Adam style is as severe as the French prototypes which had absorbed some of the ancient spirit of Rome and Greece. As early as 1763 Grimm wrote, "For some years past we are beginning to inquire for antique ornaments and forms. The interior and exterior decorations of houses, furniture, materials of dress, work of the goldsmiths, all bear alike the stamp of the Greeks. The fashion passes from architecture to millinery; our ladies have their hair dressed *à la Grecque*." Men of thought joined in clamouring for simplicity, and Diderot lent his powerful aid in heralding the dawn of the revival of the antique long before the France of Revolution days.

But eyes other than French were fixed on the remote past. The excavations of Herculaneum and Pompeii had given a new stimulus to archæological research. In this country Sir William Hamilton, as early as 1765, promoted the publication of the magnificent work, "Greek, Roman, and Etruscan Antiquities," illustrated from his collection. It was a specially valuable exposition of the system and methods and æsthetic value of classic art, especially plastic art; and in promulgating this sumptuous illustrated disquisition on the ancient potter's art Sir William Hamilton laid modern workers in the same field under a heavy debt. Incidentally it may be mentioned that Sir William was the husband of the beautiful Lady Hamilton.

So that in the midst of this eighteenth-century classic revival Josiah Wedgwood was but the child of his age, and, associated in partnership with Bentley, a man of refined and scholarly tastes, he entered into the new spirit with willing mind. Adroitly seizing classic models, Wedgwood in his art adapted all that was most suited to modern requirements. Pope translated Homer into English verse, and Wedgwood translated classic designs into English pottery.

WEDGWOOD JASPER VASE.
Subject—representing the Apotheosis of Virgil; surmounted by Pegasus cover.

By the courtesy of Messrs. Josiah Wedgwood & Sons.

Wedgwood's jasper ware is of various colours—blue in various tones, sage-green, olive-green, lilac, pink, yellow, and black, and, of course, white, which is its natural body without the addition of metallic oxides. It is capable of taking a polish on the lapidary's wheel. In use it was mainly employed for ware of a highly ornamental character, though it was also employed for utilitarian objects, such as tea and coffee services, dishes, and flower vases, and in plaques it was used as interior decorations in fireplaces and in furniture. We illustrate (p. 241) a jasper ware diced pattern *Tea Set*, which shows how wide a field Wedgwood covered with his new ware.

It is usually found with a ground of one colour, such as blue, lilac, *et cetera*—one of the seven—and the ornament applied in relief is, as a rule, white. It was Wedgwood's appreciation of antique gems that suggested the idea of reproducing them in earthenware, and in the period prior to Bentley's death, in 1780, cameos, portrait medallions, and plaques were mostly made.

There are two classes of jasper ware—*solid jasper* and *jasper dip*. The difference is similar to that between solid agate and surface agate. Solid jasper is coloured throughout. That which is coloured only on the surface is jasper dip. This latter gives more delicate effects, and was employed, after 1780, in the important series of classic vases which required translucency and greater delicacy in the white reliefs, which is especially effective in the filmy garments and flowing draperies of the classic figures.

Considerable progress had been made in Staffordshire since Elers left in 1710, but it is the Elers method of stamping the ornaments and applying them to the body of the ware that Wedgwood adopted. But there was more than enough originality of invention in this jasper ware to carry his fame to the confines of Europe. Blue and white porcelain in imitation of his jasper was made at Sèvres, and other continental factories, such as Meissen, Furstenburg, and Gros Breitenbach, made similar echoes of this wonderful English jasper ware of Josiah Wedgwood.

No illustrations can do justice to the charm and tender colour of some of the finer examples of this Wedgwood jasper ware, varying from pale lemon colour to delicate mauve as a ground, and having translucent diaphonous draperies in white standing in relief in the groups of figures.

To the sense of touch fine old specimens of this jasper ware are as soft as satin. Usually the dull matt surface of this ware is left without polish, though it is so dense and hard as to receive a high polish, which was occasionally employed in the inside of basins and cups and on the bevelled edges of some of his cameos.

His classic subjects were no feeble echoes of ancient art, but were executed from designs by a band of great artists working together and saturated with the spirit of the new classic revival. John Flaxman, James Tassie, John Bacon, William Hackwood, Thomas Stothard, George Stubbs, William Greatbach, were all employed by Wedgwood. And distinguished amateurs such as Lady Diana Beauclerk and Lady Templeton supplied him with designs, and it is interesting to note that Mrs. Wilcox, an accomplished painter of figures and borders on his Etruscan ware, was a daughter of Fry, the mezzotint engraver and founder of the Bow porcelain factory.

We illustrate (p. 245) a fine jasper vase representing *The Apotheosis of Virgil*, the cover surmounted by a Pegasus. The square pedestal has griffins at the corners. A companion vase, *The Apotheosis of Homer*, changed owners at eight hundred guineas, and is now in the possession of Lord Tweedmouth.

Wedgwood himself regarded his copy of the celebrated Barberini vase, which was lent to him by the Duke of Portland, as his masterpiece. This vase is a cameo glass vase, which was discovered in the middle of the seventeenth century in a marble sarcophagus on the road to Frascati, two miles from Rome. This vase belongs to the early part of the third century. It was bought by Sir William Hamilton for £1,000, and subsequently purchased by the Duke of Portland. This vase, of rich dark blue glass, almost black, is decorated with opaque white enamel cameos in relief cut with the most extraordinary skill, and it stands as a superb example of classic art. Strictly speaking, Wedgwood's copy of this was at best a copy in one material of the technique of another. But if it be not the highest art to copy thus in intricate detail, yet it must be admitted that such masterly elaboration had never before been attempted by the potter, and the early copies of Wedgwood (he set out to make only fifty) stand unequalled as specimens of potting by the hands of trained workmen directed by genius.

Wedgwood and his influence.—As a final word on Wedgwood and his influence, something should be said as to the charge laid against him that he inaugurated the factory system as applied to pottery. There is no doubt that he organised what was before his day a somewhat chaotic industry. And it is certain that he trained his workmen to become specialists, and that the system of the division of labour was the order of the day at Etruria. But how else could such an output as his be handled? It has been advanced that the quaintness of the peasant potter and his later development was submerged, and that all individuality was lost under the new system. There was a growing tendency to develop mechanical perfection and to introduce labour-saving appliances, but this was the spirit of the oncoming modern age. Other factories, his contemporaries, were adopting the same principles, and those who think Wedgwood unoriginal or uninventive are quite willing to credit him with all the inventiveness and originality necessary to overturn the old system. The truth lies between these two extremes. Wedgwood, in common with his contemporaries, not unwillingly embraced all the newest devices known. It was Sadler and Green, of Liverpool, who together in one day by their invention printed as many tiles as it would have taken a hundred painters to do in the same time. Similarly all over the country artisans in the china trade were becoming specialised. There were the enamellers at Chelsea and other places, and a little examination will show that Wedgwood did not inaugurate this modern factory method, but without doubt, in common with all other master potters, he had to go with the times. Trade rivalry was very strong, and competition was not unknown when every potter in Staffordshire was jealously watching the latest improvement of his neighbour. But to saddle Josiah Wedgwood with the responsibility of stamping out original talent is beside the mark. His life-work stands impregnable against petty assault. "In a word, no other potter of modern times has so successfully welded into one harmonious whole the prose and the poetry of the ceramic art."

WEDGWOOD MARKS.

wedgwood

1.—This mark occurs upon a very early specimen of "Queen's Ware," a teapot, painted with flowers, &c., supposed to have been made by Wedgwood at Burslem: each letter apparently stamped singly with printers' type.

WEDGWOOD

WEDGWOOD

Wedgwood

2, 3, 4.—These marks, varying in size, were, it is thought, used by Wedgwood up to the accession of Bentley as his partner, 1768–9, and are found upon specimens said to have been purchased about that period.

5.—The circular stamp, without the inner and outer rings, and without the word Etruria, is doubtless the earliest form of the Wedgwood and Bentley stamp, and is found upon a set of three early painted vases, in imitation of natural stone, with gilt serpent and scroll handles. No other example of this mark is known: it may have been an experimental one, afterwards changed for No. 6, and never in general use.

- 145 -

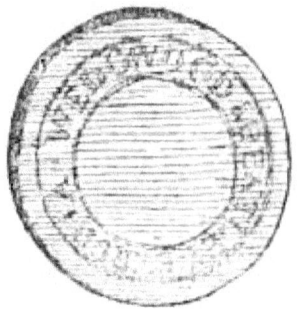

6.—This mark, with the word Etruria, is made upon a wafer, or bat, and fixed in the corner, inside the plinth of old basalt vases, reversing for candelabra and some large specimens; it is sometimes found on the pedestal of a bust or large figure.

7.—The well-known circular stamp, with an inner and outer line, always placed round the screw of the basalt, granite, and Etruscan vases, but is never found upon the jasper vases of any period.

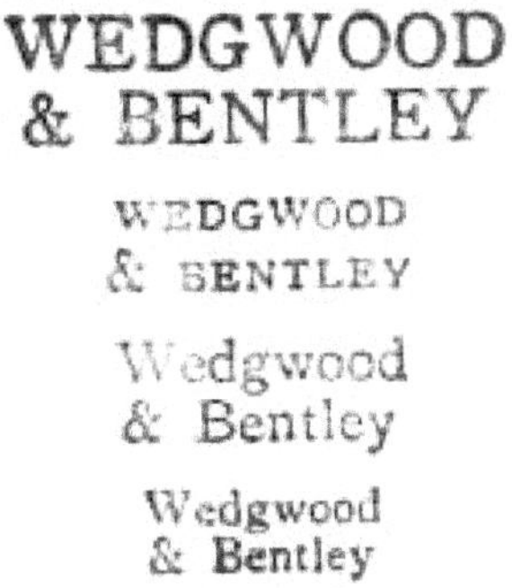

WEDGWOOD & BENTLEY

WEDGWOOD
& BENTLEY

Wedgwood
& Bentley

Wedgwood
& Bentley

8, 9, 10, 11.—These marks, varying in size, are found upon busts, granite, and basalt vases, figures, plaques, medallions, and cameos, from the largest tablet to the smallest cameo for a ring (the writer has one, only half an inch by three-eighths of an inch, fully marked); also found upon useful ware of the period.

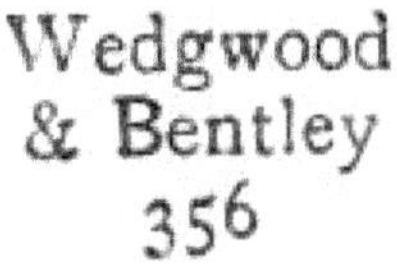

Wedgwood
& Bentley
356

12.—Marks upon the Wedgwood and Bentley intaglios, with the catalogue number, varying in size. Very small intaglios are sometimes marked W. & B. with the catalogue number, or simply with number only.

13.—This rare mark is found only upon chocolate and white seal intaglios, usually portraits, made of two layers of clay; the edges polished for mounting.

It may be noted that the word "and" in every Wedgwood and Bentley mark is always contracted "&," that no punctuation or other points, excepting those in marks No. 5, 6, 7, and 13, are ever used.

Wedgwood
Wedgwood
Wedgwood
WEDGWOOD
WEDGWOOD
WEDGWOOD
WEDGWOOD

14, 15, 16, 17, 18, 19, 20.—Marks, varying in size, attributed to the period after Bentley's death, and probably used for a time after Wedgwood died. These marks and others were used by chance—a small piece often bearing a large stamp, and a large one a minute stamp.

WEDGWOOD & SONS

21.—This rare mark exists upon some large square plateaux in cane-coloured jasper. It may have been one adopted upon the change of partnership in 1790, but little used. The circular announcing the change says: "The mark 'WEDGWOOD' will be continued without any addition."

WEDGWOOD
ETRURIA
WEDGWOOD
ETRURIA
Wedgwood
Etruria

22, 23, 24.—These marks rarely found upon pieces of very high character—usually upon dark blue stoneware, vases, and glazed ware. Adopted about 1840, but soon disused.

WEDGWOOD
(*in red, blue, or gold*)

25.—The mark upon Wedgwood PORCELAIN made from 1805–1815. Always printed either in red or blue, sometimes in gold. An impressed mark cannot be used with certainty upon soft-paste porcelain, being so apt to diffuse out in firing.

WEDGWOOD
WEDGWOOD

26, 27.—These marks, varying in size, are still used at Etruria for the modern jasper and useful ware of all varieties.

WEDGWOOD

28.—The manufacture of fine porcelain was revived at Etruria, 1878, and is still continued. This mark, *printed* in black and other colours, is used.

ENGLAND

29.—The word ENGLAND was added to the mark WEDGWOOD in 1891, to comply with the new American Customs Regulations, known as the McKinley Tariff Act.

The occurrence of three capital letters, ANO, REP, &c., in addition to name appears on ware after 1840. The first two letters are workmen's marks, and the third is a date letter, *e.g.*, O = 1855, P = 1856, and so on, as in hall-marks on silver.

PRICES.

	£	s.	d.
WEDGWOOD.			
Oval. Ganymede feeding Eagle (6¼ in. by 5¼ in.), marked Wedgwood & Bentley Christie, June, 1906	40	19	0
Oblong oval. Marriage of Cupid and Psyche (6 in. by 7¾ in.), marked Wedgwood & Bentley. Christie, June, 1906	54	12	0

Busts, *Minerva* and *Mercury*, black basalt, 18 in. high. Christie, November, 1906	16	16	0
Oval portrait, in jasper, white on blue ground, of Captain Cook (10 in. by 8 in.), marked Wedgwood & Bentley. Sotheby, February, 1907	16	16	0
Jasper vase, blue, with Venus and Cupid in relief, handles coiled with serpents. Christie, February, 1908	33	12	0
A pair of splashed mauve Nautilus Shells, marked Wedgwood. Sotheby, December, 1908	3	10	0

The above prices are for ordinary collectors' examples of old Wedgwood. But exceptional pieces bring exceptional prices. The largest known example of a blue and white jasper plaque (11 in. by 26 in.) sold for £415 at Christie's in 1880, and the fine jasper vase *The Apotheosis of Homer* (now in the Tweedmouth Collection) realised 800 guineas.

CHAPTER VIII
THE SCHOOL OF WEDGWOOD
1760–1810

William Adams (of Greengates) (1789–1805)—John Turner (of Lane End) (1739–1786)—The plagiarists of Wedgwood—The Wedgwood influence—The passing of classicism—Table of Marks—Prices.

Potters who followed Wedgwood may be divided into three classes. Men such as John Turner and William Adams, who were competitors with him in friendly rivalry, each striving to emulate the successes of the other, and each doing original and independent work. Indebted, and greatly indebted to Wedgwood as these potters were, they produced work equal with his in technique. The blue jasper of William Adams, if anything, is rather finer than that of his master. John Turner, of Lane End, made jasper from a different formula to Wedgwood, being more porcellanous in character. These men, his friends and intimates, and Palmer, of Hanley, who was first to apply bas-reliefs to his black vases, in 1769, may be said to represent original research, as compared with uninventive copying.

The second class, which includes contemporaries such as Elijah Mayer, and Palmer, of Hanley, who must be included here (in spite of his streak of originality above alluded to, and his fine use of gilding to granitic ware), and Neale, his brother-in-law, and Voyez, the modeller, and Hollins, may all be said to be plagiarists who lived largely on Wedgwood's jasper and basalt ware, as well as several schools such as Hartley Greens (of Leeds), and Swansea and Spode, and many others who followed his cream-ware designs. In regard to Palmer and Neale and Voyez the case is very strong, as they are stated to have forged the mark "Wedgwood & Bentley" in some of their medallions; but against the others the case must not be pressed too closely, as they undoubtedly displayed a fertility of invention and an originality after they had once learned the Wedgwood manner. Leeds, in particular, having caught the spirit that Wedgwood had transplanted from the silversmith to his dessert services, produced cream-ware rivalling that of Etruria.

Tennyson had a set of verses which illustrate this situation. He tells of him who "cast to earth a seed" which grew so tall "it wore a crown of light."

"But thieves from o'er the wall

Stole the seed by night."

Sown far and wide in every town, it won universal admiration, and, says the poet—who, by the way, was thinking of plagiarists of his own style—

"Most can raise the flowers now,

For all have got the seed."

We must make one other point; it was Wedgwood who lighted the way even to his source of inspiration. He made no secret of his indebtedness to the art of the silversmith, and in recognising in the antiquarian works of Count Caylus and Sir William Hamilton a new field, he left it open for others to go to the same original sources, nor were his contemporaries slow in doing this. So that, in a measure, this second class of potters may be exonerated from the charge of plagiarism when we find them striking out for themselves.

Chippendale, when he promulgated his "Director" giving designs for furniture, straightway started a school of cabinet-makers, who worked after his designs in every locality in England. These early pioneers in art— Chippendale, the masterly adapter of all that was best on the Continent, and Wedgwood, translator of classicism into English pottery—worked with broad and generous spirit, and their contemporaries and those who came immediately after them helped themselves liberally to the overflowing profusion of ideas.

The third class is the great crowd of lesser men, potters who claim little attention for original work, but who are remembered as producing, as an echo to the great classic revival, designs and shapes and copies of Wedgwood's ware, sometimes in stoneware for jugs, and more often in cream-ware, without an added touch of originality. In this decadent period, when not only in Staffordshire but in other parts of the country this was being largely done, and not always done well, though there are exceptions to which we shall allude later, one is reminded of the pregnant words of Goethe: "There are many echoes, but few voices."

William Adams (1745–1805).—The Adams family are renowned in Staffordshire as being among the oldest potters in the country. In connection with classic ware William Adams, of Greengates, is pre-eminent. At his death, in 1805, the works were carried on by Benjamin Adams till 1820. There is considerable confusion between contemporary members of this family, both of the same name, William Adams (of Cobridge), William Adams (of Greenfield), and the subject of the present remarks, William Adams, of Greengates, who commenced as master potter there in 1789. There were other firms, such as J. Adams & Co., or Adams & Bromley, who made jasper ware between about 1870 and 1886, and who stamped their ware "ADAMS," or "ADAMS & CO." This, of course, does not come into the realm of collecting, and this latter firm has nothing to do with the old-established family of Adams. But collectors cannot be too careful when auction catalogues describe such ware as "Adams."

The beautiful Adams blue which is of a violet tone is much admired, and in the finely-modelled classic reliefs the style is less frigid than Wedgwood, as William Adams drew his inspiration more from Latin than Greek models. As a rule his jasper is a trifle more waxen than that of Wedgwood, but never glossy. William Adams was a favourite pupil of Wedgwood, and was doubtless indebted to him for the guidance that set the young potter to work in friendly and amicable rivalry with his late master.

BLUE AND WHITE JASPER VASE.
Impressed mark TURNER.
Subject—Diana in her Chariot.
(John Turner, of Lane End, 1762–1786.)

BLUE AND WHITE JASPER VASE.
Impressed mark ADAMS.
(About 1790.)
(William Adams, of Greengates, made jasper 1787–1805.)

(*At British Museum.*)

As a modeller he was of exceptional merit, and it is known that he designed, himself, several of his finest pieces, such as the *Seasons*, his *Venus Bound*, and *Cupid Disarmed*, his *Pandora*, *Psyche trying one of Cupid's Darts*, and the *Muses*. Monglott, a Swiss artist, was employed by him on jasper vases, and it is believed that Enoch Wood is responsible for designing the hunting scenes which appear on the fine stoneware jugs and tankards similar in style to the Turner jug illustrated (p. 267). Many of his jugs had silver mounts.

In regard to marks, that usually found is ADAMS impressed. Sometimes, though rarely, the mark is ADAMS & CO.; and later his son, Benjamin Adams, had the impressed mark B. ADAMS, which appears on stoneware and blue printed ware.

To those who desire to familiarise themselves with the genius of William Adams, there is a special volume by Mr. William Turner, entitled "William Adams, an Old English Potter" (Chapman & Hall, 1904), which is a full and learned monograph, dealing in thorough manner with the productions of William Adams and of his kinsfolk, the Adams family of potters.

We illustrate one of a pair of jasper vases in blue and white by Adams, in date about 1790. The classic figure subjects, as will be seen, display a simplicity and exquisite grace of modelling and arrangement not surpassed even by Wedgwood (see p. 261).

John Turner, of Lane End (1739–1786).—Wedgwood and Turner were intimates, and in considering Turner we must regard him as a friendly neighbour, as well as a rival potter. He made some remarkably fine jasper, though it differed in its body very greatly from that of Wedgwood, being more closely allied with porcelain. It contained no barytes in its composition. In design Turner, though not imitative, followed the Greek school and produced, as a modeller himself, some exquisitely proportioned pieces. We illustrate a fine vase in blue-and-white jasper which is especially graceful in design, the severity being relieved by the delicacy of the fine subject in relief of *Diana in her Chariot* drawing a pair of goats and accompanied by flying cherubs (see p. 261). This subject, it will be noticed, is reproduced in a transfer-printed jug illustrated in a later chapter (p. 319).

But it is in the unglazed stoneware that he surpassed anything his contemporaries had done. It was about 1780 that he discovered, after hunting for clay even so far afield as Cornwall, the precise earth he wanted in his own neighbourhood at Longton. In colour it was a warm biscuit tone, and it was capable of being modelled with exactitude into fine sharp designs in relief. In stoneware jugs with classic figures in relief he set the fashion for half a century. His teapots and coffee-pots are models of graceful design. We illustrate a fine example of a *Teapot* (p. 267), with the lid perfectly fitting, made to slide in a groove, and showing in clear relief the style of ornamentation for which Turner became so renowned. The other illustration, on the same page, of an equally perfect *Stoneware Jug* with metal mounts, shows a slight departure from classic ornament. The figures are in old English costume, and are engaged in archery. It will thus be seen that even in the early days there was exhibited a tendency to depart from classic figure design and turn to equally graceful but homelier subjects. Possibly this influence may have been due to Enoch Wood, who is believed to have been employed by Turner as a modeller; but accurate information regarding Turner's modellers is not known.

Besides the above-mentioned wares, Turner also made black basalt of very high quality, being preferred by some connoisseurs to that of Wedgwood. He also was the first to introduce under-glaze printing into Staffordshire, and although he did not introduce the "willow pattern" (Spode brought that from Caughley), he made ware with this pattern printed in under-glaze blue, and his plates and dishes have perforated borders. We illustrate a fine example of this ware (p. 331).

The Plagiarists of Wedgwood.—We have seen that John Turner, of Lane End, that William Adams, of Greengates, came under the strong influence of Wedgwood, but were no more imitators, in the broad sense, than Gainsborough and Romney may be said to be imitators of Sir Joshua Reynolds. It must be allowed in art that a school may arise under the guidance of some remarkable genius who tinges the originality of his contemporaries with his own master mind. Wedgwood had the inspiration to transplant classic decoration into Staffordshire—the rest was easy; having shown the way, crowds of lesser men seized the new ideas with avidity.

Chief among the direct copyists was Henry Palmer. He had a spark of originality, as we have seen, anticipating Wedgwood by some five years in applying bas-reliefs to his black vases, and the sprinkled marbled ware touched with gold was another success of his, but here his ingenuity ended. He must have been a great thorn in Wedgwood's side, for he is said to have procured every new pattern on its appearance and copied it. Voyez, who was a modeller and not a potter, assisted in this nefarious traffic; but Voyez, in spite of his rascality, was a clever modeller, and struck out a new line in his rustic or "Fair Hebe" jugs. He was employed at one time by Wedgwood, and probably by Ralph Wood. Voyez specialised on the intaglio seals, and added Wedgwood and Bentley's names to his handiwork. On other intaglios, equally imitative, and on vases is the name PALMER or the initials H. P.

Wedgwood himself—as do collectors nowadays—was obliged to acknowledge the fine quality of the work of Palmer and of Neale, for he admitted to Bentley that they were "serious competitors," and he evidently feared their activity, as he says, "We must be progressing or we shall have them treading on our heels."

The sagacity of Wedgwood's remark is obvious, for an examination of the Neale-and-Palmer jasper and other ware reveals an amazing mastery of technique. It is finely potted and well balanced in ornament and design. If it were not for the impressed mark such vases might readily pass as Wedgwood. It is not improbable that in the middle nineteenth century the names both of Adams and Palmer and Neale were ground out of the bases of some of their finer vases by ingenious persons, who passed them off as the work of Wedgwood.

TURNER STONEWARE TEAPOT, UNGLAZED.
With ornament in relief and classic figure subjects.
Mark impressed TURNER. (Height 4½ inches.)
(*In the collection of Mrs. L. Scott.*)

TURNER STONEWARE JUG, UNGLAZED.
With decoration in relief of archery. Silver lid and rim.
Mark impressed TURNER. (Height 9 inches.)
(*In the collection of Mr. John Watson Bradley.*)

Marks—Palmer, Neale, Wilson.—In regard to marks, H. PALMER or PALMER. HANLEY is the earliest—sometimes only the initials H. P. About 1776 he entered into partnership with his brother-in-law, and sometimes the mark NEALE alone is found and often NEALE & CO. These marks are usually in circles; on one piece appears I. NEALE, with the word HANLY (spelt wrongly) beneath. About 1778 Robert Wilson joined the firm, and after 1788 his name alone appears. Stoneware jugs—drab ground with cupids in relief—baskets, and cream-ware are often found marked WILSON surmounted by a crown with the letter C above. Sometimes this is present without the name. Wilson, too, is remembered for having introduced chalk into the body of his cream-ware, which was of exceptional value in whitening the ware and rendering it more adapted for under-glaze printing. At Wilson's death, in 1802, David Wilson succeeded to the pottery, and the firm shortly after became D. Wilson & Sons. These Wilsons made pink lustre, similar to that of Wedgwood, and also silver lustre, upon some of which the name of Wilson is impressed. This brings the factory down to 1820, when it passed into other hands.

We have seen that Adams and Turner and Palmer and Neale came more or less into touch with Wedgwood as contemporary rivals. Before coming to the crowd of lesser men, or lesser-known men, we must not omit Josiah Spode, who was a colleague of Wedgwood under Whieldon; Elijah Mayer, whose black basalt was almost equal to that of Wedgwood, and whose enamel cream-ware stands artistically very high; and Samuel Hollins, of Shelton, with fine red or chocolate ware, having as dense a character as Wedgwood's imitations of the Elers ware, and Hollins in his jasper produced some fine examples with original combinations of colours.

Josiah Spode the First (there are three potters in succession of that name) made, in common with other potters, the black basalt ware from 1770, when he commenced as potter, and he produced stoneware jugs similar in character to those of Adams and Turner, following the sporting subjects in relief and departing from the ultra-classical subjects of Wedgwood. This class of jug and mug was made by many potters—its character was English, and it was evidently popular. An illustration of the type appears on page 277. Davenport, of Longport, made the same pattern; it was made at Castleford, near Leeds, and Hollins and others adopted the design in relief of a fox-hunt, with horsemen dismounted preparing to join others at the "kill," which is shown on the reverse. In fact, it was almost as much copied in stoneware as the "willow pattern" was in blue-printed ware.

But Josiah Spode is best known as devoting considerable skill in the improvement of under-glaze blue-printing cream-ware. In 1783 he brought two workmen into Staffordshire from Caughley, where under-glaze blue-printing under Thomas Turner was in full swing. Spode was not the first to introduce under-glaze blue-printing into Staffordshire; this is due to John Turner, of Lane End (whom we have described, maker of the fine jasper-ware and stoneware teapots and jugs), not to be confounded with Thomas Turner, the maker of porcelain at Caughley, who introduced the "willow pattern" in 1780, which same design was introduced into Staffordshire in 1784 by Spode—a year after his two men came over from Caughley. But this and blue transfer-printing is dealt with in a subsequent chapter.

Something should be said of Josiah Spode the Second (1797–1827), who continued the blue-printed ware, and produced a great number of stoneware jugs with decoration in relief similar to those we have alluded to, and produced jasper ware in blue and white with the familiar subjects of Wedgwood's day. To him must be given the credit of introducing colour into Staffordshire earthenware, colour such as it had never before attempted. His fine imitations of the Derby-Japan porcelain designs mark a new era in Staffordshire earthenware.

BLACK BASALT TEAPOT, UNGLAZED.
Impressed mark E. MAYER. (1770–1813.) (About 1786.)
(*At British Museum.*)

BLACK BASALT TEAPOT, UNGLAZED.
Impressed mark BIRCH. (About 1802.)
(*In the possession of Mr. F. W. Phillips, Hitchin.*)

These illustrations show the imitativeness of this school of potters and the difficulty of identification.

The Spodes brought something new into Staffordshire earthenware. The elder Spode evidently had a strong love for Oriental subjects, as in the "willow pattern," which he "lifted" from Caughley porcelain. He broke away—and others followed him readily enough—from the cupids and psyches and gods and goddesses of the old world, and followed the newer-imported ideas in Chinese taste, now the fashion at Worcester, Bow, and other china factories. Leeds and Swansea were not slow in snatching at this new Oriental style of decoration.

In the Staffordshire cream-ware jug we previously illustrated painted in under-glaze colours, somewhat brown owing to the imperfect knowledge of the Staffordshire potter in under-glaze work submitted to great heat, we see an example of painted design in Oriental style, which came shortly to be more perfectly done in under-glaze blue, as in the painted plate of Leeds ware illustrated (p. 303).

But much in the same manner work such as the painted scenery on services like that made by Wedgwood for Catherine II. was shortly supplanted by black and purple and red transfer-printing done at Liverpool, so the short-lived under-glaze blue painting on earthenware was quickly killed by Spode and the other Staffordshire potters when they rapidly developed the under-glaze transfer-printing in blue.

It was quite an original departure, and owed nothing to Josiah Wedgwood (who never employed transfer-printing in blue), though it was adopted very successfully by the firm after his death. And Josiah Spode the elder most certainly had a strong influence in the potters of his day in acclimatising the "willow pattern" in Staffordshire, and in assimilating the best efforts of Chinese decoration as applied to blue-and-white ware. And Josiah Spode the Second, with equal originality, took up the next stage in adopting the gorgeous colouring of Japan.

This brings the story of the development of Wedgwood's cream-ware up to modern times. And the same chain of development might be traced in the history of some of the other great potters whose descendants still carry on the manufacture. Cream-ware at first painted, then transfer-printed in black or red, then painted in blue under-glaze—which was killed by the blue under-glaze printing—finally emulated the rich colours and gilding of porcelain.

To return to **Elijah Mayer** (1770–1813). From 1786 he appears to have produced black basalt tea ware; his fine teapots with the seated figure at the apex are well known, and his unglazed cane-coloured ware is much prized, with its simple decorations in lines of green and blue. We illustrate ([p. 271](p. 271)) an example of a *Black Basalt Teapot*, and beneath it an illustration of a similar model by Birch, showing the imitativeness of this school of potters and how difficult it is to identify specimens. His cream-ware deserves especial attention, as his enamelling was in very artistic manner, and it stands out prominently among a crowd of imitators of Wedgwood's cream-ware borders. Every maker not only took the body of the ware, but in so doing he followed the designs by Flaxman or some of Wedgwood's other artists, still found in the old pattern-books to-day at Etruria. As an example of this imitation in detail, see the Swansea cream-ware plate illustrated ([p. 397](p. 397)).

Mayer made black glazed tea ware, and this, when unmarked, is very commonly attributed by beginners to Turner. The marks impressed are E. MAYER, and after 1820 E. MAYER & SON. At a later period the mark was JOSEPH MAYER.

Samuel Hollins (1774–1816), with his red and chocolate unglazed ware decorated with ornament in the Elers manner and made from the clay at Bradwell Wood, is deservedly noteworthy as well as for several important departures in colour in the stoneware teapots and coffee-pots which he made of green, with touches of applied ornament in blue jasper. He followed silver designs, and avoided the cold, classic forms of Wedgwood. He departed from the straight lines of the Turner teapot. He loved ornament, and there is a touch of elaboration in his design, as though attempting to shake off the severe formality of the Brothers Adam style of design, and he strongly loved colour.

Samuel Hollins was one of the proprietors in the New Hall china works, and his successors were T. and J. Hollins, who continued to make jasper ware in the style of Wedgwood. Their names are impressed on many examples.

The Wedgwood influence.—In the latter days of the eighteenth century and the early days of the nineteenth, the direct influence of Wedgwood became something more remote. But even in early nineteenth-century days there were undeniable traces of the old models and the old form of ware. Take, for example, the unmarked early nineteenth-century *Black Basalt Teapot* in the form of a barrel, with the grape-vine ornament in relief, and the pine cone at top of lid (illustrated p. 277). Undoubtedly this has left all classic form, but it has retained the technique of Wedgwood. In some of the buff-coloured, unglazed stoneware jugs which are unmarked, there is the inclination to follow the sporting subjects in relief, which Adams and Turner and Spode so successfully adopted, and the twisted snake-handle and reptilian-modelled mouth become original in treatment. In general, it may be said, that the classic influence remained for a considerable time in the stoneware of various kinds, but in the cream-ware which is the main stream of English earthenware, the forms and the ornamentation more rapidly departed from the styles of Wedgwood's queen's ware.

Hence we find two opposing influences working against each other in the Staffordshire potters' minds. The best of them in their highest flights essayed to make jasper, or to copy or emulate Wedgwood's classic style in vases and important ornamental pieces. Most of them largely made the stoneware of various colours, and also the black basalt. All of them made cream-ware, which was the staple ware of Staffordshire, in a thousand different forms. As time went on all except cream-ware began to deteriorate from the earliest prototypes, and the later forms are debased in design and inferior in potting.

SPODE STONEWARE JUG.
Rich blue glazed ground with decoration of hunting scene in white relief.

DAVENPORT STONEWARE JUG.
Same design as adjacent jug, but having white ground with subject in relief.

(*In the possession of Mr. Hubert Gould.*)

BLACK BASALT TEAPOT.
In the form of a barrel, with grape-vine decoration in relief.
(Early nineteenth century.)

The passing of classicism.—From the first there were those who were classic only by compulsion. Wedgwood was regarded as too classic for vulgar tastes. The cream-ware and the coloured figures display a ready appreciation of public wants. Even Voyez descended to rusticity in his jugs. Spode had a leaning for Oriental subjects in his blue printed ware, which was quickly adopted by Leeds. Adams leaned to landscape subjects after Claude and English scenery. Nor was this all. The cream-ware figures and the mugs and jugs provided full scope for the potter's fancy in political, satirical, patriotic, and humorous and fancy subjects. From Sunderland to Swansea the cream-ware took to itself more homely sentiments and more characteristic design. It became, during the last quarter of the eighteenth century and the first quarter of the nineteenth, as English as if the gods and goddesses had never descended into Staffordshire, and as though Wedgwood had never been.

Most of this cream-ware was transfer-printed, the Caxtons of Staffordshire had found blank spots enough to fill on their white ware, and in filling them they have left us a permanent record of popular feeling which was at the time strong enough to induce them to rush into print on every conceivable subject with queer engraved decoration and whimsically illiterate verse.

Marks.—The following are some of the names, mostly found as impressed marks, on ware of the Wedgwood school, in date from 1760 to 1835, a period of three-quarters of a century. In many cases in addition to ware bearing traces of a classic influence, the potters made cream ware with blue-printed decoration, a style which was not employed at Etruria until the second Wedgwood period, on the death of Josiah Wedgwood in 1795.[4]

The names are arranged alphabetically, and, where of interest, the class of ware associated with the potter is given.

William Adams (of Greengates)	1787–1805	Fine jasper ware of the highest quality. Stoneware and blue-printed ware.
J. Aynsley	1790–1826	Silver lustre. Transfer-printed ware. Melon- and barrel-shaped teapots.
Batty & Co.		Vases and jugs, classic figures as frieze, printed in under-glaze blue touched with vermilion.
E. J. Birch		Black basalt ware of good quality (sometimes marked with E.I.B. impressed).
Bott & Co.		Busts painted in colours. Vases transfer-printed.

J. Clementson	1832–1867	White ware blue-printed with foreign scenery. (Marked with name and phœnix.)
Clews	1814–1836	Stoneware jugs. Blue-printed cream ware. Picturesque views and subjects after Wilkie's pictures, Rowlandson's *Dr. Syntax, Don Quixote*, &c.
Close & Co. (Successors to W. Adams & Sons, of Stoke.)	from 1843	Cream ware with printed decoration in brown.
Cookson & Harding C. & H. (late Hackwood.)	1856–1862	Cream ware blue transfer-printed.
Davenport (Longport) (Firm continued till 1886.)	1793–1834	Cream ware painted and printed. Handles in form of dolphins. Plates and dishes—dragons and fret border printed in blue; ground pencilled in scale pattern.
Eastwood	1802–1830	Vases small, jasper, Wedgwood style; stoneware blue and buff. W. Baddeley, of *Eastwood*, is believed to have used this mark, frequently found.
Hackwood	1842–1856	Cream ware painted with knights and armed figures.
Harding	1862–1880	Blue glazed earthenware, white ornaments in relief. Brown glazed jugs and teapots in Rockingham style.
Harley	about 1809	Teapots, white glazed stoneware; cover surmounted.
Heath	1770–1777	
Heath & Bagnall	1777–1785	
Heath, Warburton & Co.	1786–	

S. Hollins	1774–1816	Jasper ware, white ground cameo figures in blue.
T. & J. Hollins	1802–1820	Similar ware to above.
A. & E. Keeling	1786–1828	Black basalt and cream ware.
Lakin		Cream ware blue-printed with English landscape subjects, &c.
Lakin & Poole	1770–1846	Dishes and cream ware. Centres often finely painted with exotic birds in Worcester style.
J. & T. Lockett	1786–1829	White stoneware and salt-glaze.
E. J. Mayer	1770–1813	Black basalt tea services, &c., with animals in relief; silver lustre.
E. Mayer & Son	1813–1830	
Mayer & Newbold	1823–1837	Made porcelain as well as earthenware (marked M. & N.).
Mayer & Elliott		Cream ware, blue-printed.
F. Meir		White glazed earthenware services, English landscapes printed in blue, dishes with pierced border.
Morr & Smith		
Moseley	1802–1825	Black basalt ware; teapots, &c.
Myatt	1802–1840	Unglazed red ware coffee-pots in Elers style. Engine-turned with wavy patterns. Sometimes marked with an oval enclosing letter **W**.
H. Palmer	1760–1775	Fine jasper ware, granitic vases; figures.
Neale & Palmer	1776–1778	Jasper ware strongly imitative of Wedgwood.
Neale & Co.	1778–1788	Jasper ware and classic figures.

Phillips (Longport)	1760–1830	Small dishes; salt cellars, cream ware, Oriental decoration, blue-printed.
Pratt		Vases and jugs, white stoneware, with blue figures in relief; border of vine.
Ridgway	1790–1854	Various elaborate marks used. W. Ridgway and W. Ridgway & Son. In 1836 the firm became W. Ridgway, Morley, Wear & Co.
Riley		
Rogers	1786–1829	Blue-printed stoneware. Inferior imitations of Wedgwood.
Salt	1820–1864	Figures enamelled in colour.
Shorthose	1783–1802	Black basalt vases and flower jars.
Shorthose & Heath	1802–	White glazed earthenware, transfer printed in red over-glaze. Subjects—children at play, &c. Cream ware embossed with wicker pattern pierced border. (Mark printed in red, also impressed.)
Sneyd	about 1850	Imitations of Portland vase, &c.
Josiah Spode (*the First*)	1770–1797	Black basalt ware. Stoneware jugs with sporting subjects in relief.
Steel	1780–1824	Jasper and ornamental ware, white relief on blue, dark blue figures in relief on pink ground, &c.
W. Stevenson	about 1828	White glazed ware, classic figures in relief on pale blue ground; impressed mark W. Stevenson, Hanley.
John Turner (of Lane End)	1739–1786	Fine Jasper ware of excellent quality. Stoneware jugs, &c., of warm biscuit colour unglazed. Black basalt, and under-glaze, blue-printed ware.

Walton	1806–1839	Figures-classical Lions, *Fishwife*, *Gardener*, &c.
Warburton	1751–1828	Rarely marked. Mrs. Warburton, of Cobridge, in 1751 made great improvements in cream ware prior to Wedgwood's queen's ware. In 1828 the firm was J. Warburton & Co.
Wilson	1788–1820	Stoneware jugs with classic figures in relief. Ornamental vases in Wedgwood style. Copper lustre ware.
E. Wood	1784–1790	Cream ware, basket pattern, &c. Busts.
Wood & Caldwell	1790–1818	White glazed earthenware. Figures, coloured busts, &c.
Enoch Wood & Sons	1820–1846	Figures of classic form.

PRICES.

School of Wedgwood.

ADAMS.   £   s.   d.

Jug (with old Sheffield plate lid), chocolate band with Bacchanalian subject. Escritt & Barrett, Grantham, April, 1907   2   2   0

Jug, blue jasper, with figure subjects of *Seasons* in white relief, old Sheffield plate cover. Sotheby, May, 1908   6   5   0

Sucrier and Cover, marked "Adams & Co." Sotheby, November, 1908   2   14   0

TURNER.

Female figure of a "Water Carrier" in black basalt, marked Turner. Sotheby, December, 1905   3   5   0

Teapot and Cover, blue ground with classical subjects in high relief; impressed mark, Turner. Sotheby, November, 1908   2   6   0

Teapot, of different form, similar decoration, unmarked. Sotheby, November, 1908	2	4	0
Sucrier and Cover, similar decoration; impressed mark, Turner. Sotheby, November, 1908	3	12	0
Cake Plate with classic decorations in relief; impressed mark, Turner. Sotheby, November, 1908	4	10	0
Coffee Pot and Cover, similar style; impressed mark, Turner. Sotheby, November, 1908	4	0	0

NEALE & PALMER.

Vase and Cover with medallions, wreaths and masks in relief, in gilt on mottled grey-blue ground, marked Neale, Hanley. Puttick & Simpson, Nov., '08	4	10	0
Vase and Cover, urn-shaped, with medallion and figure subject in white relief; ram's head handles, wreaths and borders in gilt on mottled-blue ground, marked H. Palmer, Hanley. Puttick & Simpson, November, 1908	3	10	0

RALPH WOOD.

Figure of Apollo with lyre. Sotheby, May, 1908	2	5	0
Figures, Boy and Girl Harvesters, square bases; one marked R. Wood. Sotheby, May, 1908	10	5	0

E. WOOD.

Bust of John Wesley, signed Enoch Wood. Sotheby, June, 1906	2	0	0

E. MAYER.

Four plaques of Cupids in relief; mark impressed, E. Mayer, and dated 1784. Sotheby, November, 1905	1	18	0

HEATH.

Plate of cream ware, crudely decorated for the Dutch market, subject—Abraham offering up Isaac (Hodgkin Collection). Sotheby, December, 1903	0	3	0

LAKIN.

Dish decorated with border of rose, shamrock, and thistle. Prince of Wales' feathers and lion over crown in centre. Made for the Prince Regent (George IV.); marked "Lakin." Sotheby, February, 1906	2	0	0
Pair of *Lakin* plates from above service. Sotheby, November, 1907	3	0	0

LAKIN & POOLE.

Mug, with mask head on front, marked "Lakin & Poole," and four shell dishes. Sotheby, June, 1906	1	6	0

CHAPTER IX
LEEDS AND OTHER FACTORIES

Leeds Marks—The best period of Leeds—Leeds Cream Ware—Blue and White Ware—Leeds Ware decorated at Lowestoft, Castleford, Jackfield, Rockingham, Sunderland, and Newcastle—Table of Marks—Prices.

Leeds claims notice mainly on account of its fine cream ware that was produced in the period from 1783 to about 1800 when the factory was at its zenith. The date which commences its known history is the year 1760, a most pregnant year in the history of pottery. Before that there always exists some doubt as to the exact date or the particular maker. "Early Staffordshire" or "Whieldon" are as definite as most collectors dare go.

In 1762 Wedgwood's cream ware was perfected, and all Staffordshire was aflame with the prospects of something that at last was to stand artistically side by side with Bow and Chelsea and Worcester and Derby and Plymouth. It did nothing of the sort, but still it was the dream of the Staffordshire potters that it should by reason of its cheapness smash the new china factories, and it seems to have had no little share in doing this.

In 1775 the Leeds pottery was in the hands of Humble and Green. In 1783 it was known as Hartley, Greens & Co., and for the next ten years some splendid examples of cream ware were produced rivalling the best productions of Wedgwood, at first imitative, but later strikingly original, and possessed of extraordinary artistic qualities. Down to the opening days of the nineteenth century the trade in cream ware was considerable. Pattern books and catalogues were issued in French and German and Spanish, and the output from Leeds was very considerable, and the continental trade very extensive, especially with Northern Europe.

From 1825 to 1832 the firm was known as Samuel Wainwright & Co. From 1832 to 1840 the name changed again to the Leeds Pottery Company, under the managership of Stephen Chapel, who, together with his brother James, held the pottery till 1847. In 1850 Warburton, Britton & Co. were proprietors until 1863, and Richard Britton & Sons carried on the works until 1878 when the factory closed.

Forgeries of Leeds Ware.—Leeds ware has appealed, on account of its artistic qualities, to so wide a circle of collectors and admirers that it has had the honour of being forged with intent to deceive. Nearly all these pieces are marked either "Leeds Pottery," "L.P.," or "Leeds P." In addition to being copied for sale to unwary collectors some of the basket and other patterns have been of recent years made in Germany for sale in this country. But to any one who has had the opportunity of handling genuine old Leeds ware the lightness in weight, the fine finish, and the peculiar colour of the body, especially the slightly green tinge in the old Leeds glaze are never to be mistaken. The modern copies lack the fine potting, and they are slightly heavier in weight, and always without exception have a thick white, glassy glaze which fills the corners of the pierced work, and shows the touch of modern haste.

Leeds Marks.—The following marks occur on Leeds ware, largely on the blue-printed ware which was after 1791, for many of the finest examples of cream ware are unmarked. However, these marks used may be a guide: LEEDS * POTTERY (often printed twice over and crossing at right angles), HARTLEY, GREENS, & CO., LEEDS POTTERY (either in two lines or in a semicircle), also the initials L.P. In its latter stage (1863–1878) R. Britton and Sons marked their ware R. B. & S. with the initial L enclosed in a circle.

The Don pottery at Swinton near Leeds, established about 1790, came in prominence about 1800, when one of the brothers Green, of Leeds, became owner. It passed through various vicissitudes of fortune, a comparison of the old pattern books show that many pieces made at the Don pottery were originated at Leeds. In 1834 it was purchased by Samuel Barker, and in 1882 it was still known as Samuel Barker and Sons.

The Don Pottery mark was both printed and impressed DON POTTERY in its early days prior to 1834, and sometimes the word GREEN appears above. Later in the Barker *régime* a demi-lion rampant holding in his paws a pennon with the words "Don Pottery" was used, sometimes with the word BARKER, and sometimes with the initials S. B. & S.

LEEDS CREAM WARE CENTRE-PIECES.
Made to take into four parts. (Height 4 feet.)
Pierced baskets, removable. (Height 2 feet 6 inches.)
(*In the collection of Mr. Richard Wilson.*)

The best period.—But it is chiefly the best period, that is, Hartley, Greens & Co., from 1781 to about 1805, which appeals to collectors of old Leeds, though a pattern book was issued as late as 1814, which still maintained the old traditions, but when Hartley died in 1820 the factory practically went to pieces. The two brothers Green and William Hartley nobly carried on the manufacture of cream ware. At first they looked to Wedgwood for inspiration, but very shortly introduced a lightness of design in the exquisite and intricately pierced patterns in the borders, and original touches in the feather edges in relief and twisted handles and the floral terminals. The gadrooned or fluted edges of Leeds plates were sometimes painted in blue. The ware is extremely light in weight, and varies in colour from a pale, sometimes a very pale, cream colour to a light buff. We have seen how Wedgwood invented punches at first for his pierced cream ware. But he at a later stage had the perforations punched *en bloc*. But in Leeds ware each perforation is done separately by hand, and the edges are sharp and cleancut. These are in the shape of diamonds, squares, ovals, and hearts, arranged in geometrical patterns. The characteristic feature of Leeds ware is the varied use of this pierced work in the rims of plates and dishes and trays and cups. This work was carried into such unlikely portions of the ware such as bases of candlesticks or plinths of massive candelabra. In conception no doubt it followed the work of the silversmith, but as it developed it acquired the character of some of the finest Oriental types of this class of ware, and in particular the Leeds potters achieved a ceramic triumph when they made, in the delicately pierced work with small apertures, something not dissimilar to the rice-grain form found on old Chinese white ware which in the case of Chinese wine-cups of white porcelain is filled with glaze. This especially fine style is at the present day being carried out by the potters at the Copenhagen porcelain factory. When held up to the light this porcelain of China and of Denmark is singularly beautiful, and looks as though it is perforated—but is not.

If Leeds at first copied Wedgwood and the Staffordshire cream-ware patterns the Staffordshire potters were not slow to return the compliment when they saw that Leeds had a note of originality, consequently we find many salt-glaze pieces of identical shape to some of Hartley, Greens & Co.'s patterns. It is improbable that salt-glaze ware was ever made at Leeds, though before salt-glaze was as well understood as it is now much of it was wrongly attributed to Leeds.

We give an illustration (p. 319) of a salt-glaze plate which has the typical perforated edge of Leeds cream ware, and is decorated with a transfer-print of a fable subject, illustrating "Hercules and the Waggoner." But Leeds very early did its own printing, and only the early examples were sent to Liverpool to Sadler and Green. At this time salt-glaze ware was in a bad way, and every effort was being made to compete with cream ware its new rival, and with porcelain which had struck the first blow at its supremacy as domestic ware. When cream ware was decorated by transfer-printing salt-glaze followed the new fashion, and leaving its lofty ideals of undecorated form it hastily assumed the enamel colouring of the English porcelain.

Leeds Cream Ware.—The various classes of Leeds cream ware may be roughly divided into two classes:

(1) *Plain or undecorated*, in which (especially by reason by the grace and lightness of structure imparted by the nicely balanced perforations) artistic excellence is reached by *form* alone.

(2) *Decorated cream ware*. Decorated with enamel colours, green, red, lilac, and yellow being usually found, or transfer-printed in the early manner of Liverpool—black, puce, or red, or later by printing in blue.

In regard to the finer specimens of the cream ware dependent on form and exhibiting especial delicacy in the treatment of the pierced work, the illustrations here given convey a pictorial representation of the great variety and fertility of the design.

The two magnificent centre-pieces represent Leeds cream ware at its highest. The favourite form of the centre-piece is that in which tiers of escallop shells are supported by dolphins or by ornamental brackets. The left-hand centre-piece illustrated (p. 291) is in the form of the trunk of a tree, supporting four tiers of leaf-shaped dishes. The piece is surmounted by a classical draped figure. It is noticeable that the brackets have every resemblance to metal design. These large centre-pieces are made to take apart. This example illustrated takes into four pieces, which fit into each other with great accuracy, showing great technical perfection in potting. It is no less than 4 feet in height, and one of the largest pieces known. Its rich cream colour, the perfection of the glaze, and the graceful proportion in the structure, and the modelled figure have won for this and similar creations of Leeds the admiration of all connoisseurs.

CHESTNUT BASKET AND CANDLESTICKS.
Pierced LEEDS cream ware.
(*In the collection of Mr. Richard Wilson.*)

LEEDS CREAM WARE CANDLESTICKS AND KETTLE AND STAND.
With fine pierced work.
(In the collection of Mr. Richard Wilson.)

The other centre-piece illustrated is 30 inches in height, and is constructed in the form of hanging baskets separate and removable. These baskets, which are of exquisite pierced work, are in three tiers supported from the central column. The top consists of a vase resting upon four winged figures. The piece is surmounted by a classical draped figure of Flora with a cornucopia.

Such pieces as these hold the blue riband of Leeds cream ware, and collectors who wish to find specimens only approximating to them in grace and beauty have to search as far afield as Russia and Sweden before they can hope to gratify their desire.

Another class typical of Leeds cream ware in its highest moods is the large class consisting of handsome cruets, baskets, and a great variety of candlesticks. The pierced work in these articles is of very fine character, and the design is happily lightened by this style of decoration. In regard to imitations of this cream ware, as has already been mentioned, they are heavier, are thickly coated with white glaze, whereas old Leeds pieces are extremely dainty and light in weight, and when the glaze is seen in the crevices where it may have run it is of a peculiar green, due to the use of arsenic.

We illustrate two groups of Leeds cream ware, exhibiting the perfection of its pierced work. The chestnut basket in the upper group is partly derived from Wedgwood's model. There is an indication in the use of the sphinx in the pair of candlesticks of one of Wedgwood's models in basalt. But the treatment here is more graceful, and the character imparted by Leeds to its cream ware is peculiarly its own.

Leeds cream ware undecorated plates have a great variety of patterns in the pierced borders, and are always attractive to collectors. Some of the Leeds plates, with blue painted feathered edge, had either a crest or printed design in middle. In regard to colour, there are fine under-glaze blue plates in which there is as strong a leaning to Oriental pagoda designs as at Bow and Worcester. We illustrate a fine plate of this nature (p. 303), similar in design to plates impressed ASTBURY of Staffordshire. Under-glaze blue-printing (black printing over-glaze was done, but not to the same extent as in Staffordshire) was introduced about 1790. The willow pattern, among others, was a favourite design, and most of these printed blue plates are marked.

It may be of interest to the collector to know that there are marks on the old blue-printed Leeds ware which tell their own story. These marks were made by the "cockspurs" placed between each plate to keep them separate in the kiln. There were three of these little tripods of earthenware placed between each plate. They made, as they had only one point at their apex, only three "spur" marks on the front of the plates in the border, and nine "spurs" at the back, in groups of three.

LEEDS CREAM WARE.
Seascape, and floral decoration in puce, green, red, &c. Painted by
Allen at Lowestoft and refired there.
(*In the collection of Mr. Merrington Smith, Lowestoft.*)

In regard to subjects in colour it may be mentioned that a good many Leeds jugs bear names and dates upon them, from about 1769 to 1786. These enamel colours are green, red, lilac, and buff, and are not dissimilar to those employed at Lowestoft. We illustrate a fine Leeds mug with the characteristic twisted handle (p. 303), having Oriental figure in colour and dated and inscribed. The following curious and gruesome verses appear on it. Inside the mug is a modelled frog, as found in Sunderland examples.

"In marriage are two happy things allowed

A wife in wedding-sheets and in a shroud.

How can a marriage state be then accurs'd

Since the last days are happy as the first."

Then follows "I. C. U. B. YY for me" (I see you be too wise for me). "SAMUEL CUDWORTH, 1777."

Leeds Ware decorated at Lowestoft.—There is a connection between Leeds and Lowestoft. It appears that some of the Leeds ware was sent undecorated to Allen, of Lowestoft, who decorated it there and refired it, disposing of it on his own account. The fine Leeds mug having the painted decoration, over-glaze of course, of a vessel, and entitled "Homeward Bound" (illustrated, p. 299), is typical of this work of Allen at its best. He appears to have procured ware from Turner and other Staffordshire potters for decoration and sale by himself. We illustrate (p. 303), a Staffordshire jug painted by Allen, of Lowestoft, representing a local scene, recognisable by the tower in the background. He inscribed it "A Trifle from Lowestoft." This is enamel work over-glaze, the key pattern at the rim is under-glaze and was done in Staffordshire.

Another Leeds jug decorated by Allen is that illustrated (p. 299), bearing the verses:—

"From hence to the deep

May division be tost

And prudence recovre

What folly have lost."

The "have" is a peculiarly Suffolk idiom. The floral scrolls are in the usual low tones of Lowestoft colouring.

Castleford (1790–1820).—This factory, some twelve miles from Leeds, was established about 1790, contemporary with the establishment of the Don Pottery near Doncaster. This Castleford factory, under the proprietor, David Dunderdale, commenced to make cream ware, black basalt, and the usual stoneware teapots with ornaments in relief. The mark employed by this factory, when it was used, is D. D. & CO., CASTLEFORD. This is impressed, and is found on various imitative ware, such as clouded tortoiseshell plates in the Whieldon manner. One of the characteristics of Castleford teapots with raised figures is the use of a blue line at the edge and the tops of these vessels depart from the straight lines of Turner and are scalloped, as in the illustration (p. 307) of a Castleford black ware jug and cover, having the impressed mark of the factory.

LEEDS CREAM WARE PLATE.
Painted with Oriental figures in under-glaze blue.
(*In the collection of Miss Feilden.*)

LEEDS CREAM WARE MUG.
With Oriental figure and set of verses.
(*In the collection of Mr. Robert Bruce Wallis.*)

STAFFORDSHIRE JUG.
Painted and inscribed by Allen at Lowestoft.
(*In the collection of Mr. Merrington Smith, Lowestoft.*)

Rockingham.—At Swinton, near Rotherham, as early as 1778 a factory was started by Messrs. Thomas Bingley & Co., who began to manufacture cream ware. The Leeds factory, apparently jealous of rivals, as in the case of the Don Pottery, soon had an active interest in this factory. In 1790 it became Greens, Bingley & Co., and the ware then made was blue printed and the highly glazed black pottery associated with Jackfield, of which we shall speak later. At this time a brown glazed earthenware became widely known and appreciated. It was cream ware which had received a heavy lead glaze richly and warmly coloured in brown. From 1796 to 1806 this glaze became extensively used, not only by Swinton or, as it afterwards came to be known, as "Rockingham," taking the name from the Marquis of Rockingham, upon whose estate the works were situated.

This "Rockingham ware," of smooth surface and fine reddish brown colour, was very popular, and a teapot was made, known as the "Cadogan," which was an imitation of the Chinese puzzle teapot. It was made without a lid and was filled by turning it upside down. An opening, very much in the manner of the safety glass inkpot, admitted the tea, and on reversing the vessel it could be poured out. Some of these teapots are marked "Rockingham," or "Brameld," or "Brameld & Co.," and sometimes "Mortlock," a London dealer for whom they were made. In 1806 the Leeds interest passed out of the firm, and the factory remained in the hands of John and William Brameld. In 1826 it assumed the name of the Rockingham Works, and used the crest of the Fitzwilliam family. China was made there from 1820, and the factory obtained considerable reputation and was still in the hands of the Brameld family till the close of the works in 1842. A gorgeous Rockingham china dessert service made for William IV. costing £5,000.

We illustrate a "Cadogan" teapot, with its rich brown glaze, and moulded in the form of a peach, with smaller peaches applied at the top. It is a remarkably un-English design, and it is singular that it became so fashionable.

Jackfield.—We mention Jackfield here, as it has become among collectors quite a generic term for all highly glazed black ware, especially little teapots and cream jugs. It is certain that Elijah Mayer and other Staffordshire potters largely made this ware, and Bingley & Co. (Swinton) among a crowd of others. Jackfield is in Shropshire. Its history as a pot works is as old as any in the country, but it is chiefly in the period between 1760 and 1765, when Maurice Thursfield carried on the little factory, that it became renowned for its black ware. It is quite unlike black basalt. It is red clay, covered with a bright and highly lustrous black glaze. This is ornamented with oil gilding, which in use has almost disappeared. Some of the ware is decorated with raised ornaments of vine leaves. The lids of teapots often have a bird, with outstretched wings. The designs were not original, and are found in salt-glaze and in Whieldon ware, and some of this so-called "Jackfield" ware may be attributed to him.

Newcastle and Sunderland.—On the Tyne, the Wear, and the Tees there were a group of potters working at Gateshead, at Hylton, at Stockton-on-Tees, but mainly at Newcastle and Sunderland. There is nothing exceptionally artistic in any of these productions. Some of these transfer-printed mugs were made by Dixon & Co., of Sunderland, to commemorate the building of the Iron Bridge over the Wear, which was begun in 1793 and completed in 1796.

ROCKINGHAM TEAPOT.
Known as the "Cadogan" pattern. In form of peach. Having no lid and being filled from bottom. Copied from Chinese rice-spirit pot.
(*At Victoria and Albert Museum.*)

BLACK BASALT JUG.
Castleford Pottery. Impressed mark D D & Co. (Height 6 inches.)
(*In the collection of Mr. F. W. Phillips, Hitchin.*)

Among the names found on this ware are impressed: SEWELL, or SEWELLS & DONKIN, or SEWELLS & CO., sometimes with the addition of ST. ANTHONY'S. These were made at St. Anthony's, near Newcastle, in date about 1780 to 1790.

FELL, or FELL NEWCASTLE, made at St. Peter's, Newcastle, about 1815.

SCOTT, or SCOTT BROS., made ware at Southwick, Sunderland, 1789–1803, when they were succeeded by MOORE & CO.

J. PHILLIPS, HYLTON POTTERY, appears on some Sunderland pieces. This firm was established as early as 1765.

FORD is another name in connection with the South Hylton works about 1800.

Dixon, Austin & Co., sometimes with the addition of Sunderland, is found at the beginning of the nineteenth century.

W. S. & Co., with the word Wedgewood (having an additional "e") was the mark used by William Smith & Co., of Stockton-on-Tees, or even "Wedgwood & Co." Against this firm Messrs. Josiah Wedgwood & Sons, of Etruria, obtained in 1848 an injunction to restrain the use of their name.

Another equally confusing mark to collectors is that of a firm near Pontefract, who marked their ware "Wedgwood & Co." sometimes with the word name of the factory, "Ferrybridge," and sometimes "Tomlinson & Co." Their ware is mainly cream ware of an ordinary type.

In regard to the productions of Newcastle and Sunderland these are best known by the familiar mugs and jugs having a nautical flavour, with ships in black transfer decoration, and never without verses appropriate to the *clientèle* of sailors, for whom they were made. These mugs and jugs are frequently decorated with pink lustre at the rims and in bands around the body. A feature which associates these northern factories with Leeds is the frequent use of a modelled frog crawling up the inside of the vessel, which was intended as a practical joke on the person who was lifting the jug to his lips. These frog mugs were previously made at Leeds, and the one illustrated (p. 303) has a frog so affixed in the inside.

The ware, as a whole, is rather crude in its potting and slightly inferior to similar Staffordshire ware, but all these northern factories are now closed, and the quaint doggerel, the queer nautical allusions, and the strain of patriotism found on much of this humble earthenware always appeal strongly to the collector.

MARKS USED AT LEEDS, CASTLEFORD, ROCKINGHAM, NEWCASTLE, AND SUNDERLAND.

Leeds.

From 1783, Hartley, Greens & Co.

1825–1832, Samuel Wainwright & Co.

1832–1840, Leeds Pottery Co.

1840–1847, Stephen and James Chapel.

1850–1863, Warburton, Britton & Co.

1863–1878, Richard Britton & Sons. After which the works closed.

Don Pottery (at Swinton near Leeds).

1790–1834, at one time in hands of John Green, of Leeds Pottery.

SB&S 1834–1850, Samuel Barker, and

1851–1882, Samuel Barker & Sons.

Late Marks used by the Barkers during above period:—

In addition to the lion with pennon the word Barker was added later, when the mark was *printed*.

Another *printed* mark was an eagle and ducal coronet, used when the firm became Samuel Barker & Sons in 1851. But was shortly discontinued, and the lion-printed mark again used.

D D & C?
CASTLEFORD

Castleford (near Leeds), 1790–1820. David Dunderdale & Co., and the impressed mark in margin is found on some of the productions of the Castleford Pottery.

Rockingham.
The name of the factory at Swinton, established 1757. Came into the hands of the Bramelds in 1807. Ceased, 1842.

ROCKINGHAM

BRAMELD

The "Cadogan" lower glazed teapots sometimes bear the impressed mark "Mortlock," the London agent for whom some of them were made.

The crest of the Fitzwilliam family was printed as a mark after 1826, and is also found *printed* on porcelain made at the Rockingham factory.

FELL.

SEWELL.

ST ANTHONY'S.

SEWELL & DONKIN.

Newcastle-on-Tyne
. Fell of Newcastle (about 1815), impressed cream ware mugs and jugs with this mark. Various figures appear underneath, denoting the particular pattern.

Sunderland.
Messrs. Sewell, established about 1780, after Sewell & Donkin, used these marks.

Other Sunderland makers—Dixon, Austin & Co., Dixon & Co., Scott Brothers & Co. (established 1788), Phillips & Co. (established about 1800), J. Phillips, Hylton (established, 1780), Dawson (about 1810)—impressed their names on ware.

PRICES.

	£	s.	d.
LEEDS.			
Coffee Pot and Cover, with mask under spout, twisted handles, decorated in colours. Sotheby, June, 1906	2	2	0

Basket dish, with stand and covers with embossed and open work. Sotheby, June, 1906	2	2	0
Jug, painted with flowers, inscribed "John Barnes, Chadlington, 1769." Sotheby, July, 1907	2	10	0
Teapot and cover, painted with portraits of George III. and Queen Charlotte. Sotheby, November, 1908	2	8	0
Teapot and cover, printed in red, with lady and gentleman taking tea, with negro servant at side; on reverse, a shepherd and sheep. Sotheby, November, 1908	1	10	0
Jug, printed with transfer medallions of ladies seated in a garden, blue and black bands at rim. Sotheby, November, 1908	1	14	0

CASTLEFORD.

Loving cup with handles, painted with fruit and roses, made for David Dunderdale. Escritt & Barrett, April, 1907	3	15	0

JACKFIELD.

Figure of *Diana* (height 10 in.). Escritt & Barrett, April 1907	3	5	0
Jugs, brown glazed, two. Sotheby, November, 1907	1	1	0

ROCKINGHAM.

Small "Cadogan" Teapot, marked *Brameld*, richly gilt upon brown, and another without gilding. Sotheby, June, 1906	1	14	0
Milk jug modelled as cow, brown glaze; Figure of Horse; Jug, brown glaze, with twisted handles, marked *Rockingham*. Sotheby, June, 1906	2	5	0
"Cadogan" Teapot, rich brown glazed; impressed mark. Sotheby, May, 1908	1	2	0

SUNDERLAND.

Sugar Basin and Cover and six cups and saucers, painted
with figure subjects on yellow ground, marked Sewell.
Sotheby. November, 1905   1   13   0

NEWCASTLE.

Frog mugs and jugs vary in price from 10s. to £2, according
to the style of decoration.

CHAPTER X
TRANSFER-PRINTED WARE

Its origin—Liverpool—Its adoption in Staffordshire—What is Transfer-printing?—Over-glaze printing—Under-glaze printing—The Staffordshire Transfer-printers—Other Transfer-printers—Leeds, Swansea, Sunderland, and Newcastle—The Mission of black Transfer-printed Ware—Types of Blue-printed Ware—The Willow Pattern—Table of Marks—Prices.

Before the year 1756, all ware, whether it be porcelain or delft or earthenware, was painted, or, to follow the term used in popular phraseology, it was "hand painted." It is an essentially English art, and something which stands with salt-glaze and with Wedgwood's jasper ware as being famous throughout Europe.

The subject of transfer-printing is surrounded with a certain amount of conjecture in regard to its invention. Quite a dozen persons were credited with having originated it. Mr. William Turner, in his volume, "Transfer Printing on Enamels, Porcelain, and Pottery," published by Messrs. Chapman and Hall, in 1907, has thoroughly investigated the various claims set up for the discovery of transfer-printing and, with no little research extending over a wide area, has for the first time settled the relative position of the various claimants and factories for which this honour is claimed. It is impossible, covering the same ground as Mr. William Turner, to say anything new on transfer-printing, and we must express our indebtedness to him in making use of his original investigations and embodying them in this chapter on transfer-printed ware.

In regard to over-glaze printing, including copper enamels such as Battersea, porcelain such as Worcester, and earthenware such as Liverpool delft—it was at Battersea where enamels were first printed in 1753; Liverpool, with Sadler and Green's invention, comes second with printed delft tiles in 1756. A year after, in 1757, we have Worcester with transfer-printed porcelain. This Worcester printed ware is well known from the early transfer-printed design known as Hancock's "Tea party" and the "King of Prussia" jugs and mugs.

After Worcester all the other porcelain factories followed with transfer-printed ware. There was Derby in 1764, and Caughley in the same year.

It will be seen that, so far as Liverpool is concerned as representative of the earthenware factories (cream ware being printed here to the order of the Staffordshire potters), earthenware over-glaze printing is slightly ahead of the porcelain factories. But in under-glaze printing porcelain stands easily first. Worcester commenced under-glaze printing in the same year (1757) that over-glaze was employed there, and Derby is the second in the field in under-glaze printing in 1764.

SALT-GLAZED PLATE.
Transfer-printed in red. Fable subject—*Hercules and the Waggoner.*

LIVERPOOL TRANSFER-PRINTED JUG.
Medallion representing *Diana in her Chariot.* (Height 9¼ inches.)
(*In the possession of Mr. S. G. Fenton.*)

It has already been shown that Liverpool did the printing on the Staffordshire cream ware for the potters who sent it there to be printed, and the same method was followed by Leeds. But there came a time when it was no longer necessary to ask Liverpool to employ a secret process for the decoration of Staffordshire or Leeds work. The secret known at Worcester, and Derby and Battersea, was not many years a secret. The Staffordshire potters undertook to do their own printing, and every pottery soon learned the new process of transfer-printing, and it was not long before improvements were made and newer forms of printing adopted.

Its adoption in Staffordshire.—Allusion has been made to the awkward form of the square tile decoration of fable subjects at Liverpool as applied to circular plates. But Staffordshire in its adoption of the new process made the transfer fit the object to be decorated. In the illustration of the salt-glaze Staffordshire plate with the black transfer-printed design of "Hercules and the Waggoner" from *Æsop's Fables* (p. 319), the engraver has departed from the four corners of his circumscribed tile, and we may put this piece down as of Staffordshire printing.

It is often largely a matter of conjecture as to what was printed at Liverpool and what was printed elsewhere (with the exception of Worcester, where the engraving and printing were more delicate).

The Staffordshire jug showing a full-length portrait of His Royal Highness Frederick, Duke of York, having on the reverse the Dragoon in the uniform of the period, tells its own story as regards date. Frederick was the second son of George III. and was born in 1763 and died in 1827. As this portrait represents him as being advanced into manhood and as at that date—say about 1786—the Liverpool printers had been at work twenty years, the transfer-printing may very reasonably be attributed to Staffordshire.

But it is not always easy to fix the date of the printing, and determine whether by that time Staffordshire had embarked on its own transfer-printing in black; of course, blue transfer-printing is later. The difficulty usually arises in connection with black transfer-printed ware. Liverpool was still engaged in printing for Staffordshire potters as well as printing cream ware of its own potting, and Leeds was producing similar transfer-printed over-glaze ware, so that in unmarked pieces there must always be an uncertainty in coming to a definite conclusion. In all probability the jug (illustrated p. 323) and bearing the inscription "Success to Trade" and having a typical eighteenth century rural subject on the reverse entitled "The Faithless Lover," was actually printed by Sadler and Green at Liverpool.

Another finely decorated printed jug is that illustrated (p. 318), the subject representing *Diana* on crescent moon driving a pair of goats in her chariot. The date of this piece is about 1780 to 1800, and is strongly suggestive of Wedgwood cream ware. It will be observed that the design is identical with that in the Turner jasper vase (illustrated p. 261).

JUG, TRANSFER-PRINTED IN BLACK.
Emblems and inscribed "Success to Trade."
Subject on reverse—"The Faithless Lover."
(Height 7 inches.)

JUG, TRANSFER-PRINTED IN BLACK.
Portrait of Duke of York, and mounted dragoon on reverse.
(Height 7 inches.)
(*In the possession of Mr. Hubert Gould.*)

What is Transfer-printing?—A piece of pottery may be plain or undecorated, it may be painted, or it may be printed. The process of printing consists of affixing an engraved print from a copper plate and transferring an impression to the pottery to be decorated. It is this latter process which claims our attention in this chapter. When transfer-printing was first used, subjects such as portraits (King of Prussia), costume subjects (series of actors and actresses on Liverpool delft tiles), fancy or pastoral scenes (such as *Æsop's Fables*, &c.), were produced in black, puce, or reddish brown. These were at first culled from contemporary volumes with engraved copper-plate prints as illustrations. We find Wedgwood in quite early days searching London for suitable prints of views and similar small subjects for decorative purposes. Probably at first the copper plates which had been used in books were bought up by the potters, and did service again for their ware. Later they employed engravers, who no doubt copied or adapted other people's engraved work to suit their purpose, and as the art advanced it gained in originality, and a band of engravers worked for the potters in designing subjects strictly applicable to the limitations in the technique of earthenware.

This process of transfer-printing is roughly as follows. The copper-plate is inked, and a sheet of tough tissue paper, wetted with a mixture of soap, is applied to its surface and printed in a press. The paper is taken off, showing an impression or print, which is carefully laid on the surface of the piece of earthenware to be decorated. The inked design on the paper transfers itself to the earthenware.

Over-glaze Printing.—The difference between over-glaze and under-glaze decoration always seems to puzzle the beginner, but the explanation is simple enough. A piece of pottery is produced by the following steps. The clay is "thrown," that is, it is spun into shape on the potter's wheel, or it may be made in a mould. When in this soft state, say in the form of a basin, it could be crushed by the hand into the shapeless mass of clay whence it sprung. It is next put aside to dry sufficiently to allow handling. It may receive some of its decoration at this stage as it is possible to paint on the more or less damp clay, but as a general rule that is left till the next stage.

It is now placed in the "biscuit" oven and receives the most intense heat, and is here stacked in fireproof saggers or boxes to protect it from the flames, and it is fired for about three days before being taken out in the state known as "biscuit." Wedgwood's jasper ware, black basalt, and all unglazed stoneware stop at this biscuit or unglazed stage.

It is next dipped in liquid glaze and goes again to be fired, this time into the "glost" or glaze oven, which is lower in temperature. After coming from this second oven it is no longer "biscuit" in appearance, but is covered with a skin or coating of glass or glaze, which has amalgamated with the body underneath.

It is now ready for painting with enamel colours or for transfer-printing, which obviously is "over-glaze" decoration.

Lastly, after this decoration has been made, it goes to be fired for a third time, and is put into the enamel or "muffle" kiln, which is the lowest temperature of the three.

In effect, then, the "over-glaze" decoration is on top of everything, and obviously, when the piece is scratched in use, this decoration wears away first. This at once gives the reason for another process, known as under-glaze decoration, where the work receives the protection of the glaze.

As a postscript to this description of the three firings, it may be noted in passing that, in true porcelain, such as Chinese, Dresden, and Bristol (all hard pastes), the body and glaze are fired at one operation, the glaze receiving as high a temperature as the body.

CHINESE BLUE AND WHITE PORCELAIN PLATES.
Painted in dark blue under-glaze. Painted in light blue under-glaze.
The types from which English potters made their copies.
(*In the collection of the Author.*)

CHINESE BLUE AND WHITE PORCELAIN PLATES.
Painted in rich blue under-glaze. The "Willow pattern" and the
"Aster pattern."
The types from which English potters made their copies.
(*In the collection of the Author.*)

Under-glaze Printing.—This is printing which is transferred to the ware, either porcelain or earthenware, when in its "biscuit" state *prior to being dipped in glaze*. Blue was the most frequent colour used in under-glaze transfer-printing, as of course it was the earliest colour used in the painted under-glaze decorations at Worcester and Caughley. There are other colours, obtained from metallic compounds, used both on porcelain and earthenware under the glaze, and owing to the temperature required for firing in this manner the range is limited, being usually confined to cobalt blue, green, brown, lilac, black, and a few others. But blue is the chief under-glaze colour to be considered in connection with under-glaze transfer-printing. There was a great demand for deep blue and for a lighter blue, both of which came to the Staffordshire earthenware printers and potters from English porcelain factories such as Caughley, where Thomas Turner, an apprentice at Worcester under Robert Hancock, made in 1780 his famous under-glaze blue "Willow-pattern"; or the idea may have been derived straight from the Chinese blue porcelain under-glaze of Nankin, so much in vogue in middle eighteenth-century days.

Staffordshire Transfer-printers.—It has been shown how the Staffordshire potters at first turned to Liverpool, and readily sought the aid of Sadler and Green in the decoration of their salt-glaze and their cream ware, in order to compete with the porcelain factories with Worcester and Caughley at their head. But trade secrets found their way into Staffordshire.

The over-glaze printing as practised by Sadler and Green was soon mastered, and later the under-glaze blue printing was imported by workmen from Caughley.

Among the Staffordshire potters the following are the principal pioneers in regard to transfer-printing in its various developments. William Adams, of Cobridge, in 1775 first introduced transfer-printing into Staffordshire. John Turner, of Lane End (not to be confounded with Thomas Turner, of Caughley) was the first to print under-glaze blue in Staffordshire. Josiah Spode, about 1784, introduced his under-glaze blue "willow pattern," a copy of the Caughley pattern. William Adams, of Greengates, in 1787 brought out his under-glaze blue, which in richness and mellowness has never been surpassed; and Josiah Wedgwood, although he never deserted Liverpool for some of his patterns, had a press at work at Etruria, in 1787; and Thomas Minton, now a master potter at Stoke, formerly an apprentice at Caughley with Thomas Turner, designed the celebrated "Broseley Dragon" pattern tea service for porcelain in 1782 (following the willow pattern, 1780), and produced in the late years of the eighteenth century, about 1793, some fine blue-printed ware at Stoke.

These may be termed the earlier exponents of transfer-printing in Staffordshire, but there were others whose blue-printed ware was of great merit in Staffordshire, and Leeds and Swansea, held no insignificant place.

SPODE EARTHENWARE.
Transfer-printed under-glaze blue.
"Bridge pattern" Plate and "Willow pattern" Jug.

CREAM WARE DISH WITH IMPRESSED MARK "TURNER."
With pierced border and band of embossed wickerwork.
Centre printed in blue with "Willow pattern."
(*At Victoria and Albert Museum.*)

Other Transfer Printers.—Staffordshire did not long have the monopoly of under-glaze blue-printed ware. Leeds and Swansea both produced similar work, and in both cases there is a strong attachment to Oriental design. Black transfer-printing was also executed at both these factories, and at Swansea some exceptionally fine engraved work was turned out (see illustration of Swansea plate, p. 397). At Sunderland and Newcastle the black transfer-printed mugs and jugs with the *Wear Bridge* and with nautical subjects became quite the vogue, and in these two factories the jugs and mugs often had a frog modelled in the interior, and pink lustre decoration was used in combination with the transfer design usually at the borders or at the rims.

The Mission of Black-printed Ware.—In the designs and inscriptions of the black transfer-printed ware the Staffordshire potter used his jugs and his mugs as a medium to record events and to ventilate grievances, not in "imperishable verse," but in the fickle body of the clay. This class of ware from 1760 to 1860 stands for a century as typically English in character. It reflects the political, social, and religious events, and in matter-of-fact, humorous, or satirical fashion. The black transfer-printed or earlier period, (though some of this class come down as late as the railway mugs of 1830), may be said to depict events and chronicle popular sentiment in black and white. The blue transfer-printer strove to be decorative, and mainly represented scenery and topography, and much of it was bound down to formal designs of Oriental nature.

At first fable subjects, as on Wedgwood's cream ware, were employed, and it has been seen how the square tile form was discarded by the engraver who made his engraving fit the object to be decorated. This perfect mastery of the technique of transfer-printing is shown very clearly in the old blue Spode service of the "Tower" pattern (illustrated, p. 335). It will be seen how, as the shape of each vessel differed, the engraver has altered his bridge to fit the new circumstances. At one time, on a broad, flat dish, it appears as a wide bridge, and in the circular plate the trees appear at greater height and the viaduct assumes a more circular form. In the jug of the same design the bridge is narrow, as though spanning a deep ravine.

To enumerate the classes of ware with black transfer-printing is to make a catalogue of the principal events which stirred the heart of the people. It must be borne in mind that this school was working side by side with the makers of fine stoneware and of jasper ware with classic subjects, but it is, after all, to the black-printed ware that one turns most lovingly as being more human.

It will suffice, perhaps, if we quote a few examples and stir the enthusiasm of the reader to pursue the collection of these really historic records which have something more endearing in them than the relics of Napoleon or the shoestrings of some of the Stuart monarchs.

There is a fine flavour of patriotism, of conviviality, and of homely sentiment in some of the following:—

On a bowl, salt-glazed ware, with Admiral Vernon and his fleet is inscribed "The British Glory revived by Admiral Vernon. He took Porto Bello with Six Ships only. Nov. ye 22 1739." A cream-ware jug printed, with medallion portrait of Earl Howe, is inscribed "LONG LIVE EARL HOWE, Commander-in-Chief of the Victorious BRITISH FLEET. In the ever memorable engagement on the Glorious First of June, 1794." On a cream-ware jug about 1800 with a view of Greenwich Hospital, and entitled "The Sailor's Adieu," the following lines are inscribed: "What should tear me from the arms of my Dearest Polly but the undeniable calls of my country in whose cause I have engag'd my Honour and my Life." This in date is the last year of the eighteenth century.

OLD SPODE BLUE PRINTED WARE.
"Tower pattern."
(*In the collection of Mrs. Herman Liebstein.*)

"The Sailor's Farewell and Return" are rather frequent, and Charles Dibdin's verses appear on some of these jugs and mugs. There is one interesting jug in the form of a sailor seated on a chest, coloured earthenware about 1770, with a breezy inscription, "Hullo, Brother Briton, whoever Thou be, Sit down on that chest of Hard Dollars by me, and drink a health to all sailors bold."

Another cream-ware jug, partly printed and touched by colour representing a man-of-war towing a frigate, has the inscription:

"A sailor's life's a pleasant life;

He freely roams from shore to shore,

In every port he finds a wife,

What can a sailor wish for more?"

A red earthenware mug with white slip may be mentioned here as having a characteristic motto:

"From rocks and sands and barren lands

Good Fortune sets me free;

And from great Guns and Women's tongues,

Good Lord, deliver me."

A Staffordshire blue-printed jug, made in 1793, shows the execution of Louis XVI. At the beginning of the nineteenth century there was quite a burst of Napoleonic jugs and mugs and busts, and some of Gillray's caricatures find themselves on earthenware. There is one lustre earthenware jug printed and coloured with caricatures entitled "Jack Frost attacking 'Bony' in Russia" and "Little 'Bony' sneaking into Paris with a white feather in his tail." This is in date about 1813.

A cover of an earthenware jar has the inscription printed in violet within a wreath, "Peace! May its duration equal the years of War."

The relations between England and America received attention at the Staffordshire potters' hands. There are cream-ware mugs and jugs and plates with portraits of Washington in date from 1785 to 1790. On one the inscription runs, "Success to the United States, America."

Prize-fighting, bear-baiting, cock-fighting, racing, coaching, all received their records on the earthenware of the late eighteenth century. Stag hunting, fox hunting, coursing, come as ready subjects to the transfer-printer. Cricket is recorded in earthenware on a printed mug representing the "Grand Cricket Match played in Lord's Ground, Mary-le-bone, June 20 and following day between the Earls of Winchester and Darnley for 1,000 guineas." The date of this is 1790. Even the velocipede and the balloon are not disregarded.

This list is but a rough outline of the mission of the transfer-printer in recording current events on his earthenware, for the pleasure of his own contemporaries and for the information and delectation of succeeding generations of collectors who may be something other than connoisseurs of pastes and bodies, and have learned to read aright the story of the china-shelf and enjoy to the full the secret pleasures in the byeways of collecting.

Types of Blue-printed Ware.—The black over-glaze transfer-printing came into Staffordshire in imitation of the transfer-printed delft tiles of Liverpool. But it rapidly acquired a strength and originality of its own. It lacked the delicacy of the transfer-printed black porcelain of Worcester, but its virility more than made up for its artistic defects.

Under-glaze blue-printed ware was an imitation from the porcelain printed at Caughley. Here again it may be said to have outstripped by new departures and broader effects the under-glaze blue-printing of the early china factories. In common with them its inspiration was from the Chinese. We illustrate (p. 327) four examples of Chinese porcelain plates, which are types of the Oriental china designs which served as models both for the English porcelain makers and for the earthenware of Staffordshire.

The lower left-hand plate is evidently the Chinese design from which the English potters derived the well-known and favourite "willow pattern." After Thomas Turner, of Caughley, had printed it on china in 1780, and Josiah Spode in 1784 had employed it on his earthenware in Staffordshire, all the other potters commenced to make the same design with slightly different details, mainly in the fret border. The other plate on the right hand is the well-known "aster" pattern, so frequently adopted by English potters in blue-printed cream ware. The two upper octagonal plates show the two styles of dark blue and light blue under-glaze painting employed by the Chinese; and the Staffordshire potter, true to his models, followed in his under-glaze blue-printing these tones. The period when the rich deep dark-blue-printed ware was in vogue is from the early nineteenth century to about 1825. Light blue printing was employed from 1790 till the deep blue supplanted it, and when the craze for deep blue had spent itself the light blue again became fashionable until printing in colour in the middle period of the nineteenth century came to be largely practised.

In the treatment of the border in the Oriental example we illustrate, it will be noticed how Josiah Spode and others, including the fine school at Leeds, who were printing in under-glaze blue in 1790, and the potters at Swansea, followed this decorative treatment. Spode in particular had a great fondness for Chinese subjects. We illustrate (p. 345) a blue-printed dish by him, where, as was his wont, he introduced, quite incongruously, a Gothic castle. The fine, rich colouring of this dish is most noticeable.

In the Spode earthenware *Jug* and *Plate* illustrated (p. 331), it will be seen that the plate, known as the "Bridge" pattern, closely follows the design of the Chinese porcelain plate (p. 327), and the jug is decorated with the familiar "Willow" pattern. Another variation of the "Willow" design is found on the *Turner Cream-ware Dish*, illustrated, having a band of embossed wickerwork and a pierced border. This piece has the impressed mark TURNER.

A similar Oriental influence is seen in the dark blue transfer-printed dish by William Adams, of Greengates (see illustration, p. 341). The inclination here is towards figure subjects, and the decorative use of the exotic bird, as shown in the centre panel of this dish, finds a place on some of Mason's early blue-printed dishes. Of the colour of the dishes of William Adams, of Greengates, it may be remarked that for richness of tone in the under-glaze blue he introduced in 1787 they have never been surpassed.

What is the Willow pattern?—The name "willow-pattern" has been so frequently mentioned in connection with the subject of old English earthenware and china that it will be of service to state something of the details of the history of this particular pattern, which seems to have unaccountably seized hold of popular imagination.

DISH, TRANSFER-PRINTED IN DEEP BLUE, BY ROGERS.
Subject—the Naval Fight between the *Chesapeake* and *Shannon*.
(*In the collection of Miss Feilden.*)

**DISH, TRANSFER-PRINTED IN BLUE.
Mark impressed "ADAMS" (of Greengates).
(*In the collection of Mr. Russell Allan.*)**

By the courtesy of Mr. Percy W. L. Adams.
From "*William Adams. An Old English Potter.*"

The Caughley pattern, which some authorities believe was engraved by Minton when he was an apprentice there, was closely followed by Spode, Adams, Wedgwood, Davenport, Clews, Leeds, the Don Pottery, and Swansea. The differences are slight mainly in the treatment of the fretted border, either a lattice-work or conventional butterfly being used, and details of the fence in the foreground differing.

The term "Willow" is applied in a general way to many of the copies of the blue-and-white Oriental porcelain imported from China during the last half the eighteenth century.

But the "willow pattern," to which a story is attached, is of the same design as the Chinese plate illustrated (p. 327), which Caughley copied. This popular adaptation appears as a decoration on the covers of this volume.

Whether the story was invented by some ingenious person to fit the plate we do not know; but there is strong probability that this is so. On Chinese plates the *dramatis personæ* are missing. The willow has ever been a sad tree, whereof such as have lost their love make their mourning garlands. "I offered him my company to a willow-tree ... to make him a garland, as being forsaken," says Benedick in *Much Ado about Nothing*.

This is the love-story that is told concerning the "willow" plate. Chang, the secretary of a mandarin whose house is on the right of the plate, dared to love his master's daughter, Li-chi. But the mandarin had other designs, and his daughter was promised to an old but wealthy suitor. In order to prevent the lovers from meeting, the mandarin imprisoned his daughter in a room in his house overlooking the water. A correspondence ensued, so the story goes, between the lovers, and the lady sent a poetical message, in a cocoa-nut shell, floating down the river, that she expected Chang when the willow-leaf commenced to fall. By the connivance of a gardener, who apparently lived in the small cottage on the left, overshadowed by a fir-tree, the lovers escaped, and are depicted as fleeing over the bridge—the mandarin behind with a whip in his hand, the lady in front, and Chang in the middle carrying her jewel-box! The individual in the junk, higher up, is intended to denote that they fled to the island in the north-west of the plate. They lived happy until Fate, in the shape of the wealthy lover, overtook them and burned their house to ashes. But the gods changed them into two doves, which, of course, figure prominently in the design.

This tragic story of disastrous love has clung to the willow-pattern plates, and nobody can shake the belief of owners of indifferent specimens of middle-nineteenth century days that these plates are of great value. As a matter of fact, apart from the eighteenth-century examples, anything else is not worth the attention of the serious collector.

We have alluded to the historic character of the black transfer-printed ware, but sometimes similar subjects were attempted in the blue ware. We illustrate a dish known as the "Chesapeake and Shannon" dish, depicting the famous naval encounter between these two vessels.

SPODE DISH.
Transfer-printed in deep blue under-glaze.

DISH WITH LANDSCAPE SUBJECT IN STYLE OF CLAUDE.
Transfer-printed in deep blue under-glaze.
(*In the possession of Mr. S. G. Fenton.*)

At a time when the school of landscape engravers dearly loved a classic ruin or the broken arch of a temple in the composition of the scene, it is only natural to find this class of subject on the printed ware. We illustrate a typical under-glaze blue-printed dish with fine contrasts showing very accurately what excellent decoration was employed in this engraved work. The school of Claude landscapes found its votaries, and some strong engraving by Brookes and others was done for this old blue earthenware. It is pictorial, and betrays an attempt to break new ground and get away from the conventions of Oriental design, but the border in the dish we illustrate (p. 345) shows the strong Japanese spirit which had inspired Spode, and this touch of incongruity makes it more than probable that this dish is of Spode origin.

There are many other phases of printed ware that can only be alluded to in passing. The transfer printing in outline, the colour being added by hand, was the beginning of the establishment of all the modern methods for china and earthenware as commonly in use. Something, too, should be said of "bat" printing. This was the use of a block of glue instead of transfer-paper to receive the inked impression from the copper plate and transfer it to the body of the earthenware. William Adams, of Cobridge, in 1775 first introduced "bat" printing into Staffordshire. Of the various types of engraving, such as line, and stipple, and aquatint, and, later, lithography, there is no space to deal. But enough has been said in connection with the various types of printed ware to show that when pursued in a special manner it may be found to be of exceptional interest to the collector.

MARKS.
Transfer-printed Earthenware.

Many printed examples are unmarked, both of the early transfer-printing in black over the glaze, and of the latter under-glaze blue-printed ware, but over a wide period the following names are found as marks upon various transfer-printed specimens.

It will be observed that in addition many of these potters made stoneware, following the Wedgwood influence.[5]

William Adams (of Greengates)	1787–1805	Blue-printed under-glaze (marked Adams).
Benjamin Adams (of Greengates)	1805–1820	Blue-printed under-glaze (marked B. Adams).

William Adams & Sons (of Stoke)	1804–1835	Dark blue-printed under-glaze and black over-glaze (marked Adams). (Marked "Close & Co., late William Adams & Sons, Stoke on Trent"—after 1843.)
William Adams & Sons (of Burslem)	1830–1840	Black over-glazed printing.
Wedgwood (of Etruria)	1795–1845	Blue-printed ware introduced (The second shortly after the death of Josiah Wedgwood Wedgwood in 1795. Black transfer-printed period) views after 1830.
Wedgwood & Co (of Burslem)	1790–1796	Ralph Wedgwood. Black transfer-printing over-glaze.
Josiah Spode the Second (of Stoke)	1798–1827	Blue under-glaze printing of great variety.
Thomas Minton (of Stoke)	1790–1836	Blue under-glaze printing, Oriental and other patterns.
John Davenport (of Longport)	1793–1834	Under-glaze blue-printing (marked Davenport, Longport).
Henry and William Davenport	1835–1869	
John Turner (of Lane End)	1762–1786	Oriental patterns, under-glaze blue (impressed mark, Turner).
William & John Turner (sons of above)	1786–1803	
John Aynsley (of Lane End)	1790–1826	Masonic plates printed in outline over-glaze and coloured.
T. Fletcher & Co. (of Shelton)	1786–1810	Black transfer-printed sporting subjects, sometimes *under-glaze*.

Maker	Dates	Description
Shorthose & Co. (of Hanley)	1783–1802	Red over-glaze printed fancy subjects.
Andrew Stevenson (of Cobridge)	1810–1818	Black over-glaze printing tinted in colours (marked A. Stevenson, with crown in circle).
Joseph Stubbs (of Longport)	1798–1829	Dark blue under-glaze printing (marked Joseph Stubbs in circle. Longport impressed).
James Clews (of Cobridge)	1814–1836	Black under-glaze after 1825. American views of Hudson River, &c.
John and Richard Riley (of Burslem)	1820–1827	Blue under-glaze printing. Picturesque views.
Miles Mason (of Lane Delph)	1813–1851	Rich blue under-glaze printing; Oriental subjects and birds.
Enoch Wood & Sons (of Burslem)	1820–1846	Deep blue under-glaze printing.
R. & J. Baddeley (of Shelton)	1780–1806	
J. & E. Baddeley		Transfer printing from the earliest date, both over-glaze and under-glaze. Marked I. E. B., or full names, or R. M. W. & Co.
Hicks & Meigh (of Shelton)	1806–1820	
Hicks, Meigh & Johnson (of Shelton)	1820–1836	Deep dark blue under-glaze printing. "Beauties of America," and other views.
John and William Ridgway (of Shelton)	1824–1836	

Ridgway, Morley, Wear & Co. (of Shelton)	1836–1854	
Leeds	1790–1878	Over-glaze black printing (little practised), under-glaze blue, Oriental subjects (marked Leeds Pottery).
Don Pottery (near Doncaster)	1790–1834	Under-glaze blue, Oriental subjects (marked *Don Pottery* or *Barker*—the latter after 1834).
Liverpool (Herculaneum)	1796–1841	Deep under-glaze blue-printed; Oriental subjects (marked Herculaneum).
Swansea (Cambrian Pottery)	1802–1870	Under-glaze blue-printing and over-glaze, black and brown printing (marked Dillwyn & Co.). (See group illustrated, [p. 397](#).)
Derby (Cockpit Hill Factory)	1780–1785	Over-glaze black printing of figure subjects (marked Derby Pot Works).
Caughley (Salopian)	1780–1799	Under the management of Thomas Turner. Dark blue under-glaze printing; Oriental subjects (marked in blue C).
Sunderland and Newcastle	1790–1850	Black transfer-printed mugs and jugs of crude decoration. Various firms. *Sunderland.*—Scott Brothers, Brunton & Co., Moore & Co. (1803), Phillips. *Newcastle.*—Dixon, Austin, & Co., Dawson & Co., Fell & Co. (1817), marked with F and anchor, Sewells & Donkin.
Middlesborough Pottery (Yorkshire)	1831–1850	Blue-printed ware (marked with impressed anchor and *Middlesbro' Pottery*, or with the word *London* and anchor, about 1848, or M.P. Co).

PRICES—TRANSFER-PRINTED WARE.

	£	s.	d.
Transfer-printed Jug with ship on one side and mariner's compass on reverse; another Jug with Sailor and his Lass. Sotheby, November, 1904	1	18	0
Transfer-printed Jug with portrait of Lord Nelson on one side, and plan of Battle of Trafalgar on reverse. Sotheby, November, 1904	3	15	0
Transfer-printed Jug with "Britannia weeping over the ashes of Her Matchless Hero, Lord Nelson," and a sailing ship on reverse, with motto "Success to Trade." Sotheby, November, 1904	3	8	0
Transfer-printed Jug with Subject relating to the Independence of America; *rare*. Sotheby, November, 1904	3	3	0
Twelve Plates, transfer-printed, with farmyard scenes in blue, and large dish similar. Sotheby, May, 1907	1	10	0

STAFFORDSHIRE FIGURE, SALT-GLAZED.
Touched in parts with blue. (Height 5⅛ inches.)
(*In the collection of Mr. Robert Bruce Wallis.*)

STAFFORDSHIRE EARTHENWARE FIGURE OF COCK.
Tail feathers enamelled in dark blue. (Height 8 inches.) Marked R

WOOD.
(*In the collection of Mr. Robert Bruce Wallis.*)

OLD STAFFORDSHIRE FIGURES.

DIANA.

BIRTH OF VENUS.
Modelled from the Plymouth porcelain group.
(*In the collection of Miss Feilden.*)

GROUP OF STAFFORDSHIRE FIGURES.

MINERVA.
PARSON AND CLERK.
All marked NEALE & CO.
TOBY JUG.
Finely modelled.

(*In the collection of Col. and Mrs. Dickson.*)

CHAPTER XI
STAFFORDSHIRE FIGURES

Early Period (1675–1725): Slip, Agate, and Astbury Figures—Best Period (1725–1760): Fine Modelling and Reticent Colouring, Ralph Wood the elder, Aaron Wood, Thomas Wheildon—Classic Period (1760–1785): Wedgwood, Neale, Voyez, Ralph Wood, junior, Enoch Wood, Lakin and Poole—Decadent Period (1785–1830): Walton, Scott, Bott, Lockett, Dale, and imitative school.

In attempting to classify the great array of Staffordshire figures and groups, extending over a period of a century and a half, no little difficulty has been experienced. The number of unmarked specimens is very great, and in many cases, owing to trade rivalry, models were so extensively imitated that it is impossible to say who was the first modeller. These Staffordshire figures, except in the instances of the highest modelling and restrained under-glaze colouring of the best period, cannot be regarded as ceramic triumphs. But they are highly valuable, although not from an artistic point of view, as illustrative of the character of the common folk in England, and exemplifying their tastes and their sentiments.

Ornament, even in the humblest articles of daily use, has its meaning and can tell its story, to those who read aright, of the feeling of the man who produced it; whether he took a pleasure in making the article, or whether he was a machine, human or other, producing only a thin echo of art. Practically it may be asserted that from middle eighteenth-century days to middle nineteenth-century days ceramic art was steadily deteriorating. Applied art had practically ceased to exist in the early nineteenth century. It is said that men's eyes were first opened to this fact by the cumulative hideousness of the Great Exhibition of 1851, and certainly a perusal of the illustrated catalogue of that Exhibition is a saddening occupation.

In the study of the china shelf this decadence must always be considered, and it is fully borne out by a close study of the subject of Staffordshire figures. Practically, the crude agate cat and the little mannikin of early days playing bagpipes found replicas in crudity and poverty of invention in the spotted poodle dog or the kilted Scotsman, the common cottage ornaments of a century later. And between these two dates, with the exception of an outburst which promised to develop into something really great and almost did so, there was, owing to want of artistic instinct and general lack of culture, a fairly rapid degeneration into the hideous nightmare of the Toby jug and all the awful insularities of the late Staffordshire period.

STAFFORDSHIRE FIGURE OF ELOQUENCE.
(Sometimes known as *St. Paul Preaching at Athens*.)
In coloured earthenware. (Height 18 inches.)
Similar to figure in Schreiber Collection by Enoch Wood.
(*In the collection of Col. and Mrs. Dickson.*)

Early Period (1675–1725).—The method of slip decoration has already been described, and to this period, when Toft and his school had implanted their quaint and original taste upon the common people, these early figures belong. Among the best-known figures of this early date are small *Cats* of stoneware or earthenware body, coated with white and ornamented with spots in brown slip. *Ducks* are sometimes found similarly ornamented in spots and wavy lines. These figures are only 3 inches in height. To these days belong the solid agate *Cats* made of two or three clays of different colours intermingled, and highly glazed. These are some 5 or 6 inches in height. We give an illustration of this type of ware (p. 171). *Bears* in agate ware the same nature, and small figures of doll-like individuals are also found.

The elder Astbury (1736–1743) has been credited with a series of figures of men, some 6 inches in height, playing bagpipes or other instruments. They are splashed with green and brown, and have yellow slip ornament, their lead glazing is warm and rich. The beady eyes of some of these tiny figures is suggestive of the Toft slip applied figure on some of his dishes, and was produced by the use of manganese.

Among early figures those of salt-glaze are rare and of exceptional interest, and the figure illustrated (p. 351), stands as a typical example of a class not frequently met with, and highly prized by collectors.

We have seen in the chapter dealing with Whieldon and his influence that he commenced potting before 1740 and continued till 1780, and although none of his figures is marked it is tolerably certain that he produced some fine work in which he introduced the beautiful tortoiseshell glazings, which characteristic is found on figures attributed to him. Obviously over a period of nearly half a century Whieldon ware varies in quality. The following class of figures may be attributed to the early Whieldon period, that is, before 1760. *Actor*, with turban and flowing mantle, hand resting on dagger; tortoiseshell ware, brown and green glazing; height, 5½ inches. *Diana*, with dog, on square hollow pedestal made of buff clay; brown and grey glazings, eyes of brown clay; height, 7 inches. *Venus*, with bow, on irregular base, eyes brown clay; height, 5½ inches. Figure of *Sphinx*, coloured with brown and green glazings; height, 3½ inches. *Monkey*, eyes, black; height, 4 inches. Other animals, such as *Lion*, height, 3¼ inches; *Squirrel*, height, 7 inches; *Cock*, height, 7¼ inches; *Cow*, in form of small jug with woman milking, height, 5½ inches; *Dog*, with brown glazing, height, 3¾ inches. Other figures of this early period are *Summer* and *Winter*, each 4½ inches high; sauceboats in form of *Duck* and *Drake*, coloured glazings, height, 4½ inches.

(We have illustrated several types of these figures, pp. 171, 175).

The Best Period (1735–1760).—This is known to collectors as the Wood School. Briefly, the history of the Wood family is as follows, and will be of interest to collectors of Staffordshire figures. So strong and original is the work of the modeller Ralph Wood the elder, that connoisseurs recognise the class of face in his work. Aaron Wood and Ralph Wood were the sons of the old Ralph Wood, a miller. They were both modellers of distinction. Aaron is mainly known as a block-cutter of salt-glaze moulds. Ralph Wood (1750–1772) made figures and other rustic groups at his own factory at Burslem. His models are straightforward and homely and strongly English, not greatly influenced by any extraneous classic models. He modelled the celebrated "Vicar and Moses," which for quaint humour is inimitable. It has been copied by all the potters, and much of its strength and simplicity of modelling has been lost, while its restraint in colouring disappeared in the copies upon which enamel colours were lavishly laid.

OLD STAFFORDSHIRE GROUP, BACCHUS AND ARIADNE.
By ENOCH WOOD. Enamelled in colours. (Height 24 inches.)
(In the collection of Col. and Mrs. Dickson.)

OLD STAFFORDSHIRE EARTHENWARE FIGURES.

ADONIS (after the antique).
(Height 23 inches.)
VENUS.
(Height 24 inches.)

(*In the possession of Mr. S. G. Fenton.*)

There was a strong Quaker element in Staffordshire, and the Established Church was the subject of a good deal of satire by the potter. The *Parson and Clerk* returning home after a carousal, *The Tithe Pig* and other subjects exemplify this. Fielding published "Joseph Andrews" in 1742, and it appears that parson-baiting was a familiar form of amusement. Probably there were a good many abuses in the Church that were evident. The hunting parson was often the boon companion of the drinking squire. At any rate the Ralph Wood group, entitled *The Vicar and Moses*,[6] showing the sleeping vicar, with full-bottomed wig, and Moses, the clerk, seated underneath the pulpit exhorting the congregation with uplifted hand, is a masterly piece of modelling. In colour the original Ralph Wood examples are light purplish throbbing brown in the pulpit and desk, and carved cherubs, green in the canopy behind the vicar, and who has a white cassock, and the coat of Moses is a slatey blue. The flesh tints are low in tone.

To return to Aaron Wood, the brother of Ralph Wood, he was the father of William Wood, who became one of Wedgwood's modellers, and of Enoch Wood, who went to Palmer as modeller for some years. In 1784 Enoch Wood commenced business for himself. He produced cream ware and black basalt and, what most interests us here, he made some excellent figures, including a bust of *John Wesley*. In 1790 he entered into partnership with James Caldwell. The ware is marked "Wood and Caldwell" till 1818, when the firm became "Enoch Wood and Sons," till 1866.

In regard to Ralph Wood, the elder, he appears to have engaged his son in his pottery, so that prior to his death, in 1772, we do not know which Ralph Wood modelled some of the figures; but from 1772 to 1797 Ralph Wood, junior, was responsible for the factory, and there seems to have been business connection, about 1786, between him and his cousin Enoch Wood.

Concerning the figures of Ralph Wood, father and son, it may be said that they were the first to impress their names upon Staffordshire figures. Some of the pieces are marked with impressed mark R. WOOD, RA WOOD, BURSLEM (impressed on *Vicar and Moses*). This mark is found on some of the finest and earliest Toby jugs. It is believed, though not proved, that "RA WOOD" is the mark adopted by Ralph Wood, junior.

That the Woods reflected English feeling and sentiment and did not go to the classics for their inspiration is shown by their fine model of *Hudibras* upon his horse, in the act of drawing his sword.

> "The trenchant blade, Toledo trusty,
>
> For want of fighting was grown rusty,
>
> And ate into itself, for lack
>
> Of some body to hew and hack."

The horse of Hudibras is as famed in story as *Rosinante*, the famous charger of Don Quixote, and in fine satire Butler enumerates his points.

BUST OF BONAPARTE.
Coloured earthenware. By ENOCH WOOD. (Height 9½ inches.)
(*In the collection of Mr. Robert Bruce Wallis.*)

BUST OF ALEXANDER, CZAR OF RUSSIA.
Coloured earthenware. By WOOD & CALDWELL.
(*In the collection of Col. and Mrs. Dickson.*)

It is not too much to aver that, if it were not known that the Wood model bore the title *Hudibras*, the source of inspiration would go unknown. Similarly it may not be impossible, since no title appears on the famous *Toby Philpot* jug, that it may be derived from the character of *Uncle Toby* in Sterne's "Tristram Shandy," which was published in nine volumes from 1759 to 1767. The type of blunt, jovial, rubicund Englishman was beginning to become as pronounced in Bunbury and other caricaturists as it became later on the china shelf.

Among other noticeable figures of the Ralph Wood period the pair of figures are the *Haymakers*, separate figures (7½ inches high each, impressed R.

WOOD), a youth and maiden leaning against tree trunks. A bust of *Milton*, cream ware, uncoloured, is impressed RA. WOOD, BURSLEM; height, 9 inches. *Old Age* is represented by a rustic figure of an old man leaning upon a stick and a crutch. *Neptune* and *Venus* and *Apollo* betray the contemporary classic influence.

In examining the figures of the elder Ralph Wood they will be found in parts, though hardly perceptible, to be unglazed. This is owing to the fact that he applied his glaze with a brush. In the figures of the best period the colouring is extremely delicate, and the flesh tints do not approach the rosy pink associated with other figure work. It is difficult to describe them, but they approximate to a biscuit-coloured grey. But there are the usual exceptions to all rules. In one case in particular the colouring is more pronounced—the bust of *Handel*, who died in 1759. It is marked "RA. WOOD." It is finely modelled and bright in colouring. A figure of a *Cock*, marked R. WOOD, is illustrated (p. 351). It is 8 inches in height. The body is light in colour, with light and dark brown decoration about the neck. The wings are yellow, with brown stripes, the tail brown and dark-blue enamel colours. Legs dark brown and green and splashed base. This specimen is in one piece, not having any joint at neck.

The fine coloured large figure (18 inches in height) of *Eloquence*, known also as *St. Paul preaching at Athens*, is by Enoch Wood, after a model by Sir H. Cheere. There is a similar figure in the Schreiber Collection at the Victoria and Albert Museum. But it must be admitted that some of these large figures bear a strong resemblance in technique and modelling to those of Wedgwood. The *Bacchus and Ariadne* group was most certainly reproduced by Enoch Wood, who signed it. So that the difficulty in such cases of determining which was the original model becomes very great.

The Classic Period (1760–1785).—It appears that Josiah Wedgwood, when under the influence of Whieldon and before he embarked upon his classic ornamentation under the guidance of Bentley, modelled some very fine figures which are unmarked, but exhibit considerable strength and beauty. There are three figures, *Faith*, *Hope*, and *Charity*, in date about 1770, in the Willett Collection marked Wedgwood. Other figures are the large ones of *Fortitude* and *Prudence* (height 21 inches). But these symbolistic figures betray the classic influence. They are magnificent pieces of modelling. Then there is the fine group of *Bacchus and Ariadne*, the same height. The specimen at the British Museum is cream colour, but later imitators adopted the same modelling and added colour to the decoration. A copy of this group so treated, possibly by Enoch Wood, is illustrated (p. 363).

Other busts of Wedgwood in coloured cream ware of *Voltaire* and *Rousseau* will be found illustrated on p. 233.

STAFFORDSHIRE EARTHENWARE FIGURE OF FALSTAFF.
Shield decorated in silver lustre. Marked WOOD & CALDWELL.
(*In the collection of Mr. F. W. Philips, Hitchin.*)

DERBY PORCELAIN FIGURE OF FALSTAFF. CHELSEA PORCELAIN FIGURE OF FALSTAFF.

Neale & Co. betray classic influence in much of their work, and as Voyez, the Frenchman, was their modeller, this is not hard to understand. Among their well-known figures are *Flora* (12½ inches high) and *Diana* (5 inches high), and they were large makers of Toby jugs. We give an illustration (p. 355) of a group of finely modelled ware by Neale & Co., including a Toby jug copied from the Ralph Wood model and impressed NAELE & CO., and the familiar group of the *Parson and Clerk* copied by them after the well-known Chelsea-Derby porcelain model of the same subject, and reproduced as an earthenware group by many other Staffordshire potters. It is often attributed to Ralph Wood the younger. It is interesting to compare the *Minerva* with the *Diana* illustrated above. The same classic spirit was the inspiration of the two modellers, and in the case of unmarked classic figures there always exists considerable difficulty in definitely assigning their origin.

In regard to all these coloured Staffordshire figures it should be borne in mind that, until well towards the close of the eighteenth century, they were coloured by the use of pigments under the glaze, which gave a low-toned effect of very delicate character. Later, enamel colours were used with lurid effect, and much of the beauty of the old school vanished.

Enoch Wood (1783–1840), **Wood and Caldwell** (1790–1818).—Of this school there are several fine examples. There is no doubt that the ease with which classic prototypes could be copied and porcelain figures imitated began to tell upon the originality of most of the modellers. The *Bacchus and Ariadne* (illustrated p. 363), with the vine leaf wreaths in green around the heads and the finely coloured drapery, is by Enoch Wood. There is a specimen in a private collection at Eccles signed "E. WOOD, Sculp. and HEWITT Pinxt." (the height of this example is 27 inches), in spite of the similar uncoloured group at the British Museum marked Wedgwood.

Enoch Wood is best known for his portrait busts of *John Wesley* and of *George Whitfield*. The former who stayed at his house in the Potteries sat for this bust, which is a fine piece of portraiture. This is marked "E. WOOD," and sometimes "ENOCH WOOD, Sculp., Burslem 1781." George Whitfield was probably modelled at a later date. There is a fine equestrian statuette of *St. George and the Dragon*, sometimes signed "E. Wood," similar in modelling to the Whieldon mottled tortoiseshell coloured specimen (illustrated p. 175).

There are other busts by Enoch Wood which are noteworthy. There is the fine bust of *Bonaparte* as First Consul in coloured earthenware, with blue coat with yellow border, and having marbled base. The height of this is 9½ inches, and it is marked "E. WOOD." This is in date about 1802. A bust of *Alexander I.* of Russia, in highly coloured earthenware, in military costume, marked WOOD & CALDWELL. The date of this is later than the Bonaparte, an inscription on the back on some examples runs "Alexander Aet. 35. Moscow burnt. Europe preserved 1812."

Another well-known figure by Wood and Caldwell is the figure of Quin as *Falstaff*. By the illustrations we have given (p. 371) it will be seen that this model was in direct imitation of the similar figures in porcelain at Derby and Chelsea. The colouring is different, the shield is silver lustre, the costume consists of red breeches, striped yellow and white surtout; but these colours are a feeble imitation of the finer enamel work on the china models from which they have been copied.

STAFFORDSHIRE FIGURE.
(About 1790.)
Decorated and refired by Absolon, of Yarmouth.

**BASE OF FIGURE.
(Enlarged.)
Showing painted mark "Absolon Yarm."**

(*In the collection of Mr. F. I. Burwood.*)

The group of *Toby Jugs* illustrated (p. 383), exhibit the best known models of a much collected variety of earthenware. These examples are collectors' specimens, but later models may be said to be like—

The grand old name of gentleman,

Defamed by every charlatan,

And soil'd with all ignoble use.

That it was not infrequent to take a model bodily from English porcelain is shown by the group entitled the *Birth of Venus*, which is taken from a Plymouth group of the same subject (illustrated p. 355), this apparently belongs to the Enoch Wood period.

In the figures of children we illustrate p. 387, the figures of *Flower Boys*, some 4½ inches high, are evidently inspired by some of the Chelsea-Derby figures which in their turn were under strong French influence. The middle figure of the trio is one of a pair by Wood and Caldwell. The figure of *Cupid* above is a fine specimen, standing 17½ inches in height. Cupid is fully armed with his deadly bow and arrow, which by the way are decorated in silver lustre, suggestive of the Falstaff shield of Wood and Caldwell, and at his feet are two lions crouching in subjugation, and he holds the torch of Hymen in his hand. This is a remarkably fine modelled figure representing this contemporary foreign influence upon Staffordshire figures at its best.

In regard to the strong classic influence the two figures (illustrated p. 363) are in white earthenware. That on the left, of *Adonis*, is obviously taken direct from the antique, while the *Venus* is a fine Staffordshire adaptation of a well-known classic statue in the pose and in the dolphin by her side. The only touch of colour is the darkening of the hair. It is a magnificent piece of modelling something in the nature of the classic art seen through French eyes. To find this in Staffordshire is as though one found *La Source* of Ingres in the Royal Academy of the year 1856. The date of this Staffordshire *Venus* cannot be stated. It is an important figure, being 24 inches in height and exhibits something so strikingly realistic that it must be assigned a high place among the figures.

We illustrate a Staffordshire figure belonging to this period, which is signed "Absalon, Yarmouth." Towards the end of the eighteenth century, as in the latter days of Lowestoft, a factory termed "The Ovens" at Yarmouth carried on a decorating business, receiving the ware from Leeds and from Staffordshire, and decorating and refiring it in the glost oven. The date of the figure illustrated is about 1790. On some of the pieces decorated by Absalon, the name of the Staffordshire maker, Turner, appears as an impressed mark. Turner, who carried on an extensive trade with the Baltic and Northern Europe, no doubt readily came into touch with these East Anglian decorators.

GIRL WITH TAMBOURINE.
Coloured Staffordshire figure.

COLOURED STAFFORDSHIRE FIGURES.
TAMBOURINE PLAYER (marked SALT) AND MUSICIANS.
(In the collection of Miss Feilden.)

The Decadent Period (1785–1830).—It is impossible to keep exactly to dates in any of these periods of rough classification. But in general the later period becomes more homely and a great number of mantel ornaments of a simple nature with rustic subjects were made for the homes of cottagers. These have trees as background and are Arcadian in subject. They are, when in this style, of the finnicking school of the Chelsea shepherds and shepherdesses known as of the boscage school. John Walton (1790–1839), made a great many figures in this manner, accompanied by a lamb, as well as a great number of Toby jugs. Another potter is Ralph Salt (1812–1840), whose name appears on the little *Tambourine Player* (p. 379), and probably the *Musicians* of the adjacent group are by him too. A larger figure of the *Girl with Tambourine* above is of the same period, though its maker cannot be identified.

We illustrate (p. 391) two later figures, *The Fishwife* and *Mother Goose*. Both are well modelled, and were evidently intended to meet the popular taste. The days of gods and goddesses were over, and figures and groups begin to grow commonplace. In *Mother Goose* the nursery rhyme is substituted for the mythology of the Greeks.

Among other names found on these later figures are Lakin and Poole, Dale (mark usually impressed I. DALE BURSLEM), and Edge and Grocott, who made figures of boys partly draped holding baskets of flowers. It is possible that they made the two outside figures of *Flower Boys* (illustrated p. 387).

There is to lovers of the ultra-aesthetic something which appears to be trivial and insipid in this peasant pottery of the later date. But in spite of its defects, it holds, to those who read between the lines and can add that necessary touch of human interest to their collecting, a charm on account of its quaintness. Those who have sought these old cottage treasures high and low and secured from far-away habitations snug in the hills or lone huts on the wolds, or from the dim-lit cabins of fisher folk these relics of byegone days, read into their newly acquired possessions something of the life history in their old environment, lying *perdu* these many years, perched aloft on the high mantel or hidden in the cupboard recess silently listening to the old tales of the strange men and women who live apart from the hum of cities.

Chelsea we know, Derby we know, Bow we know, with their dainty china shepherdesses minding impossible sheep, and with gallants prinked out in all the colours of the humming-bird. These were the trifles in porcelain that my dear Lady Disdain in a waft of bergamot set apart in her glazed case by Sheraton. In the days of paint and patch and of the revels at Vauxhall and Ranelagh, virtuosos drowsily passed comment on my lady's latest acquisition just to please her passing whim and wean her from the vapours.

These earthenware figures "in homespun hose and russet brown" suggest the old world nooks of other days. Give Chelsea and Bow to the town. This homely art of Staffordshire became English after all. It was found in thatched cottages "with breath of thyme and bees that hum." These boscage shepherds and shepherdesses, these rustic musicians, lusty post-boys, and the family of Toby Philpots, found kinship in the miller and the farmer, the herdsman and the milkmaid, the gamekeeper and the woodman, the ostler and the waggoner—simple, kind-hearted folk, the children of nature uncloyed by the subtleties of art. Red-cheeked lasses and wrinkled crook-backed old dames, mother and daughter and granddaughter, toilers and sufferers, who chose the warm west window seat in the sun and the ingle nook by the fireside—these were the whilom owners of the old Staffordshire figures. Somehow, nor is the fancy a foolish one, one likes to associate these diminutive figures with the old gardens of England set in sweet places where one

"Can watch the sunlight fall

Athwart the ivied orchard wall;

Or pause to catch the cuckoo's call
Beyond the beeches."

GROUP OF FINELY COLOURED TOBY JUGS.
(Date 1790–1810.)
(*In the possession of Mr. S. G. Fenton.*)

There seems to be something added to old Staffordshire figures which have steeped themselves in somnolent repose these many years till they have become invested with a subtle human interest not easily disassociated from them.

The squire had his services of Worcester and of Crown-Derby, and the nobleman relegated his cases of fine porcelain to the care of his housekeeper, to dust and to safeguard till he came again to hunt and to shoot. But the cottager's Staffordshire figures were lovingly handled when the good wife furbished up her brass candlesticks, and they insensibly became part of the environment of the cottage home.

Here, then, is the key to the charm and magic which goes to the collecting of old Staffordshire figures, even of the decadent period. There is within them and around them and about them something redolent of a sturdy peasantry, something sad, something tinged with autumn days and autumn mists because they belong to days that have faded, and almost to a race that is extinct.

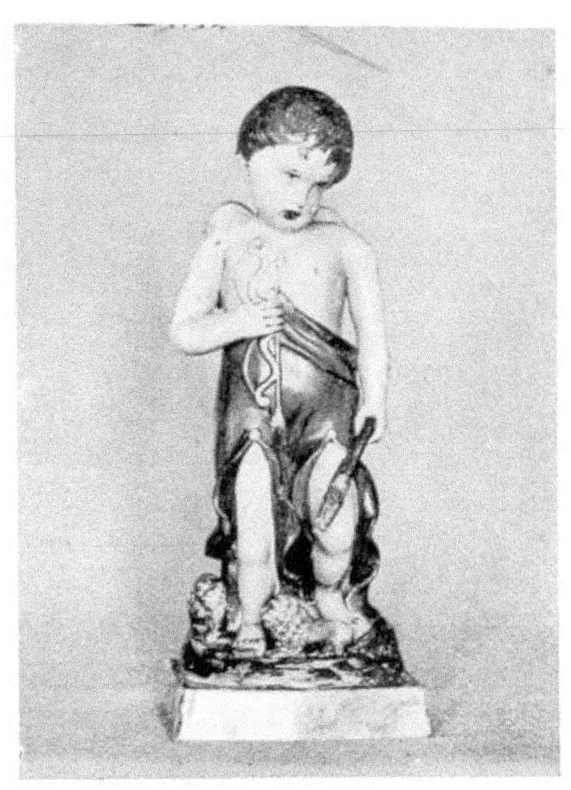

CUPID
Large coloured Staffordshire figure. (Height 17½ inches.) Bow and arrow in silver lustre.
(*In the collection of Miss Feilden.*)

**COLOURED STAFFORDSHIRE FIGURES OF FLOWER BOYS.
Pair 4½ inches. Centre figure one of pair by WOOD & CALDWELL.
(*In the collection of Miss Feilden.*)**

PRICES.

LEEDS FIGURES.	£	s.	d.
Pair of Leeds cream-ware Figures of Musicians, Youth and Girl; *rare*. Marked "Leeds Pottery." Sotheby, November, 1904	6	6	0
STAFFORDSHIRE FIGURES.			
Group of Madonna and Child (probably Wedgwood), illustrated in "English Earthenware" (Professor Church). Sotheby, February, 1906	8	0	0
Staffordshire Models of Cottages (some porcelain), encrusted with flowers. Christie, January, 1906 (59 models).	31	10	0
"Vicar and Moses," group, decorated in translucent colours. Sotheby, June 1906	35	10	0

"Vicar and Moses," group, decorated in translucent colours. Sotheby, November, 1906	8	10	0
Bacchus and Ariadne, large; brown glaze; 25 in. high. Christie, November, 1906	13	2	6
Toby Philpot jugs (four male and one female), grotesque models. Christie, November, 1906	30	9	0
Falstaff, two examples, on plinths, encrusted with flowers; 9 in. high. Christie, November, 1906	5	15	6
"Elijah," "The Widow," and "Virgin and Child"; three figures. Puttick and Simpson, March, 1907	3	12	6
Busts of *Milton* and *Handel*, impressed mark, "Ra Wood Burslem"; white: 9 in. high. Sotheby, July, 1907	6	0	0
Figure of Gamekeeper: white; 8½ in. high. Sotheby, July, 1907	2	0	0
Figure of *Lost Sheep*; white; 8¾ in. high. Sotheby, July, 1907	2	18	0
Figure of *Girl Haymaker*; white; 7¾ in. high. Sotheby, July, 1907	3	0	0
Figures, *Chaucer* and *Sir Isaac Newton*, decorated in colours; marked "Ra Wood"; impressed "Burslem." 12½ in. high. Sotheby, 1907	12	10	0
Figures, *Cobbler and his Wife*, pair, large, seated; 12½ in. high. Christie, January, 1908	13	2	6
Figures, reclining, *Cleopatra*, 8½ in. high, and *Antony*, 8 in. high. Christie, January, 1908	14	14	0
"Bacchus and Ariadne," 25 in. high; *Female*, holding dove, 25 in. high. Christie, January, 1908	16	16	0
Figures, pair, Boy and Girl harvesting, square base, one marked "R. Wood." Sotheby, May, 1908	10	5	0

"Vicar and Moses," in Whieldon colours (attributed to
R. Wood), yellow, green, brown, manganese purple,
&c. Sotheby, May, 1908   15   0   0

Shepherd and Shepherdess, seated, with dog, lamb, and
goat; shepherd playing flute; Whieldon colouring
(attributed to R. Wood). Sotheby, May, 1908   12   0   0

"St. George and Dragon" in Whieldon colouring
(attributed to Ralph Wood) Sotheby, May, 1908   14   0   0

Toby Jug, representing man seated with jug on knee
(attributed to R. Wood). Sotheby, May, 1908   6   6   0

FIGURE OF FISHWIFE.
(Late Staffordshire.)
(*In the collection of Miss Feilden.*)

FIGURE OF MOTHER GOOSE.
(Staffordshire, early nineteenth century.)
(*In the collection of the Author.*)

CHAPTER XII
SWANSEA AND OTHER FACTORIES

Swansea—The Cambrian Pottery—Opaque china—Etruscan Ware—Lowesby Pottery (Leicestershire)—Liverpool, Herculaneum (1794–1841)—Bristol, Joseph Ring (1784–1825)—Caughley or Salopian (1751–1775)—Derby, John and Christopher Heath (1758–1780)—Isleworth, Shore & Goulding (1760–1830)—Marks—Prices.

Undoubtedly the earthenware productions at Swansea are of a high artistic order. For a century, from 1768 to about 1870, the Cambrian Pottery at Swansea manufactured ware bearing various marks and comprising a wide range of examples. During part of the time a rival factory at Glamorgan, which existed from 1814, to 1839, produced "opaque china" and cream ware in common with Swansea.

Practically the history of the Cambrian Pottery dates from 1790, when George Haynes bought the factory. Fine black basalt ware was produced. There are two recumbent figures of *Antony* and *Cleopatra*, the latter in the Victoria and Albert Museum having the impressed mark SWANSEA, and the former in the possession of Mr. C. F. Cox, and marked with the name of the modeller, "G. Bentley, Swansea, 22 May, 1791." The length of these figures is 12 inches. Two somewhat similar recumbent figures of *Antony* and *Cleopatra* in colours have been attributed to Lowestoft (see "Lowestoft China," by W. W. R. Spelman, Jarrold & Sons, Norwich, 1905). But these more properly belong to the Staffordshire school, and are probably by Neale and Palmer.

Under-glaze blue-printed ware, notably "willow pattern" from Caughley, had been made at Swansea probably before Haynes bought the factory, certainly not later than 1790, when Leeds commenced similar imitations of Turner's "willow patterns." Salt-glazed ware, some marked "Cambrian Pottery," but mostly unmarked, was made and decorated in enamel colours with figure subjects, landscapes, and flowers.

The transfer-printed ware is of great variety and is excellently finished, and compares very favourably with the best of the Staffordshire cream ware similarly decorated, or with the highest productions of Leeds in the same manner. We illustrate (p. 405) a group of various types of transfer-printed ware in black and brown, and blue under-glaze transfer-printing. As will be noticed, the Oriental influence from Caughley and the china factories was very strong, but in the print of the ship there is something suggestive of Liverpool.

SWANSEA PLATES.
1. Cream ware, rim painted in green and violet with vine pattern.
Mark impressed SWANSEA.
2. Earthenware, black transfer-printed.
Mark impressed DILLWYN & CO. SWANSEA.
(*In the Royal Scottish Museum, Edinburgh.*)

SET OF FINELY PAINTED SWANSEA BULB POTS.
(*In the collection of Col. and Mrs. Dickson.*)

A very fine transfer-printed plate in black is illustrated (p. 397), showing something higher in engraving than Staffordshire had attempted. It stands, leaving out the delicate black transfer-printing done on the Worcester porcelain, as an exceptionally artistic piece of work. The adjacent plate in the illustration at once shows the source of its inspiration. It follows one of

Wedgwood's Queen's ware patterns painted in green and violet of the grape pattern, although it must be admitted that the Swansea adaptation is richer than the somewhat thinner design found on old Wedgwood plates.

One of the most interesting features in the history of the Swansea factory is the introduction by Haynes of a ware termed "opaque china," which was in reality a finer and whiter kind of cream ware, and eminently suitable for the painted decorations by W. W. Young, an artist from the Bristol factory, who painted from about 1803 to 1806, flowers and butterflies and shells with great fidelity. He was followed by another artist Thomas Pardoe, from the Derby factory, who brought more poetry into his floral subjects. Another artist named Evans painted flower-pieces with almost equal beauty. We illustrate a fine Cambrian vase painted by Pardoe, and a Swansea jug painted by Evans (p. 401).

There is no doubt that a very high standard of painting on the Swansea ware prevailed during the best period, and the illustration of a set of three Swansea-ware bulb pots (see p. 397) shows that landscape painters of no mean gifts were employed. It is this picturesque quality of decoration (dependent in a great measure on the fact that from 1814 to 1824 porcelain was made too), together with the equally fine quality of the ware itself, that has placed Swansea well to the front among the collectors of artistic earthenware.

We have alluded to Haynes the proprietor who first brought the factory into prominence. This was in 1790. But in 1802 it passed into the hands of Lewis Weston Dillwyn, and it was during this period that W. W. Young did the work we have alluded to. In 1817 the factory passed into the hands of the Bevingtons, and in 1824 it again came into the possession of the Dillwyn family, who held it till about 1850, when the firm was known as Evans and Glasson, and later as D. J. Evans & Co. until its close in 1870. During this long period the marks assumed various characters. We have at the end of this chapter given most of the more important to enable collectors to identify the period of their Swansea ware—when marked.

Another ware greatly collected must be alluded to, of which an illustration is given (p. 405). This Etruscan ware, following the early example set by Wedgwood, was an attempt to copy some of the Greek vases which were painted red on a black body.

In "Dillwyn's Etruscan Ware," made only for three years from 1847 to 1850, the body was a warm red, and the design was impressed thereon either by means of black transfer-printing or outline, and the background was then painted and the classic figures heightened. This ware is not always marked, but when the mark appears it is in a scroll, as given in the list of marks (p. 416).

Lowesby Pottery.—There is very little to be said about this pottery in Leicestershire, which was conducted under the auspices of Sir Francis Fowke about 1835. The mark is always puzzling to collectors which is a *fleur-de-lis* with the name Lowesby, both impressed. The ware usually made at this small pottery was red terra cotta coated with a dull black upon which were flowers and butterflies painted in bright enamel colours. This decoration was done elsewhere, probably in London.

CAMBRIAN VASE.
Painted by Pardoe.
(*In the collection of Mr. A. Duncan.*)

SWANSEA JUG.
Painted by Evans.
(*In the collection of Mr. A. Duncan.*)

Liverpool.—We have already alluded to the Liverpool delft, but the story of Liverpool as a potting centre is not yet complete. There was, of course, the enormous business in transfer-printing on Staffordshire cream ware established by Sadler and Green. But they made cream ware themselves as well as decorated it for others. Cream ware was produced at the factories of Chaffers, Barnes, Pennington, and others. And at a date immediately prior to the cream ware, Shaw, of Liverpool, had made "Astbury" and "Whieldon" and salt-glaze wares. So that here at once is a difficulty, and a very great one, in identifying with exactitude the origin of some of these wares. There is a great deal yet to be discovered concerning the long line of Liverpool factories, and if only as much special attention had been given to this locality as has been given to the much smaller factory of Lowestoft, original research might disentangle many a ceramic puzzle.

W. Reid & Co.—These potters made artistic earthenware from about 1754 to 1760, another firm established by Richard Abbey about 1793 continued till 1796 to make cream ware of a high order. This pottery, bought by Messrs. Worthington, was named Herculaneum Pottery.

The Herculaneum Pottery (1796–1841).—At first, when a band of Staffordshire potters came over to the new works, stoneware and black and red unglazed ware in the Wedgwood manner were made. Later a considerable amount of cream ware of pleasing character was turned out. The various marks found on the ware of this factory are given at the end of this chapter. Shortly after the end of the eighteenth century porcelain was made here, and some of the examples are of a very high quality both in potting and in decoration. From 1836 to 1841 the proprietors were Messrs. Close, Mort & Co.

Until more facts come to light and trained research is applied to all classes of Liverpool ware nothing definitely can be stated. But it is certain that some of the Liverpool ware is so fine in character as even to confuse old collectors who have never seen specimens before.

We illustrate a Liverpool plate (p. 409) with the usual Oriental design, and having no special feature about it which many another factory could not have produced. Its blue is fine and its potting is excellent, but it is not exceptional. The illustration beside it (p. 409) is of an earthenware mug some 5 inches in height which undoubtedly is a puzzle to experts. The exquisitely-painted exotic birds in rich colouring are not less perfect than those painted on Worcester vases or on Chelsea dishes. Indeed, it seems to show very strong traces of the style of Worcester painting. One is inclined to attribute it to Liverpool with the proviso that it must have been painted by some artist who had been trained at Worcester. It will thus be seen by this case that in unmarked earthenware there are exceptional difficulties in correctly placing examples where so much cream ware was made not very dissimilar in character, and where artists, as we have seen at Swansea, came over from other factories, apparently to the confoundment of the present-day collector.

GROUP OF SWANSEA WARE.
Transfer-printed in blue, black, and brown.
(*In the collection of Mr. A. Duncan.*)

DILLWYN'S ETRUSCAN WARE.
VASE.
With Warriors in Chariot and Pegasus. (Height 14 inches.)
TAZZA.
With Dancing Girl (side view and interior). (10½ inches diameter.)
(*In the collection of Mr. A. Duncan.*)

Bristol.—Joseph Ring in 1786 commenced to make a cream ware with the assistance of potters he engaged from Shelton in Staffordshire. In colour it was a warm cream due to the glaze and not to the body of the ware itself. Connected with this factory are some finely painted flower-pieces in enamel colours by William Fifield (born in 1777, and died in 1857), and his son, John Fifield. The factory changed hands in 1825, and became Pountney and Allies and Pountney & Co. until 1872. Many of Fifield's decorated pieces with floral works bear the name and date of the person for whom they were made. These are quite characteristic of the pottery, and occur after 1820 and in the Pountney and Allies period. There is a strong similarity in these chains of flowers and garlands to the Oriental ware, and its later French imitation which poses as Lowestoft. Much of this Bristol earthenware is confounded with somewhat similar New Hall porcelain, and is termed by very inexperienced buyers and sellers as "cottage Worcester." "Cottage" it may be, but it has no relationship with Worcester.

Caughley or Salopian.—The Caughley under-glaze blue-printed ware with its rich almost purplish blue is well known, but the various tints of this blue employed in the porcelain are not so well known varying as they do from this deep blue to a fairly light slate blue—but that concerns china and is another story. The Coalport factory china mark at the present day has the date 1750, proudly going back to these early days. Of Salopian earthenware not too much is known, it is eclipsed by the porcelain which Thomas Turner commenced to make at Caughley in 1772.

But earthenware was made at the factory from 1750 to 1775 by Browne, the owner of the factory, whose niece Thomas Turner married and took over the pottery in 1772. There are, belonging to this early period, some exceedingly well-modelled Caughley figures which are equal to the finest work of the Staffordshire potters. Some of these figures are 20 inches in height, and among those attributed to this Salopian pottery are the following: *Prudence*, holding a mirror, draped classical figure with figured gown; and *Fortitude*, a companion figure. *Antony* and *Cleopatra* are also believed to belong to this factory by some collectors. Caughley pottery is sometimes, though rarely, marked with the word SALOPIAN or with the initials S or C in blue under the glaze. A considerable doubt still exists as to what is and what is not Salopian or Caughley earthenware, and an opinion should not be hastily arrived at on superficial examination. Many of the early under-glaze blue-printed porcelain cups and saucers with Oriental designs similar in character to the "willow pattern" bear a mark of a blue crescent not unlike that of the Worcester factory. When such specimens in earthenware are found thus marked in under-glaze blue with the crescent they may certainly be pronounced to be Caughley, in date about 1772 to 1785. Some of the octagonal dark blue-printed Caughley earthenware plates are of similar shape to the Oriental porcelain model (illustrated p. 327), and the design especially in the treatment of the border is handled in the same manner except that Turner was fonder of more crowded detail.

COPY OF PORTLAND VASE.
In red ware Isleworth.
(Early nineteenth century.) Marked S & G. (Height 7¾ inches.)
(*In the collection of Mr. W. G. Honey.*)

FINE EARTHENWARE MUG.
Exquisitely painted with exotic birds in Worcester style (attributed to Liverpool).
(*In the collection of Col. and Mrs. Dickson.*)

LIVERPOOL CREAM WARE
PLATE. With Oriental decoration in blue.
(*In the collection of Miss Feilden.*)

Derby Earthenware.—Derby porcelain is well known. But it is not so well known that Derby earthenware is worth considering from a collecting point of view. There is a certain amount of obscurity surrounding the early ware made at Cockpit Hill. Slip ware was made in early days and delft appears to have been made there at the beginning of the eighteenth century. In 1772 the Derby pot-works, in the hands of the Heath family who were bankers, produced cream ware, though not equal to the Staffordshire products. Messrs. John and Christopher Heath, of Derby, are described as "bankrupts" in 1780, and a great sale of the earthenware in stock took place. The collector has mainly to rely on dated examples, which are very rare, or on pieces bearing local allusions to elections which may be safely attributed to Derby, but like so many of the extinct factories the ware has not received special attention in regard to its identification, nor is the task an easy one owing to cream ware being of very general manufacture.

Isleworth.—There is not much known about this factory established by Joseph Shore, who appears to have come from Worcester in 1760. The ware later is marked with the initials S. & G. after the firm became Shore and Goulding. The factory was never very large, and employed only twenty hands at the most. We illustrate (p. 409) a copy of the celebrated Portland Vase in red ware marked S. & G., and although some of the Isleworth ware appears to have been coarse earthenware to which the term "Welsh ware" was applied, some of it reverting to the old method of slip decoration, yet it must be admitted that certain pieces in red unglazed earthenware are of a high artistic character. There is a very fine teapot of this red ware in exact imitation of the Oriental style, being hexagonal in form, and having embossed decorations on the panels, the lid being surmounted with a Chinese grotesque animal, such as never was designed in Europe. The potting of such pieces as these has directed the attention of connoisseurs to this obscure factory.

There is no doubt that some of the finer pieces of Isleworth red ware have passed as Elers ware, but the former has a slight glaze and the handles are moulded. It is heavier in weight, and the teapots, &c., by Elers were undoubtedly of small dimensions.

It appears that "hound jugs" were made at Isleworth too. They were made at Brampton and elsewhere, but in those illustrated (p. 413) the mark is S. & G. They are brown stoneware with subjects of game in high relief, and are early nineteenth century in date.

In the second illustration it will be seen that the handle of the hound jug shows a later stage in its development. The reason is not far to seek, the awkward points of the hound handle were found to be in the way when Betsy Prue drew the beer. Any projection of this nature is distinctly out of place in earthenware for everyday use. This the potter readily recognised, and pattern number two was the result. Here he followed, without knowing it, the practice of the Japanese, who in their finely-carved ivory netsukes, so much collected nowadays, which were used as buttons and fastenings for dresses, always took care to leave no projecting points—the sleeping mouse has his tail well coiled around him—the dwarf mime has a smooth head and a figure as rotund as a miniature barrel.

It will be seen in this second illustration that the hound is still discernible in the handle, but probably only to those who have seen him in his former state. He has now become a clumsy, twisted handle with less meaning. It is here that his delicately balanced proportions when he was leaping over the brim with outstretched limbs—the attitude to the life of a hound when attempting to get through a fence—became a mere symbol in this later stage of his ceramic existence.

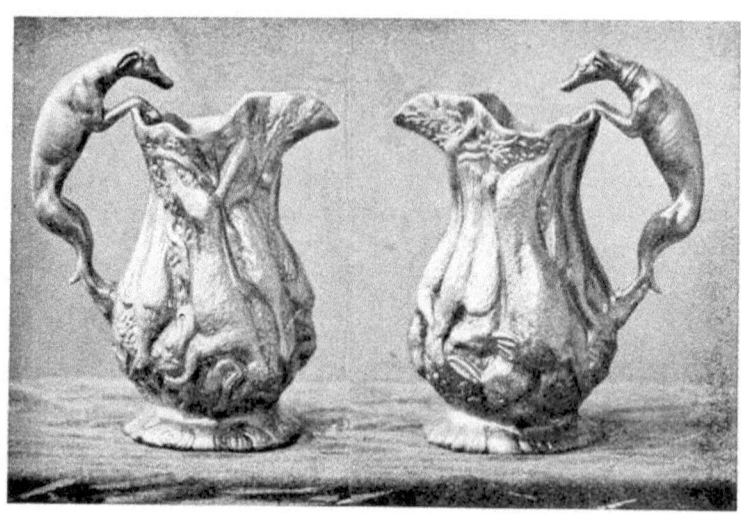

BROWN STONEWARE JUGS.
Decorated with game in high relief.
SHORE & GOULDING (Isleworth). Marked S & G. (Height 7½ inches.)
(*In the collection of Mr. W. G. Honey.*)

BROWN STONEWARE JUGS.
With sporting subjects in relief, the handles showing a debased form of the "hound" handles.
(*In the collection of Mr. W. G. Honey.*)

The pictorial history of the evolution is not a pretty one. It shows how the rushing need of the public for "more pots" destroyed the craft of the potter. It was far easier, since the demand was for pots, to turn out hasty work, and to let the modelling take care of itself. For this reason the mug degenerated into a mere commonplace mug, such as Staffordshire could produce quite as cheaply by the ton. So the factory put out its furnaces for ever.

MARKS USED AT SWANSEA, LOWESBY, LIVERPOOL, CAUGHLEY, DERBY, AND ISLEWORTH.

HAYNES, DILLWYN & CO
CAMBRIAN POTTERY
SWANSEA

Swansea.
Established 1769, works closed 1870. Cambrian Pottery, after 1780. A large number of marks employed. Sometimes the marks were impressed, but more often painted or stamped in red.

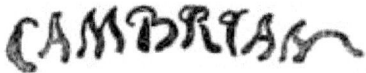   The word "Cambrian" as a mark is very uncommon.

OPAQUE CHINA SWANSEA   Used on the improved white hard earthenware invented by Haynes at the end of eighteenth century.

   Stone china was made from 1810–1830, and on some pieces this mark is found.

   Other of Dillwyn's Marks, from 1802–1817, are given here.

   Swansea *porcelain*, with its finely painted flowers, was produced from 1814 to 1817.

The celebrated "Etruscan Ware" was made by Dillwyn from 1847 to 1850, and it generally bears this printed mark.

From 1850 to 1870 the firm was Evans & Glasson, and D. J. Evans & Co., and some of the later marks printed on the Swansea ware of this period are reproduced.

This Prince of Wales' Feathers mark was often accompanied by the fancy name of the particular pattern on which it appeared.

Lowesby.
The mark of this small Leicestershire factory often puzzles collectors, and it is given here. In date it is about 1835, and it only existed for a few years.

Liverpool.
The marks of Liverpool are of exceptional interest. Sadler & Green (except in rare instances, when they signed their tiles) did not use a mark. Seth Pennington (1760–1790), celebrated for punch bowls of rich blue decoration, may have used the mark here given.

HERCULANEUM

The Herculaneum Pottery (1794–1841) (which produced porcelain too, in 1800, as did W. Reid & Co. (1754–1760) of fine quality, but unmarked).

The Herculaneum marks are various on earthenware, and when the mark of the bird, the "Liver," appears, it may be attributed to Herculaneum.

SALOPIAN.

Caughley or Salopian (1751–1775). As a china factory Caughley is well known, and is the parent of the Coalport porcelain factory.

TURNER.

In its early days nothing was marked, but from 1772 to 1775, under Thomas Turner, Salopian figures, some of large size, were made, and a great deal of under-glaze blue-printed earthenware produced. The word Salopian sometimes appears, and Turner is impressed on cream-ware plates (often ascribed to John Turner, of Lane End, Staffordshire).

S C

Sometimes the letters **S** or **C** appear in blue under the glaze.
These marks appear also in Salopian porcelain.

Bristol.
The pottery at Bristol has a history extending from seventeenth-century days down to 1820. Its delft frequently had dates inscribed, and sometimes initials of potters. Its later ware was rarely marked. But sometimes a blue cross appears, and we give a late mark, found infrequently.

Isleworth (1760–1830).
As much of the red ware of Messrs. Shore and Golding passes as Elers ware, the mark should be of interest to collectors. It is very small and impressed sometimes at the side of the piece near the base.

S & G

PRICES.

	£	s.	d.
SWANSEA EARTHENWARE.			
Dillwyn. Dinner service decorated with figures, and quantity of tea and breakfast ware similar (60 pieces in all). Leeder, Swansea, September, 1906	7	18	6
Etruscan ware Drinking Cup, formed as horse's head. Sotheby, February, 1908	2	0	0
LIVERPOOL.			
Cream-ware Punch Bowl, printed outside with figure subjects and inside with ship in full sail, in colours, and inscribed "Success to the Glory 1783." Sotheby, February, 1906	2	18	0
Bowl with ship inside, inscribed "Success to William and Nancy," dated 1776. Sotheby, November, 1906	3	0	0
Mug, with painted portrait of William Pitt. Sotheby, November, 1906	2	8	0

CAUGHLEY OR SALOPIAN EARTHENWARE.

Figures, reclining, *Cleopatra* and *Antony*, on oblong blue plinths (19½ in.). Christie, January, 1908	15	15	0

ISLEWORTH.

Ewer, decorated with Etruscan figures, rare, marked. Sotheby, November, 1907	1	2	0

BRISTOL EARTHENWARE.

Jug with inscription and landscape in blueand white. Sotheby, February, 1907	1	8	0

LOWESBY.

Basket of tortoiseshell ware, another of stoneware, another of red ware, marked "*Lowesby*," illustrated in *Queen*, January 26, 1907. Sotheby, December, 1908	2	0	0
Vase of red ware and two bottle-shaped vases, decorated with flowers in colours, marked "*Lowesby*." Sotheby, December, 1908	4	6	0

CHAPTER XIII
LUSTRE WARE

Early crude Copper Lustre (Brislington)—Gold Lustre, pink and purple Wedgwood, Leeds, Swansea, Sunderland—Platinum Lustre (termed "silver lustre").—Thomas Wedgwood (1791), Spode, E. Mayer, Wood and Caldwell, Leeds, Castleford, Swansea, and others—Lustre in combination as a decoration—"Resist" Lustre—Copper or Bronze Lustre—Marked Lustre Ware—Prices.

The collection of lustre ware is comparatively modern. In common with salt-glaze ware which was not thought much of in the auction-room some few years ago, lustre-ware has been studied and collected with avidity, and a good deal has been discovered concerning its origin.

It may be said at the outset that lustre varies very considerably in quality, and the plain undecorated platinum or "silver" lustre is being produced at the present day in teapots and cream-jugs in simulation of the old Georgian silver patterns.

So great is its variety and quality that some collectors have confined themselves specially to the collection of what is known as silver lustre "resist" style, and others have specialised in the pink or gold purple, with veined effects, of the Wedgwood school.

Lustre ware may be divided into the following classes:—

1. *Early brown copper lustre*, crude in style, made by Frank, of Brislington, near Bristol, about 1770.

2. *Gold lustre*, probably invented by Josiah Wedgwood, about 1792 (not to be confounded with gilding). The effect varies from pink to purple, and in the early pieces a combination was effected of gold, yellow, and purple, iridescent in varying lights.

3. *Platinum or "silver" lustre* (discovered by Thomas Wedgwood, the youngest son of Josiah Wedgwood, about 1791), imitations of silver ware, busts, &c.

4. *Copper or bronze lustre* (differing from the coarse early ware of Brislington), plain or undecorated.

5. Gold or purple lustre *used as an adjunct or decoration*, either around band or rim, as at Sunderland, &c.

6. Platinum or "silver" lustre *used as an adjunct or slight decoration* such as in the *Falstaff* figure (illustrated p. 371), or in the figure of *Cupid* (illustrated p. 387).

7. Platinum or "silver" lustre *in combination with other painted decoration*: (*a*) Birds, foliage, &c., painted in silver lustre on a ground of another colour; (*b*) Silver lustre "resist" style when the ground is platinum and the ornamentation is white, blue, or yellow.

8. Copper or bronze lustre *in combination with painted designs*.

PAIR OF MOTTLED PINK GOLD LUSTRE GOBLETS.
(*In the collection of Miss Feilden.*)

GOBLET AND GOLD LUSTRE MUGS WITH MOTTLED INTERIORS.
(*In the collection of Miss Feilden.*)

Early Lustre (Brislington).—Richard Frank, the delft potter, of Bristol, produced a crude ware composed of a hard body coated with a yellow dip resembling delft in character, and, upon this surface, ornamentation in copper lustre was made which gave it the appearance of burnished copper. It has been most inaptly compared with the Hispano-Mauro ware, with its rich arabesque ornamentation. There is nothing in common between the two except that they are both lustrous, and here the similarity ends. The Brislington colour was crude and the lustre ornaments extremely inartistic, and only suitable for the baking-dishes and mere utilitarian articles rudely and sufficiently decorated. Finer and thinner lustre ware found in the vicinity of Bristol can more safely be attributed to Swansea.

Gold Lustre.—As may readily be imagined, the amount of gold in the lustre decoration is very small. Gold lustre is *not* heavy English gilding. As early as 1776 Josiah Wedgwood obtained a formula from Dr. Fothergill, a Fellow of the Royal Society, of which he himself was a Fellow, which induced him to experiment with gold in order to produce lustrous effects. The Purple of Cassius was employed with great success in obtaining marbling and veining, but it was not till late in his career, about 1792, that he produced the gold lustre in its happiest combination in connection with the fine Pearl Ware shell dessert-services. We have already alluded to the thin wash of yellow and pink which was applied to these dishes to represent the interior of the shell, but the addition of gold lustre was the finishing touch, and such pieces are remarkably rare. They glow with fleeting colours as the light plays upon their surface.

In regard to this gold lustre, it should be stated that it varied, and varied most considerably, according to the character of the body not only subjacent to it, that is upon which it was placed, but owing to its filmy and translucent character it received reflection from adjacent surfaces. On a brown body the same effect is different from that on a white or cream body. This must be borne in mind to a smaller extent in platinum lustres. The warmer the body beneath, the richer the lustre and the greater its similarity to the silver which it is intended to imitate.

We illustrate two very fine mottled pink and gold lustre goblets which belong to the Wedgwood period and are very light and of very fine lustrous appearance (p. 425). In certain districts these are termed "Funeral cups," and whether they were used only on those solemn occasions or not, we cannot say.

It appears that gold lustre was sometimes used in combination with copper or bronze. In the two mugs illustrated (p. 425), the interiors are finely mottled in purple and gold, and suggest by the beautiful potting the work of the goldsmith in their sharp contour. They may be attributed to the best period, as, too, may the goblet in the centre which glows like gold. Incidentally it may be remarked that the photographs used for these illustrations cannot convey the rich and glorious colouring of these examples.

The writer knows of a cup and saucer marked "Dawson." There was a Samuel Dawson in 1802, a Staffordshire potter, and there is Dawson of Sunderland, a better-known maker of ware, which has lustre decoration, to which latter pottery this may more safely be attributed. In general effect the scheme of colour is ambitious. The centre panel is painted in red enamel colours over the glaze. The borders have a highly lustrous gold floral decoration on a ground of pink.

In regard to Sunderland and Newcastle, as a rule, the ware is crude and may be readily dismissed, but not too hurriedly. The rough bands of purple lustre inartistically painted as borders to the transfer-printed jugs and mugs with nautical subjects are well known. In broad effect on a jug or a punch bowl, this class of pink or purple lustre decoration is seen at its best. On a jug of this nature with bands and rough spongings of purple lustre appear the verses—

> "The man doomed to sail
>
> With the blast of the gale,
>
> Through billows Atlantic to steer,

As he bends o'er the wave

Which may soon be his grave

Remembers his home with a tear."

It is not a happy sentiment and suggests more the landsman's views of the sea than those of the sailor. The following has a truer ring, but it was not put on jugs to be sold to sailors' wives:—

"Go patter to lubbers and swabs, d'ye see,

'Bout danger and fear and the like;

A tight water-boat and good sea room give me,

And it ain't to a little I'll strike."

Platinum or Silver Lustre.—It is not definitely known who was the first potter to adopt this decoration. Obviously it could not be earlier in date than the year that platinum was discovered as a new metal. Its chemical individuality and qualities were established by the successive researches of Scheffer (1752), Marggraft (1757), Bergmann (1777). In 1784 the first platinum crucible was made by Achard. In 1800 Knight, of London, published all that was known concerning the use of platinum in manufacture. Thomas Wedgwood, the youngest son of Josiah, employed it as early as 1791, but it is claimed that John Hancock (born 1757, died 1847), first employed gold, silver, and steel lustres at Messrs. Spode's factory at Stoke for Messrs. Daniel and Brown, who were decorating Spode ware at that date. That is his own account when he was eighty-nine years of age. But he was employed at Etruria. At any rate Hancock did not retain the secret, for among contemporary potters John Gardner, of Stoke, Sparkes, of Hanley, and Horobin, of Tunstall, seem to have practised it. At the beginning of the nineteenth century other potters were making lustre. In 1804 John Aynsley, of Lane End, and in 1810 Peter Warburton, of Lane End, who took out a patent for "decorating china, porcelain, earthenware, and glass with native pure or unadulterated gold, silver, platina, or other metals fluxed or lowered with lead or any other substance which invention or new method leaves the metals, after being burned, in their metallic state."

Pieces of silver lustre occur with the name Wood and Caldwell impressed on them. This was the style of the firm from 1790 to 1818. Such pieces may have been made during the last years of the factory's existence. But we know that it was made in 1810, for a painted lustre jug bears the inscription "Richard Bacchus, 1810." Another name which the writer has seen impressed on plain silver lustre ware of Early-Georgian shape is E. Mayer, who commenced as a potter in 1770, and died in 1818. It thus appears that at present, until more marked pieces turn up, the exact date within a few years of the manufacture of platinum or silver lustre in its first form is not determinable.

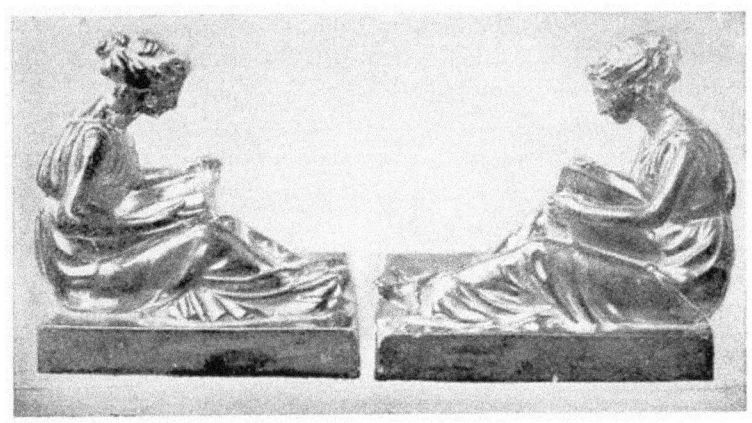

PAIR OF SILVER LUSTRE FIGURES.
By WOOD & CALDWELL. (Height 6¼ inches.)
(*From the collection of Mr. W. G. Honey.*)

SILVER LUSTRE JUGS.
1. "Resist" style, with stencilled decorations.
2. Bird painted in red, foliage in green in panel, silver lustre painted bands and borders.
(*In the possession of Mr. Hubert Gould.*)

Among makers known to have produced silver lustre are Robert Wilson, of Hanley, who was in partnership with Neale prior to the manufacture of this ware. His brother David Wilson, in the opening years of the nineteenth century, made silver lustre goblets and figures. There is a mounted figure of a hussar with uplifted sword attributed to the Wilsons, at the British Museum. The Wilsons also made copper or bronze lustre ware. Lakin and Poole is the name of another firm, and Spode, and it is believed Davenport embarked on this popular ware also. It is known, too, that Leeds made silver lustre ware of fine quality, that has stood the test of time; and gold lustre in imitation of Wedgwood's "Pearl Ware" lustrous decorations was made in early nineteenth-century days. Swansea is credited with similar productions of gold and gold-purple lustre on a marbled ground, although none of its silver-lustre ware is marked.

Probably the earliest use of silver lustre was when it was employed as an adjunct to figures in subsidiary portions in lieu of gilding. But most certainly it began to simulate the silver ware at an early date. This early type is undecorated, and was also used in busts or statuettes of classical form. We illustrate a pair of silver-lustre figures by Wood and Caldwell. There is another pair of children in silver lustre, marked Wood & Caldwell, which are colourable imitation of the figures of "children reading" made by Dwight (illustrated, p. 139).

In regard to decorated silver lustre we give two examples which are fairly typical of a large class. The illustration (p. 431) shows a jug decorated in enamel colours. The bird is in red and the foliage in green, on a cream ground. The border of the panel is in silver lustre and the rim of the jug and the bands around neck are also silver lustre.

This decorated silver-lustre ware is of two classes. The first class comprises patterns painted in silver lustre on a white ground, the foliage and birds and other patterns being in silver lustre, carefully painted over the white. As a rule in such pieces there is more white showing, and the lustre silver is palpably a decorative effect.

In the second class the silver lustre appears as a background, and the ornamental decoration is in white, covering the piece in most elaborate designs. This is known as "resist" ware, and on account of the great beauty and variety of its ornamentation, has strongly appealed to latter-day collectors. The pattern twining its way over the silver-lustre background may be white, blue, canary colour, pink, apricot, or turquoise-blue. White is most frequently found.

This second style is capable of the most intricate designs varying from farmyard and hunting scenes to ordinary conventional floral arrangements almost resembling the Japanese stencilled work in another field of art.

How "resist" ware is made.—If a white design is intended the ware is left white, but if any other colour, such as those we have mentioned, that colour is laid as a body or ground colour on the specimen to be lustred. The next step is to paint the exact design which later is to appear white, or blue, or yellow, on the surface of the vessel. This pattern is painted or stencilled on the ware with a substance composed of a glucose matter such as glycerine. The next stage is to apply the silver lustre to the whole surface which is allowed partially to dry. On its immersion in water the pattern painted previously to the addition of lustre peels off being on a soluble ground. The result is that the background of white or yellow or blue is laid bare, and the rest of the vessel is covered permanently with silver lustre. The adhesive lustre "resists" the water, adhering to the surface by means of its resinous nature, except in the pattern which peels off. Hence the term "resist" ware.

We illustrate one specimen of this silver-lustre "resist" ware (p. 431). It is of the ordinary floral conventional pattern probably stencilled on as described above. Some of the more elaborate specimens are painted. One of the finest collections of "Resist Silver Lustre" is that of Mr. William Ward, at the Kennels, Mellor, near Blackburn. It comprises examples that one may search for in vain in any of the museums. Many of the examples are marked such as "Warburton," or with the letter "W" impressed, and one specimen is marked "Leeds" a rare mark. The subjects of some of these jugs and mugs relate to the Napoleonic wars, and are dated. There is one rare jug entitled "Boney escaping through a Window," and in combination with this "resist" style are examples finely painted or transfer-printed in colours.

Copper or Bronze Lustre.—This class of lustre is generally held to be later (excepting of course the early attempts at Brislington which stand by themselves). It is held too by collectors up to the present not to offer such artistic possibilities as the "resist" silver lustre. This is amply borne out by the prices obtained at auction. But it must not be forgotten that this bronze or copper lustre varies very considerably. It may be and often is very coarse brown ordinary ware, and it may be very thin and delicate as to tempt the connoisseur to regard it with more than a passing glance.

In the highest forms of copper or bronze lustre, painted views appear in panels against the lustrous background, and such views are of a high order of merit. They may in all probability have been executed at Swansea. We illustrate a fine example (p. 437) of a large copper lustre mug with painted panel of landscape and other panels of fruit.

Very frequently in this copper lustre the jugs and mugs have ornamentation in relief which is enamelled in vivid colours. This is a fairly common form, and has been reproduced in very coarse examples, not to be confounded with the finer and thinner copper lustre at its best. We illustrate a copper lustre jug (p. 437) with serpent handle and Bellarmine mask spout, decorated in turquoise blue, and with basket of flowers in relief. The Goblet to the right is of similar decoration, and that on the left is of conventional coloured design on a mottled pink lustred band.

Marked Lustre Ware.—We have already mentioned a number of potters who are known to have made lustre ware, but the following names have been found impressed on the ware in various collections throughout the country, and may be of interest to collectors who have specimens either by these potters or by other makers not on this list. Wedgwood, Wilson, Warburton, Bailey and Batkin, J. Lockett & Sons, E. Mayer, Mayer & Newbold, E. Wood, Wood & Caldwell, Minton, Bott & Co., P. & U. (Poole & Unwin), Meigh, C. Meigh & Sons, Copeland & Garrett, and Leeds Pottery.

LARGE COPPER LUSTRE MUG.
Panels painted with landscapes and flowers in colours.
(*In the collection of Miss Feilden.*)

GROUP OF COLOURED COPPER LUSTRE.
Goblet with enamelled decoration in relief. Jug with Bellarmine mask
and spout and decorated in turquoise blue.
(*In the collection of Miss Feilden.*)

PRICES.

LUSTRE WARE.	£	s.	d.
Silver lustre Barber's jug with medallion of Barber and Customer, inscribed "William Freeman, 1809"; 6¾ in. high. Bond, Ipswich, April, 1906	5	0	0
Silver lustre "resist" pattern jug with grape and barley design. Sotheby, June, 1906	2	0	0
Nelson & Hill jug in silver lustre and decorated in red and black. Sotheby, June, 1906	1	10	0
Silver lustre jug, decorated with bird and flowers, and inscribed "J. Simpson, original Staffordshire Warehouse, 1791." Christie, January, 1908	14	14	0

Lustre decorated, Sunderland figures of *Seasons* (four) decorated in colours and purple lustre; all impressed, mark "Dixon, Austin & Co." Sotheby, February, 1908   10   0   0

Copper lustre pair of five-fingered flower vases marked Sewell. Sotheby, November, 1905   4   15   0

CHAPTER XIV
LATE STAFFORDSHIRE WARE

The School of Colour—Josiah Spode the Second (1798–1827)—Davenport (1793–1880)—Thomas Minton—Semi-porcelain—Ironstone China—The Masons—Early nineteenth-century Commemorative Ware—The revival of Stoneware—Messrs. Doulton—The twentieth-century Collector—Table of Marks—Prices.

The latest phases of earthenware are mainly concerned with the school of colourists, the chief of which was Josiah Spode the Second, who controlled the factory on the death of Josiah his father, in 1797, and took William Copeland as partner. It was this Spode who introduced into earthenware decorative patterns of Japanese colouring in which reds and yellows and dark cobalt blue predominate, following the style of the Crown-Derby Japan style. About 1800 Spode commenced the manufacture of porcelain as well as earthenware, and his richly gilded Japan patterns began to rival those of Derby. In regard to the light-blue-printed ware of a fine quality turned out by Spode, an illustration is given in the chapter on Transfer-printed Ware (p. 331). It was this second Josiah Spode who standardised the body used in English porcelain, which is to-day practically the same as Spode's formula. It may be said, roughly, to consist of the constituents of true porcelain plus a proportion of bone ash. Enoch Wood, when an apprentice with Palmer, was the first to use bone with earthenware, about 1770.

It is obvious that with these rich colours of Staffordshire porcelain side by side in the same factory, with earthenware, the latter began to assume all the decorative appearance of porcelain. A reign of colour set in. Earthenware was as lavishly decorated in colours, and as richly gilded as any of the contemporary porcelains, and in putting on these colours it lost all its old characteristic features and became an echo of porcelain.

Before leaving the Spode family, it may be mentioned that Josiah Spode the second, who died in 1827, aged seventy-three, was succeeded by his son, Josiah Spode the third, who died within two years.

William Copeland had died in 1826, and in 1833 the factory at Stoke came into the hands of W. T. Copeland, known as Alderman Copeland, as he then was, of the City of London. He became Lord Mayor of London in 1835, and in that year took Thomas Garrett into partnership. Copeland and Garrett is the name of the firm till 1847. For twenty years it was known as "W. T. Copeland, late Spode," and is now at the present day Messrs. W. T. Copeland & Sons.

The marks belonging to the firm at various dates are given at the end of this chapter. We illustrate a row of five remarkably fine earthenware vases decorated in rich colour in the Derby style, so perfectly simulating the brush work of that famous porcelain factory, that upon a hasty examination they would pass for Crown-Derby. They evidently belong to the days when Josiah Spode was turning out at Stoke more Japan patterns than were produced at Derby.

At the same time a good deal of less ornate earthenware for cottage use was being made, and specimens may frequently be met with, such as tea-sets with old-fashioned teapot and two-handled sugar-bowl made about 1825. Their homely English rural subjects are very pleasing, and show that there was still a large market in the country for simple ware without any great pretensions to foreign taste. It was the last stage of the great tradition of old English earthenware.

Davenport (1793–1880).—John Davenport, of Longport in Staffordshire, began potting in 1793. There is no doubt that he was a great potter with artistic instincts. He went to France prior to 1800, and on his return introduced a porcelain body superior to anything then produced in England. With Josiah Spode the second he claims more attention as a maker of porcelain than of earthenware. But his earthenware is highly prized by collectors. His blue-printed ware was exceptionally fine, and he followed in his plates and dishes the style of Turner and of Minton in the perforated rims. His stone china is well potted and carefully painted, and in design he was not loth to follow Mason of whom we shall speak later. Many specimens of the familiar type of jug associated with Mason's name, of octagonal shape are found in porcelain. Some collectors noticing the great similarity to Mason have been inclined to attribute these porcelain jugs to him, and doubtless, as Mason made china, many are his, but Davenport who made replicas of the Mason stoneware jugs, being a maker of porcelain too, is likely to have produced these porcelain replicas also. None of these porcelain jugs appears to be marked.

Davenport ware is strong in colour, and follows the rich designs of Spode. Some pieces of stoneware are richly gilt, and have finely painted fruit-pieces and landscapes, some probably by Steel from the Derby factory. The illustration (p. 447) of the highest flight of Mason typifies this class of landscape ware. Swansea, in common with Staffordshire, had not hesitated in painting earthenware with landscape subjects hitherto employed only by artists who decorated porcelain.

The Davenport marks are given at the end of this chapter, and are always prized when found on specimens, as Davenport did not mark his ware so freely as did Spode. From 1835 the firm became "William Davenport & Co.," and later "Davenport & Co.," and ceased about 1880.

DESSERT PLATES.
With border richly gilded with floral design.
Impressed mark MASON'S PATENT IRONSTONE CHINA.
(*In collection of Author.*)

DESSERT DISH.
Richly gilded border with landscape painted in colours.
Impressed mark MASON'S PATENT IRONSTONE CHINA.

Semi-porcelain.—This is found as a term in some of the marks of the early-Victorian period; sometimes the title "opaque china" appears. These descriptions are always puzzling to the collector. As a matter of fact they tell of the later and more modern development of earthenware. It had snatched the china glaze, it had employed the enamel colours, and had adopted the designs of the English porcelain factories. The rivalry of the Staffordshire potters and the English porcelain factories was coming to an end. This stage of semi-porcelain and semi-china represented the last word of earthenware. It now simulated porcelain in its body, with one drawback, it was not translucent as is porcelain. It was naïvely termed "opaque china." But the potters were proud of their latest achievement, and accordingly marked their wares with the above terms. As has been shown, Swansea came to the front, and Haynes in the closing years of the eighteenth century produced a hard, white earthenware termed "opaque-china," and Riley's "semi-china" about 1800 was the Staffordshire equivalent.

But, as we have seen, the Staffordshire potters not only imitated porcelain, continuing a long trade rivalry extending over nearly a century, but many of them had commenced to make porcelain themselves. Even the firm of Wedgwood succumbed to the temptation, and made porcelain from 1805 till 1815, which manufacture was revived again in 1878.

Thomas Minton (1765–1836).—Minton was one of Spode's engravers, and commenced as a master potter at Stoke in 1793.

Minton had been apprenticed to Thomas Turner, of Caughley, as an engraver, and it was he who designed the celebrated "Broseley dragon" pattern on the Caughley porcelain, and it is held by some authorities that Minton engraved the "willow pattern" too. At first, at Stoke, he made only earthenware, and his blue and white ware in imitation of the Nankin porcelain won him distinction. About 1800 porcelain was made and was continued throughout the nineteenth century. His son, Herbert Minton in 1836, took into partnership John Boyle, who joined the Wedgwoods in 1842. Herbert Minton raised the quality of the productions, being one of the greatest of the Staffordshire modern potters.

In the latter half of the century Mintons obtained a world-wide reputation. From 1850 to 1870 a band of French modellers and painters executed some fine work, but this trespasses on the field of porcelain.

Among the earthenware of Minton some of the early pieces such as plates and dishes enamelled in colours with Chinese subjects, are marked with the letter M in blue and a number. Some of the earliest-known examples in earthenware of the celebrated "willow pattern," such as plates with perforated edges (similar to that illustrated, p. 331) and baskets, are by Thomas Minton.

Ironstone China.—This again is a term used by Mason and others in regard to an earthenware body for which the firm of Mason, of Lane Delph, took out a patent in 1813. It is a ware, heavy in weight, and possessing great strength. In pieces of important size, such as punch bowls of huge proportions, and posts for old-fashioned bedsteads this was of no little value. We have already alluded to the Mason series of octagonal-shaped jugs of pleasing shape, undoubtedly following the Spode scheme of colour in Japanese style, but lacking the finer finish of Spode ware. Although undoubtedly original in design, these jugs were easily excelled in potting and colouring by copyists such as Davenport. But Mason's blue in his imitations of old Nankin ware is exceptionally fine. There are dinner-services consisting of a great number of pieces painted in under-glaze blue which are very rich in tone, and stand comparison with any of the blues of Staffordshire, not excepting those of Adams and Minton.

We illustrate a large vase obviously a replica of a Chinese model, and enamelled in very rich colours. It shows a remarkable facility in potting, and although strongly coloured conveys without caricature the decorative qualities of the Chinese potter.

"GRANITE CHINA" VASE.
Richly decorated in colours. Grass-green ground. Panels with landscape in Japanese Imari colours. Rich blue base and top heavily gilded. Dragon handles salmon-pink colour. (Height 2 feet.)

BASE OF ABOVE VASE.
Showing mark "Granite China. Staffordshire Potteries.
Fenton Stone Works. C J M & Co."
(*In the collection of Dr. H. Bournes Walker.*)

The vase is two feet in height. The ground is grass green. The panels have painted landscapes in Imari colours. The base and the top are a rich blue heavily gilded, and the dragon handles are a salmon pink. Obviously this, although imitative, is a very ambitious piece.

The mark of this vase stamped on the bottom (illustrated p. 451) is interesting. An outline design represents the pottery works. It is marked "Fenton Stone Works C. J. M. & Co." and in the outer rim is the inscription "Granite china," "Staffordshire Potteries."

The initials C. J. M. stand for Charles James Mason, who together with G. Miles Mason applied for the ironstone china patent in 1813.

Among other ware, similar to the early cream ware is a body termed "Mason's Cambrian-Argil." This evidently is in direct rivalry to the Swansea cream ware marked "Cambrian." Earlier jugs by him are rarely marked, and are not of the octagonal form, though the sides are prismatic, and usually seven in number. They are of a buff-coloured, soft, and chalky body, but the decorations are obviously his in similar style to his series of stoneware jugs. The handle of this earlier form is not of the snake or lizard form, but follows in design the metal handle of teapots of the period.

That the Masons could and did produce earthenware of a very high, artistic quality is shown by the illustration (p. 447) of three pieces marked with the impressed mark running in one line across the back of the examples "MASON'S PATENT IRONSTONE CHINA." The gilding in the floral design in the borders is well done, and the landscapes in the centre are finely painted. They are in the brush work patiently stippled with as much minuteness as the work of Birket Foster. A dessert service of which this forms portion, is a very desirable acquisition, and represents stone china at its high-water mark.

The various marks used by the Masons are given at the end of this chapter. In 1851 the pottery was purchased by Francis Morley, and it was incorporated with Ridgway, Morley, Wear & Co., and at a later date passed into the hands of Messrs. C. E. Ashworth and Taylor Ashworth, who to this day revert to the original patterns of the Mason jugs which have become so deservedly popular. Most of these old patterns are being produced, although of course they have not the charm for the collector whose interest ends with the original period under Mason.

"Stone china" became a term used by many other potters who produced strong and durable earthenware, heavy in weight, and extremely suitable for domestic use. Mintons had a series of patterns in this ware decorated in Oriental style in colour. The most popular of these is one termed "Amherst, Japan," following the old anglicised versions of Japanese Imari designs and colours. This was at the date when Lord Amherst was in the public eyes. It will be remembered that he headed an embassy to China, and was requested to perform the *ko-tou*, or act of prostration, nine times repeated with the head touching the ground. Sir George Staunton and other members of the Canton Mission protested, and the mission was admitted to the Emperor's presence on their own terms, which consisted of kneeling upon a single knee. Lord Amherst was later appointed Governor-General of India. There are a great many potters whose names are found on earthenware of mid-Victorian days. They cannot be said to exhibit much originality in design, and their value as collectors' specimens is infinitesimal.

PLATES, TRANSFER-PRINTED IN BLUE UNDER-GLAZE.
Impressed mark "IMPROVED FELSPAR. C. MEIGH & SON."
(Date 1850.)
(*In the collection of the Author.*)

SET OF STAFFORDSHIRE EARTHENWARE VASES.
Floral decoration in gold on rich blue ground. Flowers in enamel
colours on white panels in imitation of Derby porcelain style.
(*In the collection of Miss Feilden.*)

We illustrate two finely-potted stoneware plates, by Messrs. C. Meigh and Sons, made about 1850. They are printed in blue with designs of English primroses twined with peacock feathers! Here is East and West in strange combination. Fortunately the plates are not in colours or the result might have been disastrous; as it is they are very pleasing for the blue is of a very excellent tone. There is nothing hasty about the potting; the finish and the minor details suggest work of the old days long gone. It is evident that in the treatment of the design the inspiration came from the Japanese potter whose influence was beginning to make itself felt in pictorial art even so far back as the middle of the nineteenth century. Whistler's peacocks and the dawn of the later æstheticism were at hand.

Nineteenth Century Commemorative Ware.—It has been previously shown how fond the potters became of recording events and creating figures of popular heroes in earthenware. The story is continued in the nineteenth century, which covers, one is apt to forget, the last twenty years of the reign of George III., includes the ten years of George the Fourth's reign, and the seven of William IV., commencing the Victorian Era in 1837 on the accession of the late Queen.

So that the term early nineteenth century is not the same as early Victorian; as a matter of fact a good deal of very good porcelain and earthenware comes well within the nineteenth century, but very few examples that appeal to the artistic collector belong to the early-Victorian period.

The nineteenth century as a whole was crowded with incident, and in the class of earthenware with which we are now dealing the record is a full one. From Nelson to Garibaldi; from Maria Martin the victim of the Red Barn murder to Moody and Sankey, the American revivalists; from Napoleon crossing the Alps to George III., as the King of Brobdingnag, looking at Napoleon through a telescope; from Burns's *Souter Johnny* to Dickens's *Sam Weller*; from punch bowls, inscribed "Rum and Water" and "Health to all," to figures of Father Mathew, the temperance reformer—all sub-heads are touched, and although the artistic may be absent the human touch is ever present.

There are jugs and mugs with a portrait of "Orator Hunt," with inscriptions "Universal Suffrage," "No Corn Laws," dating from 1818. A lustre mug has a print with a dragoon represented as riding over a woman, and has the legend, "Murdered on the plains of Peterloo, near Manchester, 16th August, 1819." The woman carries a flag inscribed, "Liberty or Death."

A puzzle jug of Staffordshire earthenware is inscribed, "Hatfield shot at George III., 1800. God save the King." The trial of Queen Caroline produced a crowd of figures and mugs and plates with portraits and verses. The Crimean War had its ceramic record. There is a Newcastle earthenware butter-dish printed and coloured, with an English soldier greeting a French soldier, and motto, "May they ever be united."

NELSON JUG.
Portrait of Admiral Nelson, inscribed "England expects that every man will do his duty." On reverse, female figure and children, inscribed "Behold the Widow casting herself and Orphans on benevolent Britons."
(*In the collection of Miss Feilden.*)

NELSON JUG.
With portrait of Admiral Lord Nelson. Aged 47. Inscribed "England expects every man to do his duty." On reverse, plan of Battle of Trafalgar.

The transfer-printed jugs and mugs with nautical subjects we have already alluded to in a previous chapter. The unfamiliar uniform of the late eighteenth and early nineteenth century "Jack Tar" is a study in costume. This silent ceramic world of old three deckers and ships of the line and barques and brigantines is all that is left of a fleet of ships which have long since sailed their last voyage—an armada of non-existent craft as ghostly as the phantom ship of Vanderdecken.

Nelson jugs are of many types; we illustrate two varieties (p. 459). Some of them are as early as 1797, and others as late as 1820.

The top jug illustrated is of Staffordshire cream ware, and is in date after Trafalgar (1805), made to commemorate this victory. The portrait of Nelson has an inscription over it, "England Expects every Man to do his Duty." On the reverse is a plan of the Battle of Trafalgar with the disposition of the ships and a slight description which ends in the sentence "in which Action the Intrepid Nelson fell covered with Glory and Renown."

The lower jug is of the same period and the portrait of Nelson is more authentic. It is transfer-printed, the uniform being slightly touched in colour. On the reverse there is a female figure and two children, and the sad human touch in the inscription, "Behold the Widow casting herself and Orphans on benevolent Britons." This is, indeed, the reverse of the medal. The glory of war is exalted unduly. But the awful reality does not always come home so pointedly as in this homely jug, which in its way records the "simple annals of the poor." We are reminded of the lines of that forgotten poet, Amelia Opie, and of the wood-engraving by Dalziel in Willmott's "Poets of the Nineteenth Century," published in the sixties. "The Orphan Boy's Tale," who tells how pleased he was—

> "When the news of Nelson's victory came,
>
> Along the crowded streets to fly
>
> And see the lighted windows flame!"

The shouts of the crowd rejoicing drowned the widow's tears. In simple, but none the less poetical, language the child continues:

> "She could not bear to see my joy;
>
> For with my father's life 'twas bought,
>
> And made me her poor orphan boy."

It is undoubtedly such human touches as these on the domestic crude ware which stir the heart's blood quicker than all the gods and goddesses ever turned out in Staffordshire.

The age of steam and steel and its inventions did not come unheralded. We illustrate a plate of one of the earliest steam carriages (p. 463). The plate is of Staffordshire origin and evidently was intended to be sold in Germany as a "present from London," as the inscription runs, "Dampf Wagen von London nach Bristol. Ein Geschenk für meinen Lieben Jungen" ("Steam Coach from London to Bristol. A Present for my dear boy"). In date this is about 1827 as the accompanying engraving, entitled the "New Steam Carriage," is from a periodical publication of that date.

TRANSFER-PRINTED PLATE IN COLOURS.
Inscription—"Dampf Wagen von London nach Bristol.
Ein Geschenk für meinen Lieben Jungen." (Staffordshire, about 1830.)
(*In collection of Author.*)

"NEW STEAM COACH."
From an old print dated 1827.

Equally interesting is the Staffordshire blue-printed *Jug* marked at back "Liverpool and Manchester Railway" showing the famous *Rocket* steam-engine invented by George Stephenson. The date of this is 1830. A fine *Cyder Mug* printed in black with touches of colour shows an early passenger train. The luggage, as will be seen, is on the roofs of the carriages. The aristocratic company at the rear are seated in their own carriage, the ladies of the party are noticeable by their old-fashioned poke bonnets. There is something very interesting in these old railway mugs and jugs. They are modern, that is in regard to technique and artistic beauty, but the subjects are of sufficient interest to make the ware important enough to find a treasured place of honour in the collector's cabinet.

Lambeth Stoneware.—Mention should be made of the revival of artistic stoneware at Lambeth about 1850 by Henry Doulton, of the Lambeth pottery. An attempt was made to make vessels for ordinary use as ornamental in character as the old Flemish stoneware. Some of the early pieces are in brown stoneware with incised decoration filled with blue-glaze. Tankards and vases and jugs were made of very pleasing character. Under Sir Henry Doulton great advances were made, and mugs with hunting subjects and many grotesque brandy bottles of stoneware were made. Light brown stoneware flasks modelled to represent Lord Brougham, and impressed "The True Spirit of Reform," and "Brougham's Reform Cordial," are often of

Lambeth origin. In date these are about 1830, other factories made similar ware, including the Derbyshire potteries.

Of the Doulton and Watts period which commenced 1815, from 1815 to 1832 some fine Napoleonic stoneware was turned out. There is, in particular, a small stoneware, brown jar of Napoleon made about 1825, which is finely modelled and an excellent portrait. In the Reform days of the early thirties they produced, to supply a public demand, many spirit jars with more or less grotesque models of Earl Grey, Lord Brougham, William Cobbett, and Lord John Russell. In the museum at Messrs. Doulton's at Lambeth are some fine examples of the early period.

We illustrate a strongly modelled jug with Bacchanalian subject in high relief (p. 471), showing the excellence of some of this early work at its best.

The Twentieth Century Collector.—The story of the triumphs and sometimes of the decadence of English pottery cannot be ended without a passing reference to the wondrous ware being produced at the end of the nineteenth century and now. It should appeal to-day to the prescient collector. It will appeal to the collector fifty years hence.

Under the name of the Lancastrian Pottery Messrs. Pilkington, at Clifton Junction, near Manchester, have during the past few years produced some of the most beautiful ware ever seen in this country. At the exhibition of this ware in London in 1904 they astonished all experts. The indescribable variety of exquisite colours, ranging from faint pink and sky blue to the richest purple and dark green and amber, showed at once that modern scientific methods and painstaking research had rediscovered the lost glazes of the old Chinese potters.

The starry crystalline glazes so well known in the Copenhagen porcelain have been faithfully reproduced, recalling the patterns traced on the window-pane by frost—sometimes brilliantly coloured blue or green against a background of pale lavender blue, at other times having a sheen like bronze. Other crystalline glazes are the *Sunstone* in which brilliant prismatic and golden crystals are disseminated through rich green yellow or olive brown glazes. The fiery crystalline glazes display brilliant red crystalline formation through purple and grey glaze in dazzling patches.

STAFFORDSHIRE BLUE PRINTED JUG.
Marked at back "Liverpool & Manchester Railway."
Showing the famous *Rocket* locomotive invented by George Stephenson.
(Date 1830.)
(*In the collection of Miss Feilden.*)

CYDER MUG.
Printed in black with touches of colour.
(*In the collection of Mrs. M. M. Fairbairn.*)

Opalescent clouded, or curdled, or veined, or serpentine glazes have countless variations of colours—copper-green, turquoise-blue, or deep lapis-lazuli broken with white curds, or opalescent veinings, or fine lines of variegated colour shot through the glaze from top to bottom—this alone suggests a dream of colour schemes, and the wise collector will realise without further ado that we are in a period of great ceramic triumphs in pottery of this nature.

Texture glazes of chicken-skin, fruit-skin, and orange-skin are highly prized, and vellum or egg-shell glazes splashed and marked like Nature's own handiwork in the most beautiful birds' eggs. Or there are metallic effects of peculiar beauty and golden lacquer glazes resembling the old gold lac-work of Chinese and Japanese artists so cunningly imitated by Martin, the French cabinet-maker, in his Vernis-Martin, so beloved of collectors of furniture and fans.

Of purple glazes of the transmutation class some of the richest effects have been obtained in colour and in splashed effects. Wine purple, mulberry, and other alluring tones have burst upon an astonished circle of connoisseurs. Of the *flambé* specimens it is not too much to say that their like, for which the Chinese potters were so famous, have never been seen before in Europe.

The Havilands of Limoges, Copenhagen, and Sèvres, and Berlin potters, as well as the artists in the Rookwood Pottery in America, have worked in the same field; but it is pleasant to think that English potters have produced greater variety, including Lancastrian lustre ware of wealth of glowing colour not surpassed by the Hispano-Moresque potters nor by the lustrous majolica of the Italian renaissance. To the scientific activity in wresting from the past the lost secrets of the old Chinese potters, a great tribute of praise should be accorded to Mr. William Burton and his brother, Mr. Joseph Burton.

Other workers in the same field of glazes are Mr. Bernard Moore, of London, whose glorious *flambé*, rich red, and *sang-de-bœuf* glazes are of unsurpassed beauty. Mr. William de Morgan has for many years been known for his lustrous tiles and work of fine originality and strength. Another pottery known as the Ruskin Pottery conducted by Mr. W. Howson Taylor at West Smethwick, Birmingham, is a bright spot in recent ceramic enterprise, and has won distinction for ware which is of great beauty.

In bringing the story of English earthenware to a conclusion, it is the hope of the writer that the ground has been sufficiently covered to provide an outline history of a complex subject. It may be that much appears that might have been omitted, and that much is omitted that might have appeared within these covers. But it must be allowed that personal tastes play an important part in selection either by the collector or by the student. But in matters of fact and in the mass of details relative to the potters and their wares no pains have been spared to make this little handbook worthy of its subject.

DOULTON STONEWARE JUG.
(Date about 1845. Height 10 inches.)
(*In the collection of Mr. W. G. Honey.*)

MARKS FOUND ON LATE STAFFORDSHIRE EARTHENWARE.

The first half of the nineteenth century in earthenware included a variety of types: (1) the last output of the classical school; (2) cream ware transfer-printing in under-glaze blue; (3) the school of colourists in imitation of English porcelain.

In the following list a great many names appear of potters not well known nor worthy of more than passing allusion. But their trade marks often puzzle collectors.

Adams.
One of the oldest firms in Staffordshire.

Adams & Co.

Early mark for cream ware, plain and enamelled, 1770–1790.

ADAMS & CO. Mark used for solid jasper ware, 1780–1790.

ADAMS Mark for printed ware, stoneware, and jasper, 1787–1810.

Mark used for deep blue-printed ware, 1804–1840, so much collected by American connoisseurs.

 or

Spode.
Josiah Spode the second, who introduced Derby-Japan patterns into earthenware. The name is found impressed, or printed, or painted in colours on back.

At the introduction of ironstone china other marks were introduced, and they were printed on the ware.

Similarly the "new fayence," another of Spode's improvements, was printed on ware of that character.

Other marks, both impressed and printed, in the ware are SPODE, SON & COPELAND, or SPODE & COPELAND.

From 1833 to 1847 these, among other trade marks, were used.

From 1847 to 1856 this mark was used.

The present day mark of Messrs. W. T. Copeland & Sons.

Davenport
LONGPORT

Davenport (1793–1886). These marks are found on the earthenware, stamped or printed, in small letters in red, and other Davenport marks, such as that with the anchor and the stone china design used after 1805, are frequently puzzling to collectors, especially when partially obliterated.

Minton. Established at Stoke, 1790.

M & B
FELSPAR PORCELAIN

B B
New Stone

In 1800 porcelain was made, and was continued throughout the century and at the present day.

From 1790–1798 blue and white earthenware in imitation of common Nankin largely made. In 1798 semi-porcelain was made. Felspar china, similar to Spode and stone china, in common with other Staffordshire potters, was largely produced. From 1836–1841 the firm was Minton & Boyle, and afterwards Minton and Hollins, and at the present day Minton is one of the best-known English firms. Not many of the early earthenware pieces were marked, and it is difficult to distinguish Minton's firm from some of the fine blue-printed ware of Adams and of Mason.

This B B mark appears on all stone china of Minton from 1845–1861, signifying *Best Body*.
The name Minton was not stamped nor impressed on the ware till after 1861. About 1823 the *Amherst Japan* pattern was made, and has a printed mark in a scroll. It is frankly imitative of Spode and the Derby-Japan style

A rhomboidal mark with the letter **R**, sometimes "R^D," signifying that the design is "Registered," and having **M & Co**, is not confined to Mintons, as other potters used the same mark with their names or initials underneath. It is quite late and on ware not likely to appeal to the collector.

Mason.

The marks of Mason are found, after 1813, either impressed in a straight line or having the mark under a crown and in scroll, on his celebrated ironstone china printed in blue.

MASON'S CAMBRIAN-ARGIL

MASON'S PATENT IRONSTONE CHINA (*impressed*)

M. MASON

MILES MASON

His semi-porcelain or Cambrian-argil bears the name on the ware, and was intended to compete with Swansea.
An illustration of the mark on stone china, marked "Fenton Stone Works, C J M & Co," is given on page 451.

It should be mentioned that the blue-printed mark with a crown and scroll does not necessarily mean that the ware (especially in the hexagonal set of jugs) is old. It is still used at the present day by Messrs. Ashworth, who are reproducing some of the old and favourite patterns. Collectors are advised to buy one of these jugs as a model to compare it with the older work.

P. B & Co.

The mark of Pindar, Bourne & Co., of Burslem, who made red terra cotta spill vases decorated in colours and gold with arabesque designs, about 1835. In 1880 the factory passed into the hands of Messrs. Doulton.

ROGERS

Mark of Dale Hall Pottery, John Rogers & Son, 1815–1842. Notable for light blue printed "Willow" and "Broseley Dragon" series.

J E & S
DALEHALL

J. Edwards & Son, Dale Hall, 1842–1882.

W B.
W & B
W B & S
CLEWS

W. Brownfield & Son (Cobridge) 1808–1819. Bucknall & Stevenson and A. Stevenson alone during part of above period.
James Clews, 1819–1829. His mark was a crown above his name.
Robinson, Wood & Brownfield, 1836.
Wood & Brownfield, 1836–1850. *W. Brownfield*, 1850–1870. *W. Brownfield & Sons*, 1871 to present day. China has been made since 1871.

We append some of the marks of this firm, including the Staffordshire knot, which has been used by other Staffordshire potters.

Ridgway, founded in 1794.>
J. & W. Ridgway and Ridgway & Sons, 1814–1854.
Many of these marks have puzzled collectors, as only the initials are used in many cases.
The firm subsequently became T. C. Brown-Westhead, Moore & Co., and has had a distinguished career in the ceramic world, gaining honours at the various international exhibitions.
(*See Table p. 349*).

These marks are found impressed in ware of Messrs. Powell & Bishop, 1865–1878, of Hanley. They are often confused with Pindar, Bourne & Co., when only initials are used.

Another form is a Caduceus, the emblem of Mercury, impressed in the ware and sometimes printed.
(*Messrs. Powell & Bishop.*)

A seated figure is another trade mark which has given rise to a good deal of speculation among tyros in collecting.
(*Messrs. Powell & Bishop.*)

Heathcote & Co. is a mark found in early nineteenth century ware. The blue-printed earthenware was of a fine quality.

Late Nineteenth Century Earthenware.

The three marks of the Lancastrian Pottery, the Ruskin Pottery, West Smethwick, and of the earthenware of Mr. William De Morgan, are known to connoisseurs of what is great in latter-day English earthenware, and they are given here for the information of collectors who may be interested.

PRICES.

	£	s.	d.

LATE STAFFORDSHIRE.

Spode (Earthenware).

Spode felspar, ice pails and covers painted with flowers and richly gilded. Puttick & Simpson, March, 1907 — 12 1 6

Davenport (Earthenware).

Toby Jug, marked "Davenport." Sotheby, November, 1904	3	12	6

Minton (Earthenware).

Set of Chessmen, in form of mice, drab and ivory coloured, decorated with black and gold. Kings and Queens crowned, Knights with swords, Bishops with croziers, and Castles with warder on top and a mouse imprisoned below. Sotheby, July, 1908	2	0	0

Mason.

Vases, pair, large, decorated in gold with kylin tops. Debenham, January, 1906	8	5	0
Ironstone china dinner service (197 pieces) floral decoration in colours. Christie, March, 1906	53	11	0
Vases, pair (12 in. high), mazarin blue ground, decorated with Oriental birds, &c. Bradby, Perth, September, 1906	7	7	0
Ironstone china bowl, decorated in flowers blue, red and gold. Puttick & Simpson, January, 1907	5	0	0

EARLY VICTORIAN.

Staffordshire (Earthenware).

Red Barn (scene of well-known murder of Maria Martin), very scarce. Sotheby, February, 1907	2	10	0
Jug, with portrait of Lord Nelson, marked Hollins. Sotheby, November, 1908	1	19	0
Jug with figures of Volunteers, and a smaller jug with portrait of Wellington. Sotheby, May, 1907	3	0	0

Three Jugs, brown ground, with Madonna and Child in relief, marked "Meigh," and three jugs with Tam o' Shanter subjects marked "Ridgway." Sotheby, May, 1907   1   3   0

FOOTNOTES:

[1] "Guide to English Pottery and Porcelain in the British Museum," R. L. Hobson.

[2] "Staffordshire Pots and Potteries," G. W. and F. A. Rhead.

[3] These have been recently arranged and catalogued by Mr. Frederic Rathbone.

[4] Compare this with the List of Marks on Transfer-printed Ware, pp. 347–35.

[5] Compare this with the List of Marks of the School of Wedgwood, pp. 279–282.

[6] See coloured *Frontispiece*.